Two Years Before the Paddlewheel

Charles F. Gunther, Mississippi River Confederate

Two Years Before the Paddlewheel

Charles F. Gunther, Mississippi River Confederate

Edited by
Bruce S. Allardice and Wayne L. Wolf

State House Press

Buffalo Gap, Texas

Library of Congress Cataloging-in-Publication Data

Gunther, Charles Frederick, 1837-1920.
  Two years before the paddlewheel : Charles F. Gunther, Mississippi River Confederate / [edited by] Bruce S. Allardice and Wayne L. Wolf.
    p. cm.
  Includes bibliographical references and index.
  ISBN 978-1-933337-52-4 (pbk. : alk. paper) — ISBN 1-933337-52-4 (pbk. : alk. paper)
  1. Gunther, Charles Frederick, 1837-1920. 2. Unionists (United States Civil War)—Confederate States of America—Diaries. 3. Unionists (United States Civil War)—Confederate States of America—Biography. 4. United States—History—Civil War, 1861-1865—Personal narratives. 5. Confederate States of America—Social life and customs. 6. River life—Mississippi River—History—19th century. 7. Refugees—Southern States. I. Allardice, Bruce S. II. Wolf, Wayne L., 1947- III. Title.
    E458.7.G86 2012
    973.7'13—dc23

                                                                2012022955

Copyright © 2012, State House Press
All Rights Reserved

State House Press
P. O. Box 818
Buffalo Gap, Texas 79508
325.572.3974 • 325.572.3991 (fax)
www.tfhcc.com

No part of this work may be reproduced in any form without written permission from State House Press, except for brief passages by reviewers.

Printed in the United States of America
Distributed by Texas A&M University Press Consortium
800.826.8911
www.tamupress.com

ISBN-13: 978-1-933337-52-4
ISBN-10: 1-933337-52-4
10 9 8 7 6 5 4 3 2 1

Cover illustration Naval battle of Memphis, and Federal occupation of Memphis, *Harper's Weekly*, June 28, 1862.

Book designed by Rosenbohm Graphic Design

Dedication

I'd like to thank Wayne Wolf, my coauthor, for bringing Charles Gunther's 1862 diary to my attention; Don Frazier, Amy Smith, and the staff at the McWhiney Foundation and State House Press for their wonderful work on this manuscript; and the Chicago History Museum for giving us permission to use the 1861 portion of Gunther's diary. But the person we should all thank is Charles Gunther, who, at great personal risk, kept this diary of his experiences during the greatest cataclysm in United States history.

—Bruce S. Allardice

No book can be written without the help of those who share their time, expertise, and love to make it possible. To my wife Lynn, for her inspiration and historical fervor, this book is dedicated. But I also must thank my mother, Vivian, for her nearly ninety years of love and support; Don Frazier for his scholarly interest in pursuing this book to add to the knowledge of Mississippi River traffic during the Civil War; and to my coauthor Bruce S. Allardice for the hours spent researching his part of the book. They are all true historians.

—Wayne L. Wolf

Contents

Introduction: The Life of Charles F. Gunther	xi
Diary, January–April 1861	19
Diary, May–August 1861	71
Diary, September–December 1861	127
Diary, January–April 1862	183
Diary, May–August 1862	237
Diary, September–December 1862	285
Notes	331
Select Bibliography	333
Index	337

The River Flows North

Up the Mississippi the steam packet inched,
Carrying cotton and rice, sugar and dreams,
Slowly as the soldiers on board flinched,
Union troops emerged from the feeding streams.

A chase was on and young nerves frayed,
Steady the rudder, stoke the coal, stack the cotton tightly baled,
Sharpshooters scrambled to hidden nests, green recruits prayed,
The smoke belched, waves parted, and womenfolk wailed.

This day the South would win,
Yankees fell back, abandoning the race,
The precious cargo arrived to rebels dangerously thin,
Sunken grooves of starvation soon etched every rebel face.

The young purser knew that Dixie was slipping,
No oysters or fruit from river ports came forth,
Dreams of a new nation fading under hunger now gripping,
The river, muddy and shallow, now flowed North.

—Wayne L. Wolf

Introduction
The Life of Charles F. Gunther

Karl Friedrich Guenther (later Americanized to Charles Frederick Gunther) arrived in America on June 21, 1842, on the ship *Herculean* with his parents Johann Martin and Anna Marie (Frey) Guenther. He was five years old when he made the journey from his birthplace in Wildberg, Württemberg (Germany), where he was born on March 6, 1837. The family settled first in Lancaster County, Pennsylvania, where his father, a soap and candle maker, found employment. At age ten Charles held his first job: a government mail carrier, traveling up to forty miles a day on horseback. Charles and his family relocated to Peru, Illinois, in 1850, joining the growing German-American community there. After receiving his early education in both public and private schools, he began a remarkable career that would take him from clerking in a general store, to the employ of a druggist, and to the banking house of Alexander Cruickshank, where he rose to the rank of cashier. As bank cashier he came into contact with many of the merchants and steamship owners involved in Peru's blossoming ice trade with the southern United States. In late 1860 he headed south himself and found a position with the Memphis, Tennessee, ice supply firm, Bohlen & Wilson. Soon after the outbreak of the Civil War, with the ice trade halted by the war, he accepted a purser's job aboard the steamship *Rose Douglas* and served the Confederate cause ferrying troops, supplies, and equipment up and down the Mississippi, White, and Arkansas Rivers. Captured by the Union troops in late 1862, he was quickly paroled by Federal authorities and returned to Peru, Illinois, once again reuniting with his parents, whom he never forgot in the almost two years he was "trapped" down South.

But Charles Gunther's wandering spirit got the best of him. After a short stint in his old banking profession, he accepted a salesman's position with wholesale confectioner Charles W. Sanford of Chicago, providing him with extensive travel opportunities throughout the United States and Europe. Studying the art of candy making in Europe, learning more marketing strategies from the confectionary firm of Greenfield & Young in New York, and fully utilizing the persistence derived from his German roots combined with the versatility and creativeness of his Yankee upbringing and the enterprising marketing skills of his western ethos, he opened his own confectionary business in Chicago in 1868, across the street from the new retail giant, Marshall Field & Company. The Charles F. Gunther Candy Company was the first high-grade confectionary store in Chicago. In 1869 he married Jennie Burnell of Lima, Indiana, and started a family that bore him two sons: Burnell and Whitman.

Again showing grit and persistence, he rebuilt the business after it was destroyed by the 1871 Great Chicago Fire and shepherded the company as it became the largest and most successful candy company in the United States.

While many entrepreneurs would have been satisfied to run the largest confectionary business in the United States—with annual business of a half-million dollars by the turn of the century—Charles Gunther was never one to be limited in his desire to do more. He developed the caramel candy his candy company became famous for and decorated his store to appeal to both adults and children by adding crystal chandeliers and electric lights. Sweets of all kinds released an aroma that drew passersby to the counters and created a setting more reminiscent of the Arabian Nights than of a typical retail store at the end of the nineteenth century. Gunther's enterprise raised him in the estimation of his fellow merchants, who eagerly recruited him to join an 1879 commission to Mexico for promoting commerce with the United States' southern neighbor and extending business opportunities south of the border. In 1893, as the Columbian Exposition was coming to Chicago, Charles Gunther was not sitting idle. He turned his avid interest in archaeology, history, and historic preservation into a crusade to save history, own it, and display it to all who would come. He purchased the notorious Civil War Libby Prison, had it dismantled,

Gunther's mausoleum, in Rosehill Cemetery, Chicago

The home of the Gunther Candy Company in downtown Chicago, advertising "Chocolates and Bon-bons—Candy that cannot be equaled—Sold all over the world" (from postcard in author's possession).

GUNTHER'S CONFECTIONERY 212 STATE ST. CHICAGO.

A wonderful interior view of Gunther's Confectionary at 212 State St., Chicago. The cases filled with various candies netted Gunther $500,000 per year (from postcard in author's possession).

and brought it to Chicago to house his ever-expanding collection of relics, war trophies, and world curiosities. He possessed one of the largest collections of Washington and Lincoln relics, rare portraits of American statesmen, medieval Bibles, ancient papyrus and parchment manuscripts, maps, original music scores, and Indian Bibles and artifacts. Lovingly watched over by his family, his collections continued to grow, added to as his firm continued to profit.

As acknowledged during Gunther's lifetime, his collection ranged from the sublime to the ridiculous. Its rarities included priceless objects, such as the table on which Robert E. Lee wrote his acceptance of the Appomattox surrender, and the bed that Abraham Lincoln died on. Mixed in with these authentic items was a broad array of the odd, the incredible (the alleged mummy of the biblical Pharaoh's daughter who discovered Moses in the bulrushes), and the bogus (e.g., the skin of the "serpent" of the Garden of Eden!). Visitors to Gunther's candy store and to the museum he later sponsored marveled at the assembled relics—and, in an early example of product synergy, stayed to be tempted by the sweets displayed elsewhere on the premises. Fortunately, the Great Chicago Fire never repeated itself, since, as one friend observed years later, "he had enough guns and munitions [in his collection] to start a third world war."

After Gunther's death, the Chicago Historical Society (Gunther had been a member) paid the large sum of $150,000 for the bulk of Gunther's collection of curios. Wide publicity about the purchase attracted other donations to the Society, particularly materials relating to Gunther's beloved President Abraham Lincoln. The Gunther purchase provided the Chicago Historical Society (today the Chicago History Museum) with the basis of its vast collections, many of which are displayed at the museum today. The Society built a new museum, located at Clark Street and North Avenue, to display this expanded collection.

Gunther's wife also used her social connections, status, and wealth to fund numerous charities and church functions. They worked as a couple to expand their business and their charity to the city they loved, and to provide a Yale education to their sons.

There was one other area that the ever-energetic Charles Gunther could not ignore: politics. An active Democrat, he was twice elected as a Chicago alderman and in 1901 became Chicago City Treasurer. In 1908, at age seventy-one, he ran for governor of Illinois, proclaiming that "the state needs a business administration by a practical business man." Gunther lost to former vice president Adlai Stevenson in the Democratic primary that August. He remained active in politics and social clubs including the Union League Club, the Iroquois Club, and the Germania Club, until his death on February 10, 1920, at the age of 82, from complications of pneumonia.

One of the most interesting periods of Gunther's life, however, was his two years as a purser aboard the *Rose Douglas*. With the outbreak of the Civil War in 1861, every able-bodied man between 18 and 45 years of age (as well as some younger and older who successfully hid their age) either volunteered for war service or were conscripted to serve the cause.

Unable to escape North due to the fortified Union and Confederate lines, and perhaps hopeful that he could resume the ice business after a short skirmish between the two sections of the country, he accepted the least dangerous service he could by becoming the purchasing agent and acting purser aboard the *Rose Douglas*, commanded by Capt. James Maginnis. The diaries he left to posterity covering the years 1861 and 1862, meticulously kept on a daily basis, chronicled his exploits on the Mississippi, White, and Arkansas Rivers, carrying Southern troops for Generals Sterling Price, Van Dorn, and others: the dangers he faced, the sights and privations he saw among the country folk, the scarcity of goods, food, and provisions for a South increasingly deprived of the necessities of life. He watched as the Union stranglehold gripped the Confederacy and eliminated its hopes of freedom.

It was an exciting time as Gunther witnessed history, met many of the principal players of his day, used his human relations skills to aid the South (while personally sympathizing with the North), struggled for his own survival amid the uncertainties of war, and continued to educate himself, make new friends, explore new opportunities, and live life to the fullest. These diaries present the innermost thoughts of a Northerner trapped in a Southern existence, wrestling with his role and emotions and always planning and plotting to learn from whatever situation presented itself.

Both diaries, newly discovered in the vaults of the Abraham Lincoln Bookshop and the Chicago Historical Museum, provide an amazing two-year, day-by-day look at the Civil War from the eyes of a civilian pressed into service. As the *Rose Douglas* plied the rivers, transporting essential troops and supplies, Gunther's entries reflect on the mood of the people and the feelings of the soldiers and river folk he comes into contact with. He is a witness to the changing face of the South: a land punctuated with scarcity, destruction, inflation, false hopes, and newspaper accounts that dramatically skew the results of battles and events. The South won great victories in the press, routing Union troops through the sheer genius of their generals. But these accounts deluded the people into a false sense of security. Gunther, on the other hand, saw reality. He observed the blockading of the Arkansas River that trapped the *Rose Douglas* for weeks, preventing it from reaching port, loading its deck, transporting its goods and personnel, and making a living for its crew. He saw Confederate bank notes become virtually worthless as the price of butter, wheat, coffee, and other necessities rose faster than anyone could afford, even on the rare occasions when the items were available. Gunther passed his time reading, visiting friends, and trying to catch fish for dinner. Even ammunition was scarce; he could not shoot game to break the monotony of corn for breakfast, lunch, and dinner. He displayed bouts of depression when news was unavailable, when letters did not reach him from home, when he could not get news of his whereabouts through to his parents, when trade dried up, and when he suffered from bouts of malaria contracted in the swamps of the Mississippi Delta. The two years of diaries present a unique view of the everyday life of a would-be new nation struggling to survive in the face of the overwhelming might of the industrial North. When Union naval forces captured New Orleans in May 1862, Gunther saw the beginning of the end for his riverboat service. When Memphis, Tennessee, fell to Federal forces in June 1862, he knew the fate of the *Rose Douglas* was sealed. Finally, his ship was captured at Van Buren, Arkansas, by troops under the command of Union general James G. Blunt. His beloved *Rose Douglas* was then burned. Gunther accompanied General Blunt north to begin his return to Illinois, his parents, and his civilian life in Peru. For Gunther, however, capture was a relief. He felt that he could finally rejoice in his liberation from Southern service and write in his diary his true feelings (which he had kept to himself for fear Confederates would see his entries and brand him a traitor to the cause). Thankfully, he took with him to Illinois two years' worth of his daily diaries: meticulous handwritten records of events copied into the little books he had purchased in New Orleans. Perhaps he hoped that someday his years of hardship, his eyewitness testimony to history, and his true Union sentiments would be revealed.

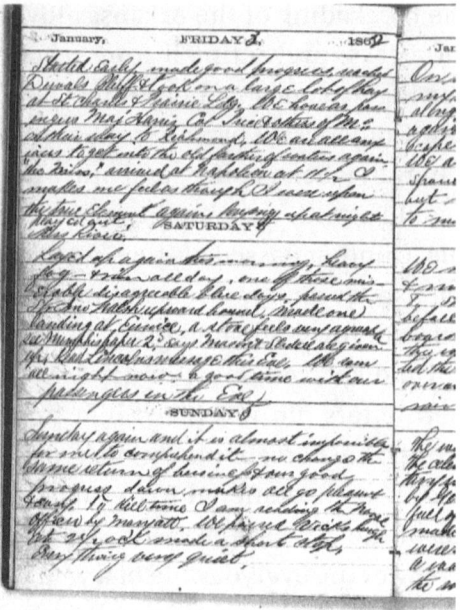

Gunther diary

Notes on Method

The diaries that follow have been transcribed, keeping as much as possible to Gunther's spelling, punctuation, and grammatical oddities in their original, historical form. Only occasionally are spellings corrected, locations identified, and errors corrected. These changes do not alter any content, but assist the historian in traveling the same path that Charles Gunther followed. His is a remarkable first-person account of the war, never before published, which tells his story: the story of a Unionist fighting for the Confederacy.

Diary
January–April 1861

As Charles F. Gunther begins his diary, his personal situation seems grim. After having gone south to work in the Memphis ice trade, he has been laid off (probably due to the seasonal nature of the trade) and, with a friend, has decided to seek a teaching position in northwest Arkansas. As will be seen, the educated young German-American cannot find suitable employment and is forced (much to his chagrin) to earn his keep as a common laborer. Wielding an axe for slaughtering hogs, he hopes to return to Memphis and (eventually) to the Illinois he is homesick for.

January 1861
Gunther's pocket diary for 1861 was of a type published annually by Denton & Wood, Cambridgeport, Massachusetts.

> [Tuesday, January 1, 1861] Today we are making some headway up the Ark. River the day is pleasant and were it not for past recollections I would not think of New Years Day, we have nothing of any account that transpired, a little more than ordinary dinner for the boat and that is all—Houston keeps the crowd alive and playing poker is all the go among the passengers but not much money is either lost or won. Asa and I amuse ourselves reading and talking over matters of the past. Illinois issues.

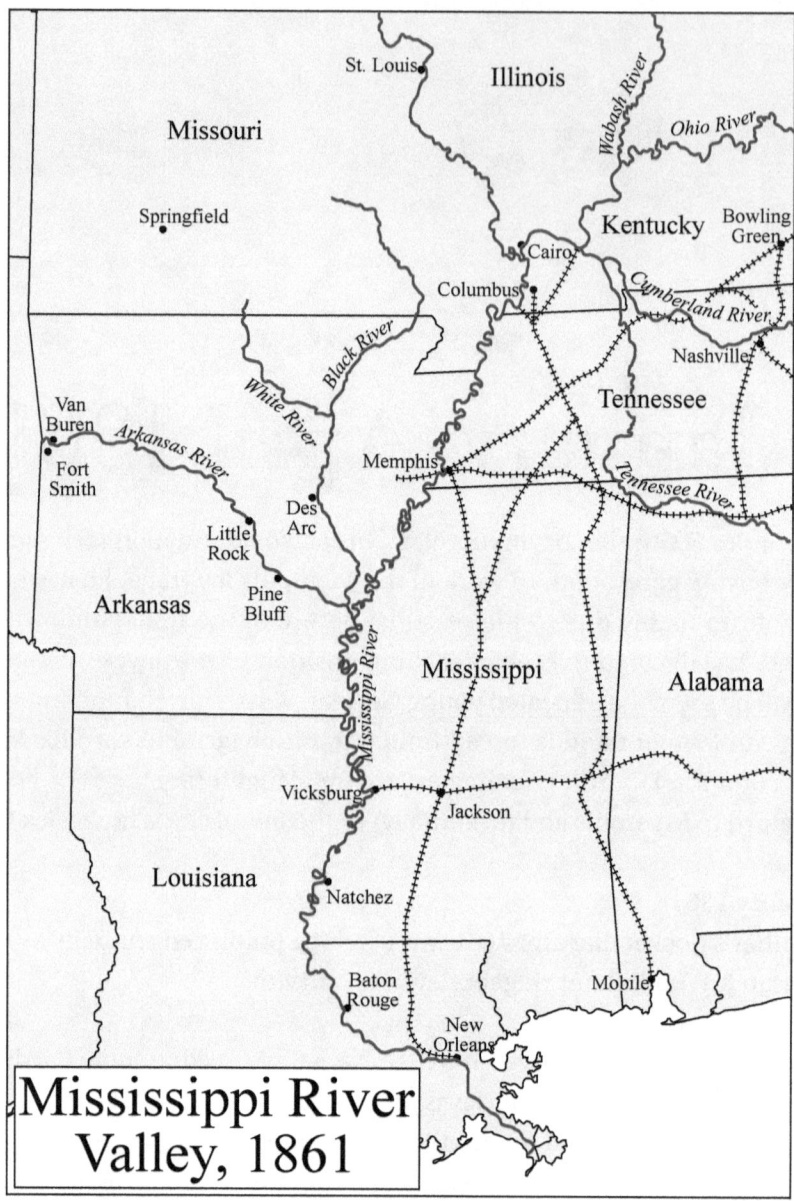

Mississippi River Valley, 1861

Charles F. Gunther spends most of the next three months with his good friend "Asa." Internal evidence suggests this was Asa Mann Hoffman (1838–87), whom he had known back in Peru, LaSalle County, Illinois: the son of prosperous farmers John and Mary (Mann) Hoffman. Asa returned to LaSalle County after the Civil War to clerk at a local store. Like Gunther, Asa became an active Freemason.

The reference to "Houston" suggests that Gunther traveled aboard the steamboat *Frontier City,* captained by Sam Houston, which was one of several steamboats arriving at Little Rock on January 4. The *Frontier City* sank in the Arkansas River a few days later.

> [Wednesday, January 2, 1861] This is a cold cloudy + disagreeable morning and I must say I felt rather bad to think that we are not going above Pine Bluff but as luck would happen it rained all day and the river is rising slowly. We made considerable headway, reached Pine Bluff at 2 o'ck and laid up for the night. I went through the city + I must say it was a regular Arkansas city not up to my expectations. There are a great many poorly set up low frame houses + no fence around the Court House square in fact the whole place looks neglected + a great want of taste among the citizens. The boys all went up to a dance in the Eve I stayed at the boat all eve, reading and had a game of cards with several others.
>
> [Thursday, January 3, 1861] This is a bright and sunshiny day. We left Pine Bluff at 8 and are making good progress toward Little Rock. The country on each side of the river looks well settled and the rail zig zag fences, pine trees + sun shine gives part of it a home like appearance or old Peru Creek scene. There is nothing of any difference to mention, some fun with the passengers. Retired late.
>
> [Friday, January 4, 1861] As usual we tied up at night + started this morning at daylight. The day is fine, but rather chilly. The scenery is about the same as before not much difference from below. We see lots of geese + ducks. They were shot at numerous times by the passengers but got none, too shy. We arrived at Little Rock about 1 o'ck. The city has a better appearance than any other

Little Rock Arsenal and army barracks, 1861, from Harper's Weekly, *March 9, 1861*

on the river. A good landing, walked the place some with Asa + stayed on boat all Eve. Retired early.

[Saturday, January 5, 1861] We payed our bill and got lodging and board for a few days at the George's House. I was rather disappointed with the place, very poor accommodations and awful room and bed but we have concluded to stay for a day or two and make the best of it, it is chiefly today. Asa and I walked over the city some there are some very nice residences + beautiful yards, but the business part of the city is very poor not really a good store in the place. Visited the Halls of the Legislature, now in session.

[Sunday January 6, 1861] Little Rock. This is a beautiful day and very much like a spring day at home. The numerous church bells are ringing which reminds me of the Sabbath. Asa + I walked out to the barracks, the grounds are very beautiful and everything is in good taste. I see Mr. Rose this morn he has been fined for selling his corn, rather hard—I stayed at the House most of the day. It rained some at noon. We returned early after having a chat with the landlord.

[Monday, January 7, 1861] This is a beautiful day and very much like a warm spring day at home. The sun shines quite warm. Asa + I

Arkansas Statehouse, from Scribner's Monthly, *October, 1874*

walked over the city some. We had considerable trouble last night. Asa was quite sick but better today. Loafing goes very hard, and we try to kill time the best we can + know how. We are both almost starved, for myself altogether, but I am going to raise the issue.

[Tuesday, January 8, 1861] We got up this morning as usual, about 7-1/2 o'ck. This is another bright and beautiful day. We are making the best out of our boarding house we can, it is not such as we should like, but we must make the best of it. Asa + I hunted most all day for Rose, but did not find him, but fortunately fell in with the Searcy Co. gents and all night. I borrowed $6 from Mr. Ashlee this Eve. Heard a speech in the Legislature by Col. Thompson.

The *Arkansas Weekly Gazette,* January 12, 1861, reported on the speech by Colonel John Baker Thompson (1834–62), president of Saint John's College in Little Rock. Thompson, a Virginia Military Institute graduate, soon left the college to become a lieutenant colonel of the 1st Arkansas

Volunteers. He was killed at the Battle of Shiloh. According to a local teacher, Thompson said the North was not well educated because they did not take the right view of slavery: "[As such] they rejected ... reason & common sense. I thought that Thompson knew better than that."[1]

"Ashlee" is probably William V. Ashley (1820–82), agent for Searcy County merchant Ludwick McCrory (see February 6, 1861 entry).

In the era prior to television, radio, and movies, people attended political speeches for entertainment. Gunther will attend many such speeches during his stay in the South, more to kill the time than because of any interest in what the speaker had to say.

> [Wednesday, January 9, 1861] We felt rather bad at the idea of Rose leaving us this morning, we learnt this A.M. that he had gone home. This is a fine day but looks some like rain this P.M. We see Melton and he says we will be all right with him to go along. We made the best of the day sitting around at the house. I bought a *NY Herald* the latest I could get Dec. 29th I feel the blues a little, but keep cheering ourselves up with the idea that all will be right hereafter.

Charles Gunther will spend the next month either traveling with or living with "Mr. Melton." This is probably Andrew Jackson Melton (1815–64), a Tennessee-born farmer in Searcy County, who with his brothers Richard N. (1826–98), William Crockett (1830–90), and James Leonard Melton (1832–63) farmed in Searcy County. They were sons of James Craig Melton (1788–60) and Mary Crockett.

> [Thursday, January 10, 1861] This is a beautiful + pleasant day, another spring day. I expected to start to day, but we were again disappointed. Asa + I amused ourselves by walking out to the Penitentiary and in the suburbs of the city. We feel a little dubious about our trip + expect some trouble to get a start. But however our hopes are for the better. Almost without money + no friends is a peculiar predicament to be placed in—spent the Eve at the reading newspapers.

> [Friday, January 11, 1861] This is a muggy + gloomy day it rained some all day. We left Little Rock in company with Mr. Melton for Searcy Co. the first trip of my life with an ox team afoot. Leaving the Rock at 10-1/2 after buying some bread we made slow progress and pitched our tent + made camp fires for the night, after some time we had our supper consisting of fried pork + bread + coffee, which I must say was exceedingly good for our hungry stomach + as soon as over, we laid down in tent + took a nap the first in my life in fact.

Oxen teams were the common method of transporting wagonloads of goods across rough terrain. The *Arkansas Weekly Gazette*, March 10, 1860, had a whole article on "Managing and Feeding Working Oxen," which included such tips as "Never use the whip but from necessity" and "Never speak a word to an ox without a meaning."

> [Saturday, January 12, 1861] After taking a pretty good sleep under the circumstances + firing up once during the night, we breakfasted about 6-1/2 + started on our trip northward refreshed + reinvigorated all hands around. I did not feel as sore as I expected, after traveling all forenoon + passing numerous windowless low shanties + poor inhabitants. We took a rest at 12, thus refreshing we passed along through Conway Arkansas. I see nothing particular noticeable except a turnip patch which we made use of thus traveling 20 miles we put up for the night in a empty shanty + I am sorry to say we ran out of good bread.

Gunther spends the next two months in the hilly region around Searcy County, a region of subsistence farming with few slaves and little interest in slavery.

> Prior to the Civil War, virtually every citizen of Searcy County engaged in some form of agriculture.... None could be considered overly prosperous, even by Arkansas's limited standards of the day. Most were

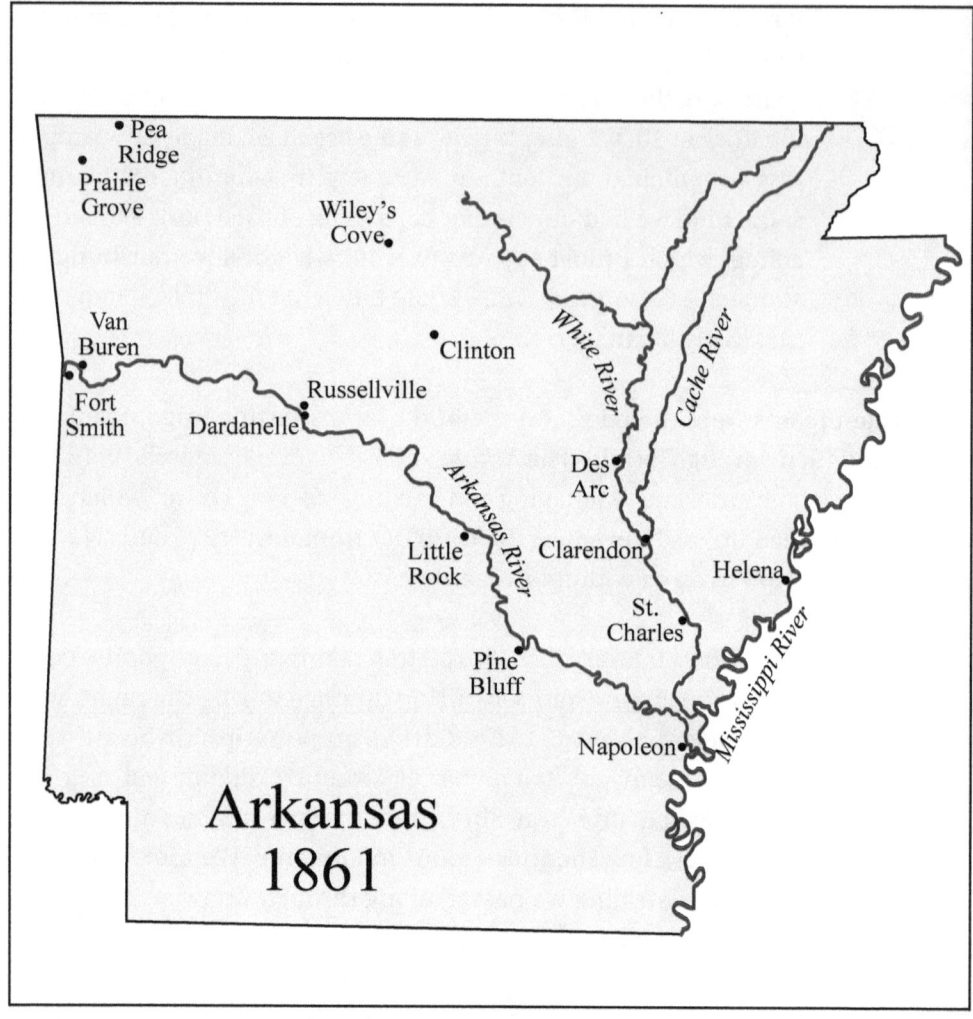

yeoman farmers, raising crops mainly for their own use and heavily supplementing their diets with wild game. About one-third of the population grew tobacco for barter or personal use, more than six percent produced butter and almost ten percent made beeswax. Corn was the predominant row crop, with little or none of the county's land in cotton or rice....

Antebellum architecture in Searcy County tended toward the functional and utilitarian. "I never saw a roof nailed on until I was nearly grown," Basil Brown Thomas, an early resident, remembered. Houses were built and topped off with 'rib poles,' with the boards laid upon them, then were weighted with 'weight poles.' Chimneys were of split logs with rock backs and jambs at the base, while stems were of wood and mud. Floorboards consisted of split logs, and house logs were rarely hewn.... Although some corn and cotton were produced as cash crops and animal pelts were sold to garner what little cash might be needed to purchase salt, tea, coffee, and other items that could not be produced on the farmstead, a barter economy predominated. Trading posts were located in most communities, but most family farmsteads were fairly self-sufficient. Politically, the voters of Searcy County were primarily Jacksonian Democrats nationally and Whig supporters in local elections.[2]

Conway County, Arkansas, was formed in 1825 and named after Congressman Henry Wharton Conway of Arkansas.

[Sunday, January 13, 1861] Oh dear what a day. I was woke up several times during the night with the patter of the rain on our shanty roof + all the horrors of a rainy day were pictured in my mind. We started about 8 o'ck + traveled all day through Conway A up hill + down. The rain continued without termination all day. I keep comfortable + body dry by having a quilt wrapped around me. Asa looks like a drowned rat. Mr. Melton + the boys don't appear to make much of its fun for them, but h_ll for us, we put up at Bradley North of the creek, + after cooking our supper we made our beds up in the kitchen floor + slept.

> [Monday, January 14, 1861] The night passed off rather hard + not as comfortable as before. Our bed clothes caught on fire but was timely discovered by Asa + extinguished. It is a wet + drizzling day, some foggy + traveling is very unpleasant, the roads however are better than I expected, hard + sandy. We traveled through Van Buren A most of the day + arrived at Hatchett's near Clinton about dark where we put up for the night + the kindness of two little girls got us up a very good supper. The first table we sat down to since leaving the Rock, thus warm + comfortable by a good fire + feel rejoiced at our good luck + what is more a good bed.

King Hatchett (1810–61), a wealthy Tennessee-born farmer in Van Buren County, kept an open house for travelers.

> [Tuesday, January 15, 1861] Contrary to our expectations, it rains to day again + o dear how it came down the whole forenoon perfectly poured down. I had my blanket around me + thus kept dry. We stopped at Clinton the county seat of Van Buren Co. it is a miserable looking place all log houses except the court house, which is very small one, it lay in a hollow surrounded by hills on all sides, after crossing several creeks we struck the hills which were very hard for the oxen to go over, thus we plodded along all day it stopped raining some at noon + we put up for the night at Copeland's shanty very poor + drank Corn Coffee for the first time they have not even the comforts of life. Slept on the floor.

With some 2,200 residents, Clinton, Arkansas, isn't much bigger today than it was in 1861. Gunther is rather dismissive of Clinton—"a miserable looking place"—but by next month Gunther is more impressed by Clinton's inhabitants, as he returns from Searcy County. See the February 22, 1861, diary entry.

"Copeland's shanty"—Probably the home of the Joab Copeland (1836–1918) who lived in Van Buren County in 1860.

[Wednesday, January 16, 1861] After passing a terrible night + little rest + sleep with the cold wind blowing in on all sides I got up sat at the fire to keep warm. Asa sat up all night + looks used up this morning. We had a scanty breakfast + like all the other meals was corn + hog. We traveled 12 miles to Mr. Melton's house, over hills + terrible rough roads, we passed over several creeks, see a mill a poor affair. Entered Wiley's Cove at 1 o'ck the land here looks very good + a little like home soil. There is a fine camp meeting ground here. We arrived at Melton's house at 2 o'ck + feel rejoiced that our journey is all most at an end. We had a good supper + went to bed early + sleep on feathers again.

Named for Chief Wiley, a local Indian chief, Wiley's Cove follows Wiley's Creek and is noted for its limestone rock formations. The village of Wiley's Cove was renamed Leslie after the Civil War, in honor of Colonel Samuel Leslie, who built a two-story home here.

[Thursday, January 17, 1861] After a good night's rest I feel quite refreshed this a.m. Mr. Melton has a good place and we all feel at home, considering ourselves strangers. I started for Big Flats at 11-1/2 Asa is unable to go can't get a saddle after 5 hours awful riding and such roads + hills indescribable in this brief space, through a drenching rain + hail storm, and a deep rarity for the sight of a habitation in a perfect wilderness. I arrived at my destination Big Flatts, at the shanty of Mr. Rose who has not yet returned home + I feel he has been foully played with. After taking some supper we sat at fire chatting. The rain continues. We [have] a good bed.

Big Flat Township is in eastern Searcy County. In 1860 the brothers Frederick (1804–71) and Silas (1815–72) Rose lived in Big Flat Township.

[Friday, January 18, 1861] After a good night's sleep in the bed 4 men in two beds and 3 men on the floor, we got up at 6 o'ck. The weather is bright + shining today I see the great place called Big Flatts, a few log shanties + very poor people. I made up my mind I did not wish to live in any such community if possible. I started for the Cove at 9-1/2 + arrived at 2 o'ck am glad to get back over such a long rough road. The ride was refreshing + pleasant in contrast to today I knew where I was going. We tried to shoot some rabbit in the Eve. Hit many rabbits but didn't get. We had a good supper + I did my duty to close the chimney. Had a good glass of milk + layed out in the Eve.

[Saturday, January 19, 1861] We got up in regular farmer style at daybreak the euphonic words of Jim Jones + Smith get up salute our ears, we manage to roll out in a cold room + get on our duds in as good a time as possible and scud for the fire. The weather is pleasant. I amused myself around the place helping to cut wood + turn the grind stone. Asa called around some of his intended school friends to see what first facts were, not very good he reported but we are bound to make the thing go, sure as we are in teacher's position, at present. We spent the Eve I working our land for the whole. Returned at 7-1/2 o'ck.

[Sunday, January 20, 1861] This is a fine day, we sat around the fire place all morning doing nothing. Mr. Melton had some corn pone and so we did not go to church which is nearby. Wiley's Cove is a valley between many surrounding hills, well settled with good people and good land as a general thing the people are very poor and have no advantages we have [at] home. No schools and no markets here and money scarce. We went up to Bradshaw's this Eve. I as usual sit at the fire during the Eve and chattered on matters and things in general.

[Monday, January 21, 1861] The weather continues clear and sun shiny. As I did not get back from Bradshaws and stayed I tried fishing with the boys in the creek but got nothing. The ground is froze up in the morning but thaws up during the day which makes the road very bad. There is nothing going on to mention, except things look very blue in this section and very scarce. We had some pop corn this Eve, and sat chatting, retired early, Melton is absent from home.

[Tuesday, January 22, 1861] I started this morning for the county seat of Searcy County, Burrowville a very small miserable looking place a few shanties and about 3 small frame houses. The courthouse is a small inferior looking building. I see nothing very interesting. Made the acquaintance of Dickerman. I left about 1 ½ o'ck, lost my saddle blanket. The view from the top of the Backbone hills is beautiful, and the mountains in the distance loom up in perfect grandeur, spent the eve as usual.

Burrowville (now Marshall) is still the county seat of Searcy County. It is located at the base of Devil's Backbone Mountain. Henry Dickerman (b. ca. 1824, Kentucky), practiced law in Bear Creek Township in 1860.

[Wednesday, January 23, 1861] I was in the expectation of seeing Dickerman today, as he promised he would come to see me. The mountain folks were washing, and I sat the greater part of the day reading. The weather is cloudy and some drizzling rain. It turned quite cold in the evening and the wind blew, and the snow came down in regular northern style. Blowing through all the cracks of the roof and house I went to bed with the snow coursing down on my face. Oh dear how I wish hot spring came here my only prayer to get out of this country.

[Thursday, January 24, 1861] This morning the ground is covered with about 3 inches of snow and quite cold very much like home winter weather. Mr. Melton and I hunted rabbits. We caught one in the stone fence alive, I skinned it and we had it for supper. I spent the balance of the afternoon helping to get out some wood from the woods. I felled 3 trees, new business—Asa came over in the eve from Bradshaw's and stopped. We had some news and newspapers up to the 15th inst. Early for this section.

There were numerous people named Bradshaw in Searcy and Van Buren Counties in 1860. It is unclear which Bradshaw household "Asa" stayed with, but the likely one is the household of James Henry Bradshaw (1845–1920: see January 26 entry) and his father John (1817–65).

[Friday, January 25, 1861] The snow did not all melt off, we went hunting rabbits this a.m. and shot one on the creek. We went up to Edding's shoe shop, a natural cobbler and a perfect genius. The sun shined warm, but the snow makes a slow progress in melting. The prospects for a school for Asa and myself look very gloomy and I fear we shall want ere we get to some other point on the river. I shall remain until I have frozen these [rabbits] and see what prospects are.

[Saturday, January 26, 1861] I managed to get up at the usual hour, about daylight. The weather continues pleasant but the snow keeps on the ground some yet. Melton and the girls went out to Burrowville I wrote a long letter to Strauss of 12 pages after dinner I may send one to James Bradshaw's house to see Asa. The home sick we both are in a peculiar position, no money + no prospects of making any, but have to trust to good fortune + providence for our safe deliverance from this land of darkness and poverty. Had a pleasant time in the Eve childing.

[Sunday, January 27, 1861] We got up something later than at Mr. M__ [Melton] this morning. Asa and I were talking over matters + things about our trip homeward. I am only waiting to hear from the Dr. to determine my future course of action. Bradshaw has a very good place, as much so as I have seen here. He is a good man in my opinion. Old Griffith son + Mrs. B. all went to town. Asa + I stayed + made up the day talking and drawing some sketches of our adventures. I left for Melton's a[t] 5 o'ck.

[Monday, January 28, 1861] This is a bright and shiny day and quite warm for the season. I helped to get out some timber for fence, and in the p.m. we killed two hogs. We had a good time a-cleaning them—a new business for me, but there is nothing like pitching in and making the best of it. Time is all I wish to fly for a month, and then for some better land of promise. I am very content under the circumstances, and not yet sick at heart.

[Tuesday, January 29, 1861] Theres's nothing to change the monotony of the usual routine of getting up in the morning. Breakfast as usual—Mr. Melton went to a house raising the boys and I hauled logs and what a time we had—such torment I have not had for a long time. The ox going generally where they pleased and I after. Tore my pants some. The weather is pleasant and quite like home. Spring weather. Retired early as usual.

[Wednesday, January 30, 1861] Today we all went to work hauling wood as it is the only day we have until the oxen leave—it is pleasant and not much like work today. I am getting quite proficient in the handling of an axe, and the way the woods has to take it it is a caution, there I am amusing myself and manage to kill time I have not seen for some time. Oh that I was in Memphis again where I expect to be next month.

[Thursday, January 31, 1861] This is a disagreeable rainy day. We are unable to do anything outside, we shelled some corn this morning and afterwards went over to see Crockett in Lane. Melton took dinner at homes the roads were very bad and unpleasant to go calling, but the object is to make calls when you cannot do anything else. There we spent the day, reading the newspapers but there was nothing of any special interest in these. I expect to see some awful secession news, but it did not [materialize].

Jacob Virgil Johnson Crockett (1816–78), a Van Buren County farmer, was probably a cousin of the Meltons.

February 1861
Increasingly, Gunther feels trapped in Arkansas. Suitable jobs don't appear, and his only old friend, Asa Hoffman, returns to Memphis. "The political world looks dark" to the loyal Gunther, as he reads of more and more states seceding from the Union. Even in northwest Arkansas, at this time largely Unionist, secession fever mounts. Although Arkansas voters reject immediate secession in a February 18 election, it becomes obvious that Gunther—a Unionist, a northerner, and of foreign birth—may face hard times if he remains. The few newspapers in this rural area usually are a week or more behind the time in the news they report, frustrating Gunther intellectually and leading him to read any book available.

> [Friday, February 1, 1861] It cleared off some today and it is quite warm. And went over to help Addaire to move—after some delay he got started, we had a great time getting the sheep and cattle started, I was on the old gray mare, she travels something like an old cow, at the crossing of the creek we had a great time. Addaire plunged in to help out the sheep and cattle and got a perfect ducking. We met Asa near Bradshaw's, he returned with us, got home in the Eve. Killed a hog and after tea read the papers, the *Voice*—a tip top paper.

> [Saturday, February 2, 1861] This is a very cold and Wintry day, a regular Northern day. The coldest I have SEEN South. Melton and I started for Russellville, and such roads I have not traveled over for an age, a perfect mud hole from Melton's to the town. There were numerous people there all regular Ark. Still the day being cold blankets were all the go, a very motley looking crowd.

I was some stared at by them, the meeting being a Union one, speeches were made by Stephenson, Campbell & Leslie. I got home at 4 o'clock, and retired early.

Russellville, today the county seat of Pope County, is adjacent to Searcy County. South Carolina born farm "Addaire"—John Kilgore Adair (1828–94).

This Union rally featured speeches by local notables. Tennessee-born John Campbell (1806–79) had been a state representative. Elected to the Secession Convention from Searcy County, he was one of only five delegates who voted against the Ordinance of Secession. Samuel Leslie (1809–90), a Kentucky-born farmer, was colonel of the county militia. North Carolina–born Andrew R. Stephenson (1797–1864) practiced medicine. Despite their speeches, Campbell and Leslie eventually supported the Confederacy. Stephenson, described as a "staunch Union man," remained loyal and gave three of his sons to the Union army. See Goodspeed's *Reminiscences of the Ozark Region*, 123, 639, for more on Campbell and Stephenson.

[Sunday, February 3, 1861] This is a moderate fine day. I have lately got rather irreligious, not being in a church since Christmas last, at Memphis. I am rather afraid to go, being a stranger and gazed at too much for my taste by the natives. I manage to assure myself reading and doing nothing and hoping that time will only pass as that is my only wish at present. We sat at Eve at the fire and retire much too early for my taste.

[Monday, February 4, 1861] Got up as usual much too early for my taste, with all the doors left open by the young ones and a perfect gust of cold wind blowing through my log chamber, pretty cold getting up. Very much like a barn, but it is nothing after you are used to it. Melton and I were out cutting logs for his log & stone fence at the creek. It was a hard job, and one of the hardest days work I have done for a long time, but anything to pass time. Retired early and nested well for that night sure.

[Tuesday, February 5, 1861] Asa came over from Bradshaw's this morning, It is a pleasant and warm day, and went down to the woods and got out a trough for the women to wash, a hard job to cut & saw and very tiresome—I was all morning or afternoon rather mending my breeches, & such mending it is, but necessity is the mother of invention and the job was well done. The Sheriff and ___ stopped at our house all night went down I had Kesner mend my boot, they must hold out.

The family of Tennessee-born George Washington Kesner (1805–63) were neighbors of the Meltons and the Bradshaws.

[Wednesday, February 6, 1861] We went down and got Mr. Cotton on the wagon [sic] and stayed around the house, did not work much today. Asa feels much for home—see Col. Campbell & Sheriff McCrory's wagon stopped for Asa, he concluded to go and would over take them the next day by horse, it took us rather by surprise. The weather is pleasant, freezing by night and thaw by day, we had a general chit chat in the Eve around the fire place, Campbell, Sheriff, Asa & myself.

Ludwick McCrory (McRorey) (1814-72), was a merchant in Burrowville.

[Thursday, February 7, 1861] After sleeping on the floor Asa and I got up early, exchanged my carpet sack for his trunk, & after breakfast he started for the wagon. It was very unpleasant for me thus to part with him but I felt it as an imperious necessity to wait for my letter from the city—and then, ho for White River. He will thus beat me 10 days home. The political world looks dark and omens of bad times, though 10 days behind the rest of creation in news. We get the papers today & I read them all Eve—the *Voice* as usual very good.

[Friday, February 8, 1861] The weather is fine and pleasant, we work hauling wood & logs, and at 3 o'ck went to Russellville to attend lodge meeting. I was examined & admitted the room is way up in the 3rd story of the court house attic, wood and common looking room but answered every purpose, the members are all good bricks and the work is very good considering I took the Lolies [?] Degree also. Secret Monitor, Masters Reliance, Knight of Constantine, and the Traders Degree, we kept up until one o'ck, and then put up at Old Burns—slept in the attic, Melton & I. I am well pleased with my visit and made some remarks.

Gunther's diary is filled with his activities in Freemasonry. At this time he belonged to the Saint John's Lodge No. 13 of Peru, Illinois.

[Saturday, February 9, 1861] We loafed around town until 12 o'ck. The weather is cloudy, started for Melton's and got home all right—I was woke up by the beautiful strains of a violin in the hands of young Burns, who played in regular Ark style, sawing on two strings at a time. We had plenty of eggs for breakfast and I made out very well for a small man, the roads have improved some & considerable dryer, we work at the Chicken House and after tea read some in the *Voice* & retired early.

[Sunday, February 10, 1861] It rained all night and came down in perfect showers, but it stopped this am. We all went to the campground meeting house there was a small congregation out, a regular Ark meeting. There is considerable Christian feeling manifested among them. We took dinner with Crocket's Melton, we had some flour biscuit, something new, and returned home—read some, and amused myself generally. I am only wishing for time to pass and next week I will be off for the happy Land of Canaan—the White River.

"Crocket's Melton" probably refers to William Crockett Melton. See January 9 entry.

[Monday, February 11, 1861] Today we went down to the field and all pitched in making rails. I have ever on excel in the art, and my work is not of much use, but it is better [than] doing nothing. Jesse is helping us. After dinner I went over to Len Melton's to stop a day or two, he had one of his hogs carried off last night by the wolves, we had a good social chat at the fire in the Eve. I was also reading Nigine's *Biblical Antiquities* a very fine book of its kind & very instructive.

Probably Francis A. Cox's 1852 work, *Biblical Antiquities*. A Baptist minister, Cox wrote numerous works.

[Tuesday, February 12, 1861] We got up a little later than usual—after breakfast we went hauling rails. I lessened the Brush leaves. After dinner I wrote an article for Melton and the Union meeting at Russellville 2nd inst. The weather continued fine & pleasant we chased up several rabbits very plenty here time is fast passing and Spring will be here my only wish at present. I think a great deal about home just now, but however I don't let it trouble my mind. A letter from home would be appreciated by me you may be assured.

[Wednesday, February 13, 1861] I left Len's this a.m. and mailed my letter to Rob Morris & to Iowa on tax business. It is cloudy today. We all went to splitting rails and worked until about 3 o'ck when the rain spit down on us. I read *Josephus* until Eve. It is very interesting & I will undertake to read it at some future day. Asa is no doubt on White River to the Happy Land of Canaan, I wish I were along with him. We have good indications of an early Spring, and some talk of planting in about 10 days.

[Thursday, February 14, 1861] It got colder today & a strong north wind is blowing. Went down to work in the celebrated rail business, worked all day more or less to keep the blood in circulation and give an appetite. It has quite a rainy appearance here yet, though but little ice if any. The times in this country continue very hard and no money is to be seen. We had a genuine Ark teacher staff with us, a fine specimen and odd genius in his way—and suitable for the big Ark region where he has taught.

[Friday, February 15, 1861] The weather being somewhat pleasant although pretty cold, I went to the store and then went to town with the horse, the roads were muddy and riding very unpleasant but I met with no success in my expected letter and no mail from the Rock. I feel rather "down in the mouth," nothing but disappointment appears to me at all my efforts. I have determined to leave for the Point [West Point, AR. See March 2 entry] the first opportunity and then good bye to north Ark. Hope on and Providence will see me though yet.

[Saturday, February 16, 1861] This is a cold and disagreeable wintry day the wind blowing with some snow. I sat in the house all morning reading *Josephus*. I undertook to help to haul some wood. But Smith hurt my hand so I concluded to quit for the day. I am getting more and more anxious to go to Memphis as time passes fast I am going to make the best of it. My hope is to get to M__ [Memphis] by the 1st boat and try my luck again in the city.

A Roman-Jewish historian, Flavius Josephus (37–100 A.D.) wrote extensively on the history of Israel and Judaism, providing contemporary insights into early Christianity. Gunther probably read William Whiston's popular English translation of Josephus's works.

[Sunday, February 17, 1861] The weather has not moderated much, but some sun shines. I have not done any of the necessary chores, but take it as easy as possible and keep my clean clothes for the lower country. I read *Josephus* all morning and talked about matters and things in the afternoon with Kesner and

Crocket. I am getting used to farm life some but don't think I would get along so well were it not for the hopes of the future—i.e., getting out of this country.

[Monday, February 18, 1861] I went down to Jno Kesner's to get my boots mended & after helped Melton to haul logs. It is cold and cloudy with a damp south wind, yet not sufficiently cold to make ice. I hauled my trunk down to the store & I intend to start for Clinton tomorrow. The election for the Convention takes place today, the first Ark election I have seen. Everything goes on quietly a big vote is polled here for No Convention and Union, there is no a single disunion vote in this precinct (Wiley's Cove).

Old-style political conflict scarred the secession movement in Arkansas. Politically, the state split into three main groups: Whigs, regular Democrats, and secessionist Democrats. Northwest Arkansas, where Searcy County is located, had been settled largely by farmers from Tennessee and the Upper South, and like the rest of the Upper South, most inhabitants were regular Democrats and (at most) reluctant secessionists. The Arkansas voters who braved the near-freezing weather on February 18 approved the calling of a secession convention by a large majority (27,412 to 15,826) but elected a majority of Unionist delegates to the convention. The seventy-seven elected convention delegates convened in Little Rock on March 4 and rejected secession by a 39-35 vote. The firing on Fort Sumter and the outbreak of the war caused the convention to later reverse itself and vote to secede. Searcy County's delegate John Campbell was one of only five delegates to vote against secession. See Michael Dougan, *Confederate Arkansas*, for the best summary of this confused political situation.

Even after Arkansas's secession, Searcy County remained mostly Unionist. Colonel Sam Leslie's militia arrested more than 100 members of a local Unionist. "peace society," and sent eighty-seven of them to Little Rock in chains. Many more Unionists hid in the mountains to avoid the draft or enlisted in the Union army.

[Tuesday, February 19, 1861] After breakfast I made ready and wished the folks all good bye. Mrs. Melton gave me a lot of snacks for on the way. Smith & I went on as far as the mill on Johns and after waiting until 11-1/2 o'ck we got started for Clinton. We traveled thus along slowly until almost dark and camped on the mountain this side of Copeland's we had a good fire eat cold lunch and hot coffee for supper made up a good fire and put up two tents for seven of us, the weather is pleasant and warm.

[Wednesday, February 20, 1861] We got up early, had breakfast and pitched tents and made ready for the start of early day's light. The weather is beautiful and fine and very much like a spring day. Traveling is pleasant today, the scenery along the road is very mountainous, and none of the land is cultivated in my opinion, and all it will be good for is to hunt. We passed through Clinton and eat lunch this side of Little Red River fork. I put up at the Hatchett's where I intend to stay until I get a chance for the Point. This is a very pleasant place to stop.

[Thursday, February 21, 1861] I got up this morning after a good night's sleep on feathers. I am now comfortably situated at Hatchett's. I went over to town to get a sign board made. I amused myself talk and sitting around I also read the Bible not of reason by G. Spring it is a fine work and has removed many doubts that I previously entertained upon the subject. The weather is bright sun shiny and warm the frogs are croaking the doves cooing & the birds are singing that spring must be at hand.

"Spring's Bible"—Gardiner Spring's popular 1847 book, *The Bible not of Man: or, The Argument for the Divine Origin of the Sacred Scriptures.*

[Friday, February 22, 1861] The weather continues bright and fine. I painted my sign board for Hatchett three times to day and dried it at the fire. I finished reading Spring's Bible, and am much pleased with it. I did nothing but sit around and paint a new business, but anything to make it pass. I am feeling much better than I did in Searcy Co. and under the circumstances enjoy myself. There is a marked difference between here and Searcy Co. among the people, for the better.

[Saturday, February 23, 1861] I was woke up by some rain and storm it did not last long however, it cleared off again & turned somewhat cooler. I was busy part of the day painting my sign and made a good job of it. It pleases all, well done. Today a week's board made, sure times here are very hard. I saw a drove of mules return from the Southern market today on their way back. I sat at the fire all Eve. King is writing under my instructions.

[Sunday, February 24, 1861] This Sunday, like most of my Arkansas Sundays, I have spent doing nothing here, being no church near. I sat reading the Encyclopedia of history, the day is fine. I see a lot of the Clinton *bon ton*, on their way to church, gay looking indeed—curls and flats—I'm making time pass very well. H__ being up and place leaving a little fun with the boys and being very play[ful]—I feel perfectly contented and am taking things easy.

[Monday, February 25, 1861] The boys started on a turkey hunt before breakfast. But got nothing. They are said to be very plenty around here all kinds of game. I painted my sign all day, and making hardly all that I did though the day. The weather is pleasant, still, too much so for me to be laying about in the sunshine. The news is good, Old Tennessee leading the van with 23,000 for union. Drovers Appleby stopped with us all night on their way home to Mississippi. We retired at about 9 o'ck I sleeping with Hicks.

Tennessee indeed voted for Union on February 11 (the news getting to rural Arkansas almost two weeks later), voting down the calling of a secession convention by 12,000 (not 23,000) votes, and rejecting secession itself by a much larger margin.

Prominent Searcy resident William Hicks (1829–69) served as county judge prior to the Civil War. During the war he raised Company A of the 32nd Arkansas Infantry, but was forced to retire due to wounds received in 1863.

> [Tuesday, February 26, 1861] This day opens bright and fine. With the sign today it is like Joseph's coat of many colors, but looks well and William H. is pleased with it. I accidently faced with Mr. McElroy and sped off in haste for West Point. I hardly time to say goodbye. Mr. H. furnished me with some meal and house and left giving them all to. We traveled about time and chipper without us sleeping under the blue canopy of heaven for the first time.

Tennessee-born Gashum H. McElroy (1824–89) farmed in Seary County.

> [Wednesday, February 27, 1861] I sleep quite well considering after having a very interesting talk with one Curtis, [illegible]— it was all laugh—We traveled some 24 miles and left Boor's family at that destination. A sing such a time I seen such an arrival. Robies and young ones—perfectly awful—Mac and I hurled another house and made __ something of home. I feel very tired walked all day but glad I got rid of our load. Solstice with a S.C. [Southern Confederacy] an interesting one.

> [Thursday, February 28, 1861] We started about 7 o'ck slept well all night We traveled through a very rough country all day. Very little out fit for anything, perfectly awful. The scenery was not interesting monotonous oak woods, hills, some beautiful water— that's all. We got some bread boxed right up at old Riley Flats, we had a very good supper and a good bed. I enjoyed the travel better today rode in a wagon most all day. I took it easy.

March 1861

This month Gunther finally gives up on Arkansas and returns to his southern base in Memphis. Old friends from Illinois are there to greet him, and he is able to spend some weeks touring the city. And after a period of unemployment the ice trade revives, and he is rehired by Bohlen & Wilson, his old ice company. However, the Memphis of 1861 differs from the Memphis of a year before. Secession and politics dominate the dinner table conversations. The ice trade, and Memphis trade in general, depends on steamboats enjoying free passage along the Mississippi River. Secession and war promise to curtail or eliminate that trade and isolate Gunther from his Illinois home.

> [Friday, March 1, 1861] We got started rather late. Our cattle got strayed off we had a good breakfast. The weather is beautiful and could not be wished for better. The sun shone great wagon. We traveled through White County all day. I passed through Searcy in the afternoon. It is a small miserable looking place but a good business point. I did not look around any for business opportunities. My point is Memphis now, sure. We camped this side of Searcy, slept without any tent on the ground of the very hard supper. We look worn I being cook.

One of the earliest towns to be founded in Arkansas, Searcy (pop. 20,000 today) was, and is, the county seat of White County. In 1861 it boasted a polytechnic military school. Today the city is home to Harding University.

> [Saturday, March 2, 1861] I slept well last night and got up about 4-1/2 o'ck. Cooked our breakfast and got started around 6 o'ck. We traveled many plantations that looked some imports some of those yesterday. One wagon got in the mud hole and stuck. We slid it out. I got my breeches torn and had to change and threw them away. The balance of the trail is beautiful and has been for a day or two past. We arrived at West Point, a small place on Little

Red River, where I put up at the Rogers House. The face is very good and the change is quite agreeable.

A small town even today, West Point was incorporated in 1858. By 1860 it boasted 350 inhabitants. Situated at the the highest navigable point on the Little Red River, the town had three general stores and served as a shipment and distribution center for White County.

Pennsylvania-born David Rodgers, age 58, kept a hotel in West Point in 1860.

> [Sunday, March 3, 1861] This is gloomy rainy day nothing doing no church but this place (West Point) I sat around and amused myself the best I could reading—and signed for boat to come. This is a small place and I don't see any elements to make it a place of any account. The people are a difficult set of looking people from those above, I have interested myself by reading Bulwer Lytton, *Ernest Maltravers* a love-sick story for its language.

Englishman Edward Bulwer-Lytton (1803–73) wrote numerous very popular novels. The originator of the literary phrase, "It was a dark and stormy night," Bulwer-Lytton's notoriously florid writing style gave rise to the modern, tongue-in-cheek Bulwer-Lytton Award for bad writing. Among his novels was *Ernest Maltravers*.

> [Monday, March 4, 1861] West Point is a dull place for me. Not such a place as I would like to live in, it is clear and pleasant today, there don't appear to be any business doing I can see except Rogers the old captain tries to make us feel comfortable at his house. There are several waiting like myself for a boat. The confounded saw mill fooled me several times when sounding—I read most all day and finished *E. Maltravers*, our board is good. I retired early this eve after a good talk with home guests.

> [Tuesday, March 5, 1861] I was woke up this morning at 2 o'ck the good tidings—a boat comes. "Greeted my ears." Up we got! Pulled on breeches and paid our bills got off cheap. I took passage on the steamer *New Madrid* small but good boat. Got up in good season and had a good breakfast. We mislied one way it arrived at Des Arc. Not so much a place as I expected see some lot of news made good progress stopped at Clarendon. I started downstairs after passengers got off.

The steamboat port of Des Arc was an important stop along the White River, shipping cotton and lumber downriver. It was captured by Union forces in January 1863. By war's end, the town's population had shrunk to 400.

Clarendon, Arkansas, located in Monroe County, hosted French hunters and trappers on its river banks as early as 1799. The military road running through the town's boundaries was part of the Trail of Tears and was by the time of Gunther's diary used for military movements by both Union and Confederate forces. Clarendon was held by Confederate forces at this time and remained in Southern hands until 1864, when Union forces succeeded in burning the town to the ground in retaliation for the Confederate sinking of the gunboat USS *Queen City* by General Joseph Shelby.

> [Wednesday, March 6, 1861] I got up this morning about 6-1/2 o'ck still we go down White River. There's nothing of any life out to mention. See some small landings canebrakes wild fowls. We got into the Mississippi River by 11 o'ck, where we met four boats on their way down—the weather cool and chilly, but a sunshiny bright. We have very good fare and quite a contrast with Arc. We made Friars Point at dark. The night is dark I retired at 10 oc. We had newspapers of the 5th and a little news of Lincoln.

Founded in 1836, Friars Point was a major steamboat port on the Mississippi River. It is the county seat of Coahoma County, Mississippi.

Memphis riverfront, from an 1871 image in Every Saturday, *September 23, 1871*

[Thursday, March 7, 1861] We made slow progress up. The Mississippi is high and swift current. I made the acquaintance of a gentleman from Alabama, we had a good time racing with the *Admiral* we burnt pitch + grease in progress and had a very heated race but got beat. We made Memphis by 2 o'ck. I called around on all my friends, they were very glad to get back. I had much to say about Memphis looked big in my eyes after coming out of the woods. I put up at Mrs. McClure's, there is not the crowd there as before.

One English observer painted this portrait of Memphis in 1861:
> This resuscitated Egyptian city is a place of importance, and extends for several miles along the very high bank of the river, though it does not run very far back. The streets are at right angles to the principal thoroughfares, which are parallel to the stream; and I by no means expected to

see the lofty stores, warehouses, rows of shops, and handsome buildings on the broad esplanade along the river, and the extent and size of the edifices public and private in this city, which is one of the developments of trade and commerce created by the Mississippi. Memphis contains nearly 30,000 inhabitants, but many of them are foreigners, and there is a nomad draft into and out of the place, which abounds in haunts for Bohemians, drinking and dancing-saloons, and gaming rooms.[3]

Forty-two-year-old widow Lydia McClure ran a boarding house on Union Street between Main and Front Row.

[Friday, March 8, 1861] I had a good sleep last night, slept with Sam. Got up this morning feeling so much better and made like home. I went around among the business community business prospects are very poor for me. I intend staying around until Mr. Bohlen gets back. The city houses look lively. I made several applications but no go. The weather is pleasant but somewhat chilly. The theater is in full blow but can't go—ain't got any currency. It is hard but honest.

[Saturday, March 9, 1861] I took a stroll around after breakfast and spent most of the day loafing at Bohlen's office. I did not look around any today. I don't see as it is much use at present. Secession is a little talked of but it is kind of dying out here I think. Cockroaches are less numerous. Times all over the city are hard. The boys about the house are about all strapped just like myself, but who cares if success only yet along.

[Sunday, March 10, 1861]. This is a pleasant day but a very dull Sunday and I don't feel much like going to church, so I pass the day partly at Loyd's and took a stroll over the city. The levee looks very empty of boats, there is a lot of freight on the levee. Several

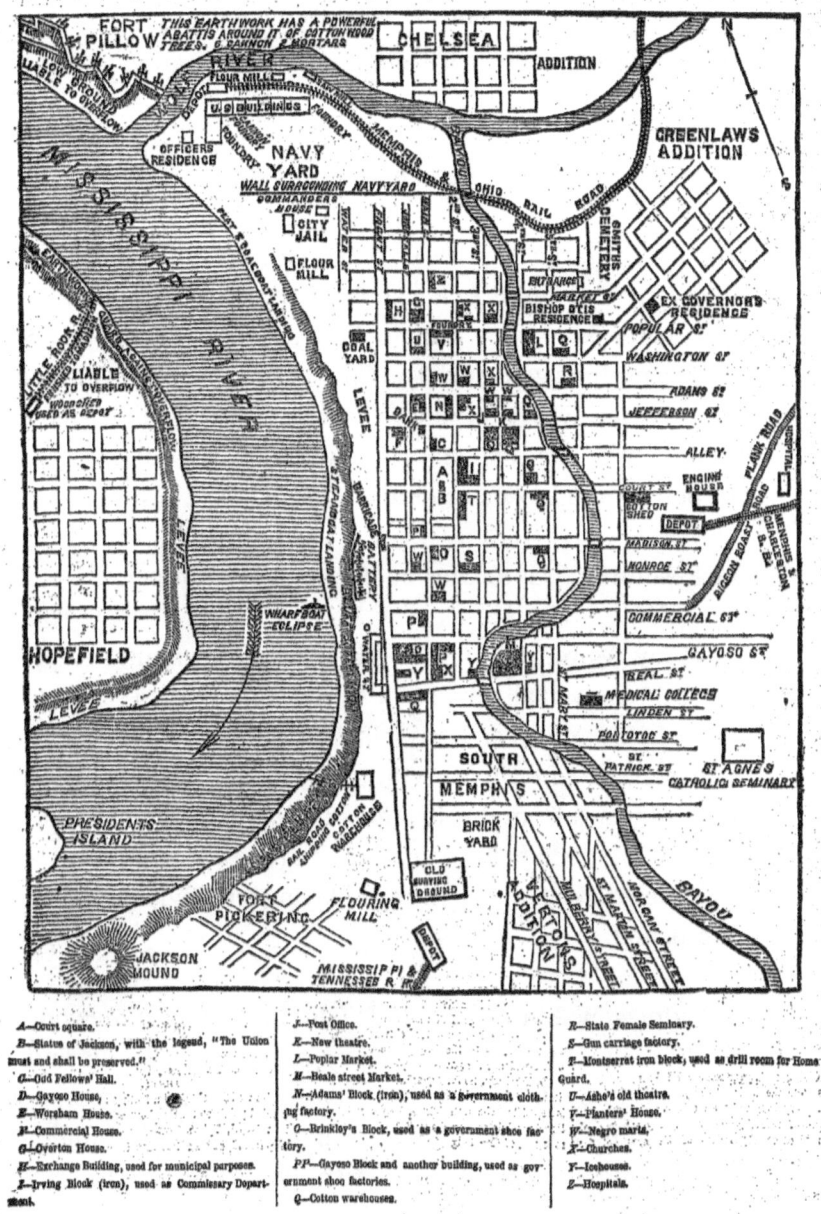

Memphis street map, from New York Herald, December 4, 1861

steamers passed down. Memphis is very quiet for a city of its kind. I see George Coates this Eve. We had a threatened shouting affair at my boarding house but it all ended in a scuffle and throw down. I retired in good season.

"Loyd" may be Stephen S. Lloyd (1819–73), treasurer of the Odd Fellows and a Memphis merchant with offices in Front Row.

[Monday, March 11, 1861] The weather continues pleasant and warm. Memphis beats all for dust, perfectly awful. I spent the greater part of my time looking around the city with Loyd. There's nothing going on. The Christies are here but I am unable to go, reason why: no money. There was an alarm of fire all the firemen were out. I spent all Eve walking around some. Visited the Senate and looked around a little.

The Senate Restaurant was located at 36 North Court Street.

[Tuesday, March 12, 1861]. I had a very poor night's sleep and feel quite unwell all day. I fear somewhat of being sick. I took a dose of pills and elected myself all day and shall take more care of myself hereafter in everything. I stayed at the house most all day. We heard from the steamers *Capitol* will be here Saturday. There's not much political excitement here at present, and secession is less talked of. The thing is playing out. I hope to God it will be crushed.

[Wednesday, March 13, 1861]. I got up feeling somewhat better this a.m. I walked around saw some of my friends and had a good time talking, but I am getting perfectly disgusted with this loafing and I hope that I will be doing something before long. Times here don't appear to brighten up any. The Christies are playing every night, I don't leave the house in the Eve. The theater is playing *Die Frau im Weiss*.

Gunther could have found employment by joining the army, as so many out-of-work Memphisians were doing. But his loyalty to the Union prevailed over his "disgust" and poverty.

The New Memphis Theater hosted Wilkie Collins's famous mystery novel and play, *The Woman in White* (*Die Frau im Weiss*) throughout the second week of March.

Formed in 1843, the famous Christy Minstrels toured the world for many decades under various names.

The local newspaper headlined their performance:

> Christy's Minstrels.—This troupe of minstrels really deserve a degree of praise beyond what we have space to give them. Night by night they have held crowded, indeed over-crowded audiences spell bound with their rich and enchanting music. As instrumentalists, we doubt whether any former company have equaled them. They touch deep the fountains of human sympathy.[4]

[Thursday, March 14, 1861] The day is clear and bright, but a fire feels very comfortable most all day. So cold already. Wind comes from the northwest. There are many boats on the levee, and business there looks brisk. The secession news is about the same, and the thing is dying out plenty. Lincoln's policy is pacific. I spent a great part of the day with Loyd. I like Memphis more from day to day, i.e., city life. I spent the Eve at the setting rooms with the boys talking but having some beer among ourselves.

[Friday, March 15, 1861] I am walking over the city trying to get something to do, but no go yet. Money is scarce. I spent my last dime for a shave. I ran across Pryor at the auction rooms. I was glad to see him and hear the news from home. I having bought a valise and borrow money to pay for it. I spent the day loafing around and went to the Masonic Lodge in the Eve. The Christies are yet here.

[Saturday, March 16, 1861] We were in expectation of the boat *Capitol*, but she did not come across as expected. I have been loafing about the city the greater part of the day. I tried __noldes & Co. today, they said "call next week." Pryor is getting hard up—no work for the moment. I got several letters forwarded from Arkansas from home. It rained some and the weather is cool. I visited my friends Harris, Pryor and myself walked around town, missing like company.

[Sunday, March 17, 1861] I got up this a.m. rather late, the day is cold, many persons are going to church but I have no inclination to go. No work, no money and prospects are such makes things gloomy, but hope reigns supreme. If only the *Capitol* arrives I will try Bohlen [& Wilson]. I was in Pryor's room part of the day and in Loyd's office. Stayed there in the Eve, thought I saw the boat come, but it was not the one, disappointment again.

[Monday, March 18, 1861] We were in hasty expectations of the boats arriving, but at last she came this Eve, we see Mr. Bohlen all night for me. There is nothing doing in the city of note, some of the newspapers still harp on the secession of the south. The *Appeal* and *Avalanche*. I spent the greater part of the day at Loyd's and the Eve at Main Street office. I am very glad I can get a job here, and so goodbye to home. It will be a great relief to me that I will see some Peru folks.

[Tuesday, March 19, 1861] I was down at the ice house the first thing this a.m. See all the folks. News is encouraging from home feel glad to think it is so. Had a good long talk with Lieut. and Capt. Almost the whole fourth Ward is down. I was around the house and bored all day. I feel fine and prospects are good for the future, business on the levee is good and many boats at the landing. I spent the eve at an auction looking on retired early.

J. G. FLOURNOY,

Wholesale Grocer

AND
COMMISSION MERCHANT,

Keeps constantly on hand a large and well selected stock of

CHOICE GROCERIES & PROVISIONS,

Suited to the City and Country Trade.

NO. 11 FRONT ROW,

Between Monroe & Union Sts.,   *MEMPHIS, TENN.*

Strict Attention Paid to Receiving and Forwarding.

BOHLEN, WILSON & CO.,
WHOLESALE & RETAIL.

DEALERS IN ICE

City Ice House, 276 Main Street,

NEXT DOOR TO CLARK'S MARBLE BLOCK,

Depot, on Levee, Water St.,

MEMPHIS, TENN.

We are now building, on the Levee, a very large Ice House, and have made arrangements to have between 5,000 and 6,000 tons of Ice the coming season. When it arrives, we shall be enabled to fill all orders, large or small, and supply our old customers and the public with ice in abundance.

Ad for Bohlen, Wilson & Co., from Tanner's 1859 Memphis City Directory

Memphis Appeal, March 19: "Bohlen, Wilson & Co.'s tow boat *Capitol* arrived last evening with fully five thousand tuns [*sic*] of ice in tow, the largest ever received in this city. The *Capitol* leaves today again for the Illinois river for a similar tow." Bohlen, Wilson & Co.'s steamer *Capitol*, built in Louisville, Kentucky, in 1854, was 235 feet long, with a thirty-five-foot beam, and reputed to be fast. The *Capitol* was one of several steamers Bohlen, Wilson & Co. used to ship ice.

    The brothers Philip Reed Bohlen and William Bohlen, in partnership with Victor Wilson, operated one of the largest ice selling companies in the South. Born in Pennsylvania, the brothers got their start cutting ice out of rivers in Armstrong County, near Pittsburg, and shipping the ice south. In 1850 they established a wholesale ice business in Memphis, in partnership with Vicksburg, Mississippi, ice merchant Victor F. Wilson. Philip (1820–92) left his large collection of books to help found the collection at the Memphis Public Library. Hallum's *The Diary of an Old Lawyer*[5] tells an amusing story about a breach-of-promise suit filed against Philip by the husband of Philip's jilted fiancée. William (1803–88) died in Memphis. When Wilson died in 1865, Huse, Loomis & Co. took over Wilson's interest in the firm, and the company changed its name to the Bohlen-Huse Machine & Lake Ice Company. In Memphis the firm had offices at 296-1/2 Main Street, Water Street, and 372 Second Street.

Irish-born Victor F. Wilson (1812–65) rose to become one of Vicksburg's most prominent citizens. His steamships brought ice down the Illinois River to points south, often stopping at Peru, Illinois, the hub of the Illinois River ice trade. Undoubtedly Charles Gunther first became involved in the ice trade due to the Bohlen, Wilson & Co. boats stopping in his home town of Peru. Wilson's antebellum Vicksburg mansion, Anchura, is today a bed and breakfast.

> [Wednesday, March 20, 1861] This is a pleasant day and business in the city looks moderate. I was in the icehouse all day doing not much of anything. Took the tally of Bohlen's men. I am now only waiting to be set to work, and trusting to luck for something to turn up. I spent the Eve walking around town and stopped at an auction shop looking on.

> [Thursday, March 21, 1861] The time passes fast and boredom accumulates from day to day. I am in hope of getting to work again. I was at icehouse all day, walked around with Michael Pyne and read newspapers, time passes well and enjoy myself the best I can under the circumstances—no money but I have no present desire to use any. Stayed at house all Eve.

> [Friday, March 22, 1861] I managed to get up as usual, 7 o'ck, there is nothing particular to mention. I am growing fat. Good living and no work. The weather is moderating i.e, getting warmer. The river business is pretty good, we are having some fun with the boys, the Ark connection home shapes things very well. That is, submit secession to the people, it meets the approval of all.

> [Saturday, March 23, 1861] There was a shower last night, but pleasant today. I stayed at the icehouse most all day. There is

nothing going on to mention. The *Appeal* and the *Avalanche* harp on secession yet, but it don't appear to have any effect among the people. Tennessee is for union every time. There is lots of grain shipped here from day to day, all for S.C. [Southern Confederacy]. I bought me a pair of shoes and threw away my old Arkansas shoes.

[Sunday, March 24, 1861] This holy Sabbath day, I am sorry to say, I have passed like all other days. I have not gone to church. No but sat around at the icehouse and stayed at Pryor's room all afternoon. I got a letter from Jonathan Schmal this Eve, he is in Chicago. Many changes have taken place at home, but sweet home is ever dear to me. I was at Loyd's office in the Eve.

German-born John Schmahl (1827–80) was a grocer in Peru and later Chicago.

[Monday, March 25, 1861] I spent the great part of the day at the icehouse with Mich—there is nothing doing of any account in the city. Business as usual, the levee is full of teams and horses among the steamboats. There is nothing new in the political world, but Lincoln's policy appears to be peace. I am for union yet, stronger and ever. I spent the Eve at house.

[Tuesday, March 26, 1861] The weather continues pleasant and business is booming up a little in the city. The bell ringers are performing in the city this week. Money appears to be scarce in the south, and times at all business houses are slim. I read the *Bulletin* (Union) and *Appeal* (secession) every morning. I went around to the senate in the Eve a few minutes and after went to the theater. Maggie Mitchell playing *The Cricket* is a beautiful play, a good deal of love, and as usual ends well.

The newspapers heralded the arrival of "Blaisedell & Pritz's Celebrated and Original Troupe of Swiss Bell Ringers and Brass Band": "This interesting and talented troupe of musicians have finished their Cuban tour, and at the close of their engagements below, will visit this city. They are expected to open here on Monday next. Due notices will be given of their entertainments" (*Memphis Appeal*, March 19, 1861). They played at the Odd Fellows Hall, with tickets selling for fifty cents.

Famed actress Maggie Mitchell (1837–1918) found in the play *Fanchon the Cricket* her signature role. One reviewer found this tale of an elfin outcast saved by a wealthy young man "by far the best domestic drama of the last few years."[6] The March 28 *Memphis Appeal* proclaimed the New Memphis Theater production "delightful… No one who is a lover of drama should fail to attend."

> [Wednesday, March 27, 1861] This is a bright and beautiful day, the city looks lively, military men are seen going to and fro, this noon the streets are alive with the people and soldiers, there were 500 MS [Mississippi] volunteers going through on their way to Pensacola, marching through the city with music and city escort. A very scary looking crowd and some fierce looking specimens of men. I spent the Eve with Ross walking around the city and at Levy's auction rooms.
>
> [Thursday, March 28, 1861] I got up rather late this a.m., and undertook to write some, but no ink. I wrote two letters at Loyd's office, to Jonathan Nielson and John S. Smith. I spent the greater part of the day at icehouse and at the boats, business in the city looks slim and is __. I went around and heard the Swiss bellringers reed brass band play. After stopped in at Levy's. There was an immense quantity of flour sold, the city was quite lively this Eve.

Gunther probably is referring to the auction house of Abraham S. Levy (b. ca. 1822, South Carolina). Levy enlisted in the Confederate army, rising to the rank of captain in William T. Avery's 40th Tennessee. He moved to Galveston, Texas, after the war, dying there in 1875.

> [Friday, March 29, 1861] There is an immense storm of wind all day, the dust flies unmerciful which makes it very unpleasant to

go out. The day is warm, but the ice business is improving considerable. The levee is full of boats. I have spent the day mostly at Loyd's office, amusing myself the best I could. There's less and less talk about secession. I sent a letter to Hays Danon.

[Saturday, March 30, 1861] This day is not so pleasant. Today business in the city is somnolent. I was at the lower house most all day. Take the tally of the men every day. I was much pleased got a letter from home. Things are all right there. I feel now contented and rejoice that I have a good situation. There's nothing of any import to record, I feel yet a little embarrassed—short of money but there is a good time a-coming.

[Sunday, March 31, 1861] This is a fine day but a shower came up in the Eve. I was down at Loyd's all morning and some at noon. I have not been to church until this Eve for a long time. Heard a good sermon this Eve at Odd Fellows Hall. My mind is not much troubled just yet at present upon religious matters, the wicked, but indispensible world at present occupies my thoughts.

April 1861

As April begins, Tennessee remains part of the Union. However, Charles Gunther feels increasingly nervous. Most of Memphis's newspapers campaign for Tennessee to join her slave state sisters in the new Confederacy, and while most residents of Memphis are not yet pro-secession, it is becoming rarer and rarer to hear expressions of outspoken Unionism in the city's streets and taverns. Gunther attempts to ignore or dismiss the political crisis, tending to the ice business or attending the theater. At this point, Gunther remains a Unionist at heart: perhaps sympathetic to the South and the southern way of life, but appalled at the political hullaballoo and fearful of the war that everyone is talking about.

The firing on Union-held Fort Sumter on April 12 brings on that war. And Gunther's diary entries subtly change. Perhaps fearful that some vigilance committee might seize and read his diary, his entries now downplay his sturdy Unionism. More and more his entries deplore the inevitable destruction the war will bring—an attitude widespread enough, and true enough, so as to cause him no trouble. Gunther's sadness at the conflict is sincere, however, and often eloquently expressed.

Later in life, Gunther asserted that he'd been trapped in the South by the coming of the war, unable to return north. As this month's diary entries show, he in fact passed up several credible opportunities that spring and summer to return with his northern friends. His need to make money, along with hopes the war would end soon, prompted his continued stay in Memphis. By the fall of 1861, as security restrictions increased, travel north became almost impossible.

> [Monday, April 1, 1861] This is a cloudy day, but the sun came out quite warm. Mr. Bohlen and I went out to the Beal St. house and looked around. This is to be my starting day for work, it is truly a pleasure that I can now go to work again, and do something for myself. We sold considerable ice at the Lower House, and the time is now coming when ice will be all the go. I spent the Eve at the Angerona Lodge, a regular meeting. Had a pleasant time.

The Angerona Lodge No. 168, Free and Accepted Masons, was chartered in Memphis in 1848.

> [Tuesday, April 2, 1861] There was a tremendous thunderstorm and lightning last night and rain all morning. The carts were unable to do anything, but this noon all have went to work again. There is nothing of any interest. Dan Rice and his show came and played all the while at the landing. There are many down to see him. I spent the greater part of the day at the ice office setting. Spent the eve at house and playing for amusement with some of the boys.

Dan Rice (1823–1900) has been described as foremost circus performer and manager of the age, a noted wit, great showman, and self-promoter. The local newspapers advertised his tour as follows:

> Dan Rice's Great Show!
> Solo Lessee and Manager Dan Rice.

Now on its return up—southern tour, from the Academy of Music, New Orleans, will exhibit at Memphis, for Five Days Only, on Jefferson street, opposite the new Post Office, On Tuesday, Wednesday, Thursday, Friday and Saturday, April 2d, 3d, 4th, 5th and 6th. Performances Afternoon and Night. Admission 50 cents; Children and Servants 25 cents. Dan Rice, Manager and Humorist, respectfully informs his numerous personal friends that he has greatly modified, additionalized, and improved the Great Show, And is prepared to give an entire new series of Spectacles and Features, by New Artists and New Horses, together with a retention of the old favorites, on a similar plan so successfully observed by him for twelve consecutive weeks in the Crescent City. (*Appeal* ad, March 23, 1861)

[Wednesday, April 3, 1861] I got up this morning as usual about 6-1/2 o'ck read the *Bulletin* and start for the Lower house. Help Loyd most of the day packing etc. The weather is moderating. There is not much business going on, Dan Rice is making a stir among a certain class. I went around but did not go in. Mr. B and I made a bargain to start employment to

Dan Rice, courtesy Library of Congress

commence April 15th, so now I am under salary again. Good. I am now going to do my best.

[Thursday, April 4, 1861] I went to work this morning with a renewed zeal and glad that I am once again working under pay, it rained some today, not much doing. The weather keeps cool and not very good for ice. The trees and shrubbery are getting green, and things having the appearance of Spring now. Dan Rice is all the attraction just now and his circus is crowded every night. I spent the Eve at the house and retired early.

[Friday, April 5, 1861] It was raining all morning and no stop to it. Business is all at the standstill. I was at the lower house all day. My mind is now content, and not occupied with the calls of the world as it was after Eve. Having a situation gives me a quiet mind again, and now my whole care is be steady and upright. I went to the circus this Eve, to see Rhoads folks, did not think the show merited to come up after. We had a little shindig at house, nonesuch as I like, but pitched in and enjoy myself as much as possible.

This circus is probably Mabies Circus, of which Daniel Rhodes was agent. This circus was touring the South in 1860 and 1861.

[Saturday, April 6, 1861] The weather is some better this morning, we are still filling the levee house. The *Capitol* arrived this noon with a full tow of ice. I was glad to see all the Peru folks again. Went down to her in the Eve she started. Got a note from Wilkins by Joe Monks. We were busy packing and shipping ice this noon and paying off Loyd's. Got my supper late. I spent the Eve walking around and retired early, being a little tired.

[Sunday, April 7, 1861] This is a pleasant day. Went down to the lower house. Stayed the greater part of the day. I have not had my Sunday suit on for a long time and had got quite a hardened sinner and running around much like a lost sheep but with time I will make a great return to my old accustomed life of attending worship every Sabbath day. There's nothing to mention of import or note.

Chilly News.—Bohlen Wilson & Co's steamboat *Capitol*, arrived at our wharf yesterday afternoon, with another large fleet of ice in tow. She will return to the Illinois river for another tow.[7]

[Monday, April 8, 1861] Still it rains, no intermission, perfectly awful. It is interfering very much with my ideas and my intended business. We all doing nothing reading war news. War—war appears to be all the say + go. Business is very dull in the city in general, something at least still onlooking. The last boat of our first tow. I spent the Eve at house and retired early.

[Tuesday, April 9, 1861] The weather is rainy yet and cloudy, streets are mushy and business is only halfway. Some folks are at the levee, the Glendale reeves regaling us with the calliope discourses of their good time tunes. Times are hard all over the south. The secession papers keep up, the cry of secession disunion all the time while the *Bulletin* battles nobly for the Union. I got some letters from home, One from Monk.

[Wednesday, April 10, 1861] Men worked all forenoon, but the rain stopped work. Rain, rain, is they say. It stops all business and practically our ice business. We had some great sensation dispatches this morning, but were all contradicted again by the *Argus* again this evening. There appears to be a great effort made to excite the hopeful and get TN out of the Union. The south is mustering all her forces for war. And the U.S. is preparing also. Trouble ahead sure.

Famous newspaper woodcut of the citizens of Charleston viewing the bombardment of Fort Sumter, from Harpers Weekly, *May 4, 1861*

[Thursday, April 11, 1861] This is a pleasant day for once. The sun is shining and the mud is drying up fast, we ship a lot of ice on the cars. I am not doing much of anything, loafing around our office. The weather is too cool for ice. The city is quiet and not much stir on the levee. The S.C. [Southern Confederacy] is all the talk and the probabilities of success is discussed. Oh I am for the Union yet.

[Friday, April 12, 1861] War, war appears to be all the cry. News has reached here that the war has commenced at Charleston. Some are doubting it, but it appears that the battle has at last commenced. God only knows where it will end, the south will fight, the Lincoln appears determined to carry out the Republican policy. The papers published extras, the long-expected event has come, let her rip. I spent the eve in house.

[Saturday, April 13, 1861] The dispatches of today are confirmed, it is reported that Sumter has capitulated. There is much excitement in the city, every body is talking about it. Extras have come out and great joy among all at the victory. I was busy shipping ice, and paying off men. There is firing of cannon, rockets, etc., a large meeting was held this eve. Speeches were made by Scruggs, Caskey and others. As much excitement and many tales of going to war.

Celebration of secession in South Carolina (from Leslie's Illustrated, *December 1860)*

The *Memphis Appeal* of April 14 reported:
>Rejoicings.—The joyful Secessionists showed their pleasure, by the pealing of cannon and the firing of guns. The Steuben Artillery on the bluff made the windows rattle from their fine cannon. The Crockett Rangers fired a *feu de joie*. Rockets in great numbers rivaled the brilliancy of the glowing stars. Speed, Donoho & Strange, C. K. Holst & Son, and other citizens illuminated. At Main and Court, and on Main above Adams, large bonfires were lighted.

The speakers at the meeting included Phineas T. Scruggs (1806–78), a local judge and minister,[8] and Rev. Thomas W. Caskey (1816–96), who gave pro-secession speeches throughout Tennessee and Mississippi. Caskey later won fame as "The Fighting Parson" for his service as chaplain of the 18th Mississippi Infantry.

[Sunday, April 14, 1861] It is cloudy today again. I was at the lower house, *Capitol* got up steam and started for Peru. Mr. Bohlen and I went along up the river some 4 miles took dinner and came back in a skiff. It rained again and has continued until this Eve, harder and harder. There are many suspicious persons around the house. I spent the Eve in hotel, wrote to Seeluck, McClenniston + more this noon.

[Monday, April 15, 1861] The proclamation of Lincoln has been passed by telegraph, and published in extras. There is a great amount of sorrow and regret felt within the city, and I feel myself like many are rejoicing that the time had come, war is the cry, it is hard that it has come to this, and not deplore it more than I do. Meetings are held this Eve and resistance is all the go. Northern men are looked upon with suspicion. Business is dull in general and prospect is worse.

The *Appeal* of April 15, 1861 reported on the secession meeting, under the headline "Uprising of the People." Next to that article was printed "Lincoln's War Proclamation," in which the president called for volunteers to put down the rebellion. As we know, there were many secret Unionists in Memphis, particularly in the northern-born part of the population. But, like Gunther, they dared not be open about their beliefs.

[Tuesday, April 16, 1861] The weather is fine today but business continues dull, ice trade poor—too cold. There's much excitement in the city, groups of people may be seen at the corners all discussing the great war question. Lincoln is determined to fight, so is the south, so fight let it be, the north is rallying to coerce us, military companies are the order of the day. The drums beat to arms. I am a little uneasy myself, there is more or less uneasiness felt among our boys.

[Wednesday, April 17, 1861] The weather continues fine. The excitement is increasing. The Crockett Rangers were out, war news is coming in from all quarters. Maryland stays in the Union. In response to Lincoln's call, there are military companies organizing and drilling every night. Drums were beating over town this Eve, all the boys in the hotel talk of leaving for the north. I am bound to stick by Memphis and defend her. Times in the city are hard. There is a great demand for specie. I spent the Eve at the South Memphis Lodge, we raised a Bro.

A largely Irish-American company, the Crockett Rangers were formed from the members of the Memphis volunteer fire department, company number 5. They became Company H of the 154th Tennessee Infantry.

Here Gunther vows to "stick by Memphis and defend her." This diary entry might have been for appearances only, in case anyone else read his diary. Gunther never made a move to join the Confederate army.

[Thursday, April 18, 1861] I got up this morning at 7, the day is fine, the excitement is unabated, extras are out at noon every day. The steamers *Lady Jackson* and *Citizen* were tied up by the citizens to retaliate for the Memphis boats taken at Cairo. There's much talk here and particularly in our office. I've not yet gone on Beal Street—too cold—the drum and fife are going through the city this Eve, and joy is expressed at Virginia going out of the Union. I spent the Eve at the hotel playing and retired early after making the acquaintance of a horse.

The report that Memphis boats had been seized by Unionists at Cairo, Illinois, was false—or at least, premature. Within two weeks, Federal forces and local vigilance committees began to inspect for war contraband all Mississippi River steamboats travelling south.

[Friday, April 19, 1861] This is another fine and pleasant day, but not much business in our line. The war excitement continues unabated. The news a riot in Baltimore and the resignation of Scott has been received this Eve, Guns are being fired. I see Otho

McLain this Eve. Jeff Davis calls for volunteers. General Pillow calls for Tennessee volunteers, drilling is going on every Eve. There was quite a parade this Eve. Some of the boys are much excited. Steamboats are taking many northerners up, and none coming down. Spent the Eve at house talking to McLain.

[Saturday, April 20, 1861] I am taking the general excitement cool and calmly. The news comes flashing in from all quarters. The *Star of the West* was taken by the C.S. There are extras issued every Eve and noon, there is a great demand for news and everything is eagerly sought for. The newsboys have a rich harvest. Business is very dull. Pryor is in the city yet. Says he is broke. I did but very little today, and spent the Eve at house.

[Sunday, April 21, 1861] This is a fine and pleasant day. The city is quiet. I went to church at Odd Fellows Hall, a very good sermon and a large congregation. There is not much of any interest except the coming war. The American flag was to be buried today, but did not take place. I was at room all afternoon writing to Hugo, the boys at house are getting scared considerable. I read the war news every morning. The enthusiasm in the north is at its highest pitch.

[Monday, April 22, 1861] I was at the lower house all day. We did not do much business. The steamboats at the levee all have secession flags flying so all over the city. Troops are drilling every night and the greatest preparations are being made for the coming conflict. It is contradicted that General Scott had resigned, I am taking things coolly, and look on the coming conflict quietly and hope there may be peace yet still. I have gloomy apprehensions.

Virginia-born General Winfield Scott, the aged commander of the US Army, remained loyal to the Union. This is but one example of the many rumors flying about that proved to be false.

[Tuesday, April 23, 1861] This is another pleasant day, everything now looks like summer. The roses are all in bloom and everything looks cheerful, while the people are preparing for a deadly conflict. A lot of troops left here for Randolph to throw up batteries. There are lots of passengers going north upon every passing boat. Nothing is talked about except war, war. I bought a *New York Herald* it supports Lincoln now and changed its position. Times look gloomy in the city. I spent the Eve at house reading and conversation.

The city of Memphis had appropriated $50,000 (a huge sum for the time) for war materials and fortifications, and local recruits were already being sent north to Randolph, Tennessee, to fortify the bluffs overlooking the Mississippi River. The diary of future general Marcus J. Wright explains the troop movements Gunther observed:

> On the 23 April 1861 being in command of the 154 Senior Regiment of Tennessee Volunteers as lieutenant-colonel, Colonel Preston Smith being absent on official business at Montgomery, Ala. I received an order by telegraph from Governor Isham G. Harris to proceed with a portion of my command and the Steuben Artillery to some point above Memphis on the Miss. River. I laid this order before the Military Board at Memphis and being furnished by them with means of transportation, subsistence stores, etc. I left Memphis at 12 o'clock at night with two companies of Infantry, Light Guards, Capt. Genette and Southern Guards, Capt. Hamilton and the Steuben Artillery and landed at Randolph 60 miles above Memphis about 10 o'clock next morning. The troops were at once encamped and a temporary organization made for the Battalion.[9]

[Wednesday, April 24, 1861] We had a fine shower last night, but fine and sunshine today. The city is quiet, some soldiers may be seen on the streets. Business is dull. I wrote a letter to Jonathan Schmal this morning. There was a man stabbed a few doors from our office. Our boys are laughing and having some fun among themselves—but that don't pay. There was excitement that Fort Pickens is taken, but it is all a hoax. I read the *Herald* this Eve and after retired.

[Thursday, April 25, 1861] Sunshine all day but no business to do, the boats are not arriving and business as usual. The *Dickey* got in the a.m. *George Foreman* leaves for St. Louis this eve. There's nothing new of any import. The military excitement is still up and uniformed men all over the city. Batteries are now being erected at Randolph. There is not anything of import in the city just at the present.

[Friday, April 26, 1861] We could get dispatches three times a day. The noon extras have got to be a perfect nuisance, and I got up to sell, but there is not so much excitement as for some days past. At Cairo, recruits are constantly arriving. Our men are all up at Randolph. The home guards are drilling every night. I spent the eve mostly at home reading. The landlady is since excited about the boarders running off, my mind is now occupied most about the thinking over the [uniform] coat.

Sixty miles north of Memphis, the fortifications at Randolph (sometimes known as Fort Wright) were constructed to control passage down the Mississippi River. The fort failed to impress English observer W. H. Russell who, in his *Diary* entry for June 20, 1861, found the earthworks

> ... rudely erected.... A more extraordinary maze could not be conceived, even in the dreams of a sick engineer. ... They were so ingeniously made as to prevent the troops engaged in their defense from resisting the enemy's attacks, or getting away from them when the enemy had got inside.[10]

The outpost was largely abandoned in July, in favor of new fortifications (Fort Randolph), nearby but at a better location.

> [Saturday, April 27, 1861] The weather continues fine but a shower came up and cleared off again this eve. I spent most of my time doing nothing. John Moss is fixing our snack at the Concord House. The excitement is high. A report of a fight at the York County PA came today. Nothing is done at Pickens yet. I bought me a *NY Herald* full of news. I was at the levee most of the eve and stopped at the drill rooms with Ross a short time and after read my paper. Mrs. McClure is having a rough time with her boarders. I paid my board this eve.

In 1860, Jonathan Moss, a twenty-four-year-old, Pennsylvania-born ice salesman, lived with the Bohlen brothers.

> [Sunday, April 28, 1861] The sun came out again and the day is fine. I did not go to any church, stopped at the levee house and spent time in that hotel reading. I spent the whole afternoon with Pryor. We talked over the past, the present and the gloomy future. P is strapped, and nothing troubles me now, but still I cannot think of the war news from above is meager. I stayed at levee all eve and read the *Home Journal*.

Begun in 1846, the weekly *Home Journal* is published today under the title *Town & Country*. Under editor George Pope Morris (1802–64) it featured poetry (much of it written by Morris), prose, and fiction.

> [Monday, April 29, 1861] The day is clear and fine. Business is dull generally in the city. There are many boats on the levee, there are various compromise rumors afloat, I sent some letters to Pennsylvania by Mr. Bohlen. He left at 4 o'ck p.m. I helped at the lower house to put up sawdust. I'm hoping I will get out at this Hell House before long. I'm glad that I

have up to date not yet joined any company. I hold myself for the reserves. I spent the eve at house reading and at Main St. office.

"Put up sawdust": Ice was commonly packed in sawdust to retard melting. [Tuesday, April 30, 1861] Nothing of any interest going on. Excitement is cooling down some. Mr. Billingsley called on me today. I was glad to see him, but did not speak long to him. My opinion is that we must all go to war before long. And things are coming to a focus. I got me a few things to send to Melton's and wrote a letter. I am satisfied that they will be pleased, as I owe them a debt of gratitude. I spent the eve at Main St. office and called at store house to see Billingsley, but he had gone.

In addition to its office at 276 Main Street, Bohlen, Wilson & Co. had three ice houses in Memphis, including the "New City Ice House" on the steamboat landing. Gunther seems to have worked at all the locations, intermittently, and occasionally stayed the night at one of the locations.

Diary May–August 1861

A busy river port city, Memphis was fast becoming a major staging and supply center for the Confederacy. In peacetime it produced and transshipped $51 million annually, via steamboat to the north and south, and via its three main railroads to the north, south, and east. The onset of the war had depressed that trade, especially the northern segment. But new lines of business had sprung up. As the Memphis Chamber of Commerce reported on August 31, 1861:

> We have, therefore, at the expense of considerable trouble and labor, examined into the relative increase or decrease of business in the various departments above named, with the view of ascertaining to what extent the manufacturing classes have been affected by the extraordinary occurrences of the past year, and present the following as the result of our investigations: In the manufacture of doors, sash, blinds, etc., we find a decrease of from 45 to 50 per cent., in steam engines, cars, fronts and miscellaneous castings; a decrease of about 20 per cent.; in brick, of fully 50 per cent.; carriages and buggies, 30 per cent.; tin ware, roofing, boilers, agricultural and ornamental iron works, wagons and drays, lath, furniture, etc., a decrease of from 10 to 25 per cent.; while

in flour and corn meal, cotton seed oil, soap, lard-oil and candles, saddlery, plantation machinery, tests, caps, and several articles of minor importance, there has been an increase varying from 20 to 60 per cent. Added to this, the peculiar circumstances of the times have given rise to the manufacture in our city of military goods and implements of war, on a most gigantic scale, and the increase in the value of productions thus created, will go far toward counterbalancing the loss sustained in other departments, if indeed it does not exceed it. From official sources, we learn that during the past two or three months from twelve to fifteen hundred persons, male and female, have been actively engaged in the production of clothing, camp equipage, cartridges, percussion caps, knapsacks, cavalry equipments, etc., to say nothing of the very considerable force employed at the various foundries and machine shops in turning out field pieces of various descriptions, shot and shell, swords, knives, and warlike implements generally.[1]

May 1861

[Wednesday, May 1, 1861] The weather is cool and pleasant. Not much business done in our line. The steamer *Manchester* got down with a law office yesterday. We are having plenty of bids at the Lower House. The boys caught some canaries today. I am expecting some letters from home today, but no letters come. I fear that mails are stopped. Great excitement with Oh dear what a miserable place my boarding house is. I am getting disgusted more and more every day. I spent the eve at Main St. house had some fun and made a bet with Moss on steamship time.

[Thursday, May 2, 1861] I got up rather late had a miserable breakfast am getting more and more disgusted with McClure's and I have left and now took my boarding quarters to Mrs.

Correll's. I am much pleased with the change, a very favorable one. I think what I fool I was for not changing before, but as usual I am not fond of changing. The military excitement is up. Several companies left for Randolph, and some companies came up from Arkansas. I got a letter from Asa, and spent most of the eve in town, and slept at the lower house.

L. Correll ran a boarding house on Court Street.

[Friday, May 3, 1861] This is another fine day but not warm it did not do but little business. The war excitement is about the same, the Foundry is casting cannon and preparations are being made for war. The shot + fire mind is yet strong and hopes of a reconciliation. Mr. Bohlen's getting here with our ice is all that troubles us at present. I spent the Eve at office + retired early.

[Saturday, May 4, 1861] Business is but little better. The city looks very empty, and one cannot help but notice the general stagnation that exists over the city. Stores closed and but few men engaged upon any work. Several companies have gone up to Camp Harris this eve. Also, some guns have gone up, from all reports there must be 6,000 men at Cairo. We look for a fight in that quarter. I was up at the main office, but no letter, I am anxious to hear from some. Retired early. No usual reading room.

[Sunday, May 5, 1861] The news depots has raised on papers from 5 to 10 cents. I bought several but think the last at this price. I have not been to church this Sunday but did go this eve. Heard a good sermon by the Reverend Mr. Stedman to the young men on the question of the day, Prepare to die in time of war, a very large crowd out. We had heavy rain today. I am pleased with my new boarding place I like it very well. I read the most part of the day. Received a letter from Wilkin this evening.

The Reverend James Owen Stedman (1811–82) was pastor of the First Presbyterian Church in Memphis from 1854 to 1868. A native of Fayetteville, North Carolina, and a Princeton graduate, Dr. Stedman was described as an "earnest, able, sound and effective" preacher. See the Princeton Theological Seminary, *Necrological Reports*, vol. 1, 33 for more on Stedman.

> [Monday, May 6, 1861] Here is a Monday again and I have not gone to work yet. The weather continues very unfavorable yet. Harris and Pryor have left this eve for St. Louis. I see them off P is hard up and had a slight difficulty before getting off. I see Rhoades folks and was glad to see them. But did not get to speak much to them. The war news is very meager and mails are irregular. I played several games of checkers with Mrs. Jonathan Moss and Miller beat both fairly and after hear McDowell make a speech—poor thing.
>
> [Tuesday, May 7, 1861] This is a beautiful day and quite warm. We packed some ice today Spent the greater part of the day assisting in the work. There's nothing sure from above. I sought to write several letters, but I can't get my writing spirit up to the place to stick. Asa left the city last eve, the strict vigilance is kept up on all suspicious characters. Mich Pyne got on a bust this eve, we had some trouble with him. I played after games of checkers, got beat by Ferris.

Regarding this "strict vigilance," the *Janesville* (Wisconsin) *Weekly Gazette* (untitled article, May 15, 1861) claimed that the Memphis "Committee of Safety" really ran the city, and that 4–5,000 residents had been driven out. The same newspaper (untitled, May 10, 1861) quoted the *Memphis Argus* as saying "most of the up-river boats are filled with laborers and mechanics for points north."

On May 6th, the Tennessee Legislature, at the urgings of secessionist governor Isham G. Harris, voted to take Tennessee out of the

Union—though not necessarily to join the Confederacy. The law scheduled a referendum on secession, to be held one month later. The legislators also created (on paper, at least) an "Army of Tennessee" and called for men to volunteer for that army.

[Wednesday, May 8, 1861] The weather is very quite and this day is dull, war rumors of every kind are plenty. Dispatches reached us last eve from Nashville today this state is out. 55,000 volunteers called out and a five million dollar loan authorized. This looks like work and we fear the worse, our hopes are now that our ice will get down, if reports are there the prospects are favorable. I spent the eve party at the upper house, playing checkers. An immense fire broke out on Front Road about 8-1/2 o'ck and consumed half Rhoades.

Governor Isham G. Harris (1818–97) of Tennessee, courtesy Library of Congress

The *Memphis Appeal*, May 8, 1861, under the headline "The Fireman's Fight," reported that the city's different (and differing) fire companies fought each other rather than the fire. The paper blamed the fight on an "excess of whisky." While the punches rained, the fire consumed several businesses near the intersection of Main and Court Streets.

Among the "rumors" floating around was this from the *Appeal* of May 4th: "Drunken Abe—We have it on very good authority, that Abraham Lincoln, since the date of his inauguration, has not been sober for a day." Needless to say, this report was false.

[Thursday, May 9, 1861] There was another fire last night, another block of buildings burnt down. The loss last night was heavy. I worked hard for Murphy getting out goods, this is a whole attracted to incindiaryism. The weather is fine and warm and ice house loafers for our boats. Excursion parties are going up to Fort Harris every day. Defenses of the city are very good now. I see a fireman's funeral now. There was a big fight among them last night. I was up at the upper house and retired early this eve.

Named after Tennessee's governor Isham Harris, Fort (Camp) Harris lies six miles north of Memphis.

[Friday, May 10, 1861] There was a heavy storm last night, the rain came down on our beds—the general excitement among the boys. This is a gloomy rainy day. Everything is dull. There's quite a party gone up to Camp Harris on the *Hartford City*. I'd like to hear from home very well. I fear mother is troubled [for] me. I hope not. I went up to the upper house this eve our whole mind is absorbed on the coming war.

[Saturday, May 11, 1861] We had a fine shower last night the day is pleasant. The steamer *Perry* got down from St. Louis. Cairo is not yet blockaded. We are all discussing the probabilities of the Cairo blockade. I cannot help but notice the stand still of all business on the levee and the city. I wrote a letter to George W. Carriston at St. Louis, massed and went up today. He got scared out. There was a fight in St. Louis today some 20 killed. Our boys are trying to get up the Marine Guards again. I went to bed early this eve.

On May 10, 1861, Federal troops under General Nathaniel Lyon seized an encampment of pro-Southern Missouri state militia at Camp Jackson, Saint Louis. When Lyon marched the prisoners through the streets of that city, residents threw stones at the mostly German Federal guards, who fired back, killing some twenty-eight people and wounding a further fifty. The "Saint Louis Riot" helped polarize the state into pro-Union and pro-Confederate sides.

[Sunday, May 12, 1861] I got up this morning rather late after breakfast I read papers all morning and took dinner Lloyd going along. I'm getting to be quite at home at Mrs. Small's. I took a pleasure trip up to Fort Harris and Camp Rector on the *St. Charles*. I see nothing of any particular note. That fort I don't think to be very strong effective. I had quite a reception of the Arkansawers at _____ - A very poor equipped ____, but some strong ones among them. Hindman made a speech, a true and patriotic Southern speech, full of zeal.

Thomas C. Hindman, courtesy Library of Congress

Thomas Carmichael Hindman (1828–68) was one of the more colorful politicians of the age. A lawyer, Hindman's energy and speaking abilities took him to the leadership of the secession forces in Arkansas—and won him a seat in Congress. When the war started he raised the 2nd Arkansas Infantry and became its colonel. Quickly promoted to general, Hindman proved less than Napoleonic, though his courage was unquestioned. Placed in command of Arkansas, Hindman's draconian measures to mobilize an army, combined with his ineptness as a field general, led to his transfer back to the Army of Tennessee. He led a division in that army until illness (an eye injury) forced his retirement. He was assassinated postwar, while sitting on his home porch, by one of his numerous personal and political enemies. General Arthur Manigault, Hindman's subordinate, found him "a man of talent," but "the cunningest, most slippery intriguer that I ever met with."[2]

Camp Rector was at Mound City, on the Mississippi River near Memphis. J. T. Small's coffee house was at the intersection of Second Street and Market.

> [Monday, May 13, 1861] This morning the long looked for steamer *Capitol* was espied by Alec coming around the bend, sending a perfect thrill of joy through all the boys to see they got by Cairo. Our fears are all dispelled, so they can do with Cairo what they wish—and let 'er rip. There are numerous troops coming over from Arkansas. The men are all making preparations for getting out the ice. The old gent feels quite well at his good luck. I spent the eve on the boat talking over the news with the boys.

> [Tuesday, May 14, 1861] The captain had everything ready for the work on the ice to commence. We made a good start and all works well. There is nothing particularly new at present, ice sales not very good yet. The war goes quietly on, and blows are expected to take place very soon. Joe Monks and I went up to town this Eve. Byass (?) cloths are not to be had I must write. I am in good spirits and having some fun with the boys.

> [Wednesday, May 15, 1861] This is a pleasant and warm day. The Washington street house is getting filled fast. Our peace men are getting scared. See so many soldiers' movements, a company came down from Hatchie River. The *Capitol* is lying opposite our office. The war preparations appear to go on, on both sides. Mrs. B feels in good spirits, though he Were rather don't diet. (?) I am yet without any definite post of business, but will go along. Spent the eve at upper house with Joe Miller.

[Thursday, May 16, 1861] Old Ben Gassaway routed us out this morning pretty early. Sat around and got breakfast rather late. Weather is fine, but rather too cold for business. We are working away on the boat. There is nothing of any interest to note at the present, only the war feeling is keeping up by the drums throughout the city. This is very hard, most of the boats are layed up, the St. Louis line is stopped.

[Friday, May 17, 1861] The weather is fine and pleasant, the work is going on the ice comes out finely, very large. No business doing. I am having some fun at boarding house I enjoy myself very much, good boarding companions to the merchant's hotel—and what is more—clean. Mr. Bowers and I have some fun, and talk over peace matters with the men. I am not working much of expect to go in next week.

[Saturday, May 18, 1861] This is a hot summer day, one of the warmest of the season. We got the *Washington* St. Louis filled by 2 o'ck, then moved over to Beale. We are making good progress with the boat. I am glad we are filling the Beale house. I paid off all the men this morn. I was a little taken back by Miller on masses bet, but I guess it will come out all right yet. We had some ice cream on the strength of it, $5 made.

[Sunday, May 19, 1861] This is a warm day. I made my usual change, and after I stayed on the *Capitol* all morning and took dinner. There is nothing of any import except war preparations are being made on all sides, and terrible times are ahead. This is truly lamentable to see all business stopped, and the American people in a final contest. I am in the expectation of having to take up arms before long.

[Monday, May 20, 1861] All had to work again on the riverboat, got all out by 5 o'ck. The Beale Street house is filling up fast.

Captain Bowers got back from Vicksburg this noon, the crew were all very much pleased to see him. I worked at the boats all day. The steamer *Prince of Wales* got up with the wounded of the *Kentucky* on board Blew up yesterday and many persons killed. Horrible! I spent the eve on the *Capitol* and at office. There was a terrible storm all eve.

The *Fayetteville* (North Carolina) *Observer* of May 30, 1861: "On Sunday morning 19th inst. the Steamer *Kentucky* exploded her mud receiver at Columbia, Arkansas on the Mississippi River by which eleven persons were killed.... defective iron caused the accident." Fuller details of the accident can be found in the *New Orleans Daily True Delta* of May 24, 1861.

Pennsylvania-born Peter Bowers (1817–92) piloted steamers for the Crescent City (New Orleans) Ice Co. He owned an ice business in Peru.

[Tuesday, May 21, 1861] We get the boat in and took my breakfast on the steamer. This is a very cold and disagreeable morning and lasted all day. The crew are unloading the boat. It is amusing to see the old hands trying to scare out the crew. There is nothing of import in the city. The *Walsh* arrived and was tied up. There was an immense crowd on the levee. A rumor prevailed that a lot of Turners [Germans] were coming up, but false—to join Lincoln. I spent the eve on the boat and at office.

[Wednesday, May 22, 1861] We got a dispatch from Orleans, ice cold, it gives us great dinner. I sent all the old hands to work again, filling the Beale Street house, yet about 3 o'ck the *Capitol* got underway and went downstream under full headway. The day is warmer than yesterday. I am in expectation of some letters, but none come. I have a very bad cold and running at the nose. Our levee is full of boats, but no business. I was up town a while and retired early.

[Thursday, May 23, 1861] I am suffering with an awful cold today. I am not doing much today, running my cold and nose most of the time, bought me some Bryan's wafers—a good thing. We are making good progress on the ice boats. The war news is of no particular interest. All are preparing for the war, in hourly expectation of some news. I wrote a letter for Mich Pyne. I spent the eve at lower house, wrote a letter to Bill and retired early.

"Bryan's Pulmonic Wafers" promised "freedom from cough in ten minutes after use."

[Friday, May 24, 1861] We got the boat emptied by 9 o'ck and all glad of so much done All the houses filled and now we are prepared to meet all demands. We have the news that the federal forces advanced into Virginia and Col. Ellsworth killed. Mr. E. was a fine officer. I have seen him several times. The weather is very pleasant and warm and the prospect of our business opening. Most of our city soldiers have left the city and not so many are to be seen now on the streets.

Colonel Elmer E. Ellsworth (1837–61), a close friend of President Lincoln, won nationwide renown prewar as the head of a famous drill team. When the war broke out, Ellsworth raised the 11th New York Infantry (the "Fire Zouaves") from New York City's volunteer firefighter companies. On May 24, 1861, he led his soldiers across the Potomac River into Alexandria, Virginia. While tearing down a Confederate flag flying atop a hotel, the hotel owner, James W. Jackson, killed Ellsworth with a shotgun blast to the chest. Gunther had undoubtedly seen Ellsworth's Zoauve drill team on one of their many tours of Chicago.

Here Gunther shifts from unloading ice to selling ice.

[Saturday, May 25, 1861] After cleaning up the Beale Street offices this morning, I commenced operations in my new line of business. It went very well and the customers commercial coming in. My

Elmer E. Ellsworth, from Harpers Weekly *May 11, 1861*

office is a lonely one away from the balance of the city. Retired from the world, my companions move in this lonesome retreat can only be books and papers, but give me books what real need I? This is a warm day.

[Sunday, May 26, 1861] This is Sunday again. Well I would hardly think it's Sunday, were it not that the shops around me were closed and the Negroes with their Sunday go-to-meeting clothes on. I have been selling ice all day and reading, the day is warm. I was awfully sucked in at the Union House for board, had to pay in advance took supper got disgusted and concluded to take only one more meal there—a miserable place. Good board houses are not known on Beale Street. Sleep at the lower house.

[Monday, May 27, 1861] I took a poor breakfast as missing hotel as I shall call it to finish my advance pay. Ice sales are not much just yet but we must keep up appearances for summer trade and wait the advent of warm weather. Beale Street is quite a business street, many vehicles and people pass continuously. I commenced boarding at Mrs. Pierce's received a note from Mrs. Daniels, to board call up to see her, but too late, it looks like a nice place, sleep down at the lower house.

The 1859 *Memphis Directory* lists two Pierce boarding houses, those of Mary Pierce, Beale St. between Main and 2nd, and Mrs. Pearce's, at Poplar near Main.

[Tuesday, May 28, 1861] Got to work again about 7 o'ck. Joe Miller came up early to play me a game of checkers. Beat him badly. The weather has been pleasant, reports are here that a battle took place at Harpers Ferry—false I think. The newspaper editors catch at any floating straw to make a dime out of the anxious people to hear news. Mich and Loyd come up this Eve. I renovated my bedding and exterminated the bedbugs. Delightful creatures, but they shall not suck my blood, sleep at Rome Street.

[Wednesday, May 29, 1861] Got up at about 4 o'ck before George, can out his ice and laid myself down again and slept until 6, this has been a dull day, the weather being cool. My station here is a quite dull one, howsoever I am improving my time by reading. I am now reading the *Eclectic Magazine* for May it is a high number and gives me great pleasure to read it—what would I do were it not that I have a great love for literature and only that of a higher type, it is a blessing to me and unspeakable worth and value.

The *Eclectic Magazine of Foreign Literature, Science, and Art* featured the best from foreign periodicals, almost all of them English periodicals. It was published from 1844 to 1907.

If Gunther had read that day's *Memphis Appeal*, he might have pondered this bit of love advice:

> Advice to Girls.—There is a practice, quite prevalent among young ladies of the present day, which we are old fashioned enough to consider very improper. We allude to giving daguerreotypes of themselves to young men who are merely acquaintances. We consider it indelicate in the highest degree. We are astonished that any young girl should hold herself as cheap as this. With an accepted lover it is, of course, all right.

[Thursday, May 30, 1861] This is a somber and rainy day. I am selling but little ice, there's not much news at present. War preparations are going on, all the signs and I am momentarily looking for the news of a big battle. I finished reading the *Eclectic* and have now commenced Roland's history. I am getting used to my place and loneliness has passed away. I spent the Eve at Main Street house and retired early.

"Roland's history" is probably John S. C. Abbott's *History of Madame Roland*, published in 1850. Madame Roland was a key figure in the French Revolution.

[Friday, May 31, 1861] We have done some sunshine and sass showers today. Business is dull generally. Mr. Bohlen got back from New Orleans. I sold—the old gentleman feels good over it. It gives pleasure to all home and we don't care whether corn costs $1 a bushel or not. I spent all my amusement time reading Roland, All the military movements take place in Virginia. I went to the Lodge this Eve, the first for some time. Brother Charles Scott is deemed a worthy brother.

Charles Scott (1811–61), a Memphis attorney, was an active Freemason, having written several books on the subject.

June 1861
Charles Gunther became involved in the ice business when he lived in Peru, Illinois, one of the centers of the Mississippi River ice trade. As one history of Peru notes:

1847 saw the beginning of Peru's ice business, which for many years was the most important of Peru's industries. The development evidently was rapid, for an historian of 1858 writes: "The ice trade (packing and shipping to a southern market) is a very important business here. Three hundred men are employed during the winter, and seventy during the summer." For years the business grew and prospered, reaching its peak about the middle seventies. At that time Peru's boats were known not only all along the Mississippi and the Illinois, but on the Tennessee, the Arkansas and the Red Rivers as well.... The pioneer in the industry was Capt. John Lowery McCormick, who came here from Pennsylvania in 1847. He had a number of interests, among them farming and trading in stock. He built some valuable buildings along Water Street, as well as his residence, which was erected in 1848. His principal interest was in shipping, in which he had been engaged in the east, and as he had had some experience in the ice business there, he was quick to see its possibilities here. Others soon followed his lead, among them the Huse and Loomis Ice & Transportation Co., the Crescent City Ice Co., and the Memphis Co., consisting of Bohlen, Huse and Graves. Some ice houses were located on the south bank of the lower slough; others near the canal cut; some on the north bank of the river in the west end of town; and others west of Peru on the banks of small bayous.... Most of the barges were wintered in nearby sloughs. They were loaded with ice in winter. The capacity of barges ranged from 600 to 3500 tons. One of the old river barges of 3500 tons capacity held as much ice as could be packed in 105 of the present day boxcars. Some years, in addition to filling all the houses and the barges, ice was stacked in large piles. Some of these were roofed over with boards; others simply covered with straw. It is estimated that over 100,000 tons of ice were harvested some winters. When conditions were favorable in the ice business there was work for all.[3]

As can be seen from the June 6 diary entry, the war hurt the business of Peru as well as that of Memphis.
Many in Peru's populous German-American community found employment cutting or loading ice. As Bailey's *LaSalle County Directory for 1858*

& *1859* claimed, "three hundred men are employed during the winter, and seventy during the summer" in the ice business.

[Saturday, June 1, 1861] This is pronounced as the warmest day of the season. I felt quite civil in my domicile and ice sales are pretty good, the streets are lively with the femines. I see some more of our military are preparing to leave. I am now only reading the *Appeal*, the only paper I get, and have to make out when I can. I went down to see the boys Rebecca.

[Sunday, June 2, 1861] This is a warm day. The sun is shining brightly. As usual I am to work selling ice, sales are good—I am getting so that I don't mind getting up early and help George out. Harpers Ferry Virginia and Alexandria are now the points to which all eyes are turned. I am reading my Roland yet, and it is very interesting. Got through with the Egyptians. I spent all Eve at office and went to bed early.

[Monday, June 3, 1861] We had quite a shower all day, something longed for by many. The day being cool—of course my trade was poor. Well I must say I improved the time reading and wrote 2 letters, one to Jonathan Wilkin Small and I fear it will probably be the last mails are stopped next week. I don't see no one the weather here is just as cool so far as at home. My hopes are now for a peace and then all will be well. I went to the main office, returned late.

[Tuesday, June 4, 1861] Senator Douglas is dead is the telegraph dispatch from Chicago. I must say I am sorry as I have spent many a dollar in his cause, and battled manfully in his behalf—cast my first vote for him. He was a giant, peace be to his ashes. This is a bright and very pleasant day, sales moderate. I went up to the main street office—and after went down to the river house—the boys are getting along very well.

Stephen Arnold Douglas (1813–61), US Senator from Illinois. Leader of the Democratic Party in Illinois. Unsuccessful candidate for president (against Abraham Lincoln) in 1860. Known as the "Little Giant," Douglas was beloved by Illinois Democrats such as Gunther.

Stephen A. Douglas, courtesy Library of Congress

[Wednesday, June 5, 1861] I got up 3 o'ck to help George out, stayed down again. Commenced sales 6 o'ck not much doing. Still better than the days previous. There's nothing new. The Confederate cabinet arrived at Richmond Virginia headquarters now of the Confederacy. Frequent skirmishes are reported with not much importance, a distribution for Jackson is being made. Jackson killed Ellsworth. This city remains quiet. Nothing going on at all times. Retired very early—tired.

[Thursday, June 6, 1861] This is a pleasant warm day, not much doing. Our streets are going to be barricaded, and batteries erected on all available points of the river, one in front of ice house. A census of all male inhabitants is going to be taken, a determined resistance is resolved upon. I received a letter from home, gave me great pleasure. Mother is troubled very much, but my last has removed all fears. Times are evidently very hard at Peru, and glad ain't there.

[Friday, June 7, 1861] This is a fine day. Business in my line is moderate only. I have nothing of any interest to note, as are city is void of everything except military preparations, barricades in the streets are in progress. And also one in front of ice house. Several companies are preparing to leave for Virginia. No new movements appear to be made in Virginia but something must turn up very soon. I retired early.

[Saturday, June 8, 1861] I am getting to like early hours. The market appears lively, and gives our street a busy appearance. This is a warm day. I was pretty busy and had a small job upstairs. I am phrasing away my leisure hours reading Roland yet. This is the day of election—for this date (Tennessee) to secede from the Union. And will ever be memorable in history. I shall now look for plenty of affairs in this section, and the scene of war transferred to the Mississippi—went to the Mission Street office in Eve.

In the June 8 referendum on secession, Tennessee voted overwhelmingly (108,339 to 47,233) in favor. For all practical purposes Tennessee had been "out" of the Union for a month, and this vote ratified the de facto secession. West and Middle Tennessee voted heavily for secession, while East Tennessee voted heavily for the Union. In Shelby County (Memphis), which in February had voted for the Union, only five Union votes were cast out of 7,000+. In Memphis itself, 5,608 voted for secession versus only five for Union.[4]

[Sunday, June 9, 1861] And Sunday is here and no church nothing that pertains to the day but work. My work is such that has no interest and notion in warm season. I have been selling ice all day. The *Capitol* came up from New Orleans. This has been one of the warmest days of the season, yet not so hot as I expected in this country, the state has gone out by a big vote. No reports from East Tennessee. I stayed at Lucas's all Eve and retired early.

[Monday, June 10, 1861] A beautiful warm day this. Business is only moderate. I am getting along as well as may be expected in my boarding house. But torn from such as I should like, it can't be helped at present. Our city looks truly forsaken. Shops closed and the many people gone. Soldiers no more looked at—got to see uniformed men. The steamer *Capitol* got up today and is going to lay up for the present. England is favoring the South in our struggle.

Memphis and its surroundings had already contributed 4,000 soldiers to the army, and as a major transshipment point many more soldiers passed through the city each day.

It looks as if most of Gunther's Illinois acquaintances from the ice business, understandably nervous and homesick, decided to return to the North while they still could. However, Gunther stayed in the South. His sympathies lay with the northern states he had been raised in. However, he did not see any good reason why the two sections could not coexist in peace.

[Tuesday, June 11, 1861] This is a warm day—ice goes moderately only. I went down to see the Peru boys before they left, sent them my overcoat and a forsent of 85th to father so paid Straus my little balance owing him—gave me great pleasure to send up my small matters knowing that it will get there safe—i.e., in good hands. Joe Thomas the battery in front of our ice house is progressing finely A bad joke on the ice house. I spent the Eve mostly at Main Street house and got in late.

[Wednesday, June 12, 1861] After loading wagons I went down to M & O [Mobile & Ohio] railroad to see the crew folks off. Sent letters. There were some soldiers going up also. The pensioners are awfully scared and glad to get off. The weather continues fine and warm. There was a skirmish at Little Bethel, Virginia. There's lots of war news, but no fighting yet. I would like to see them pitch in and have end of the matter. I went down to Main Street house to see Bowers in the Eve, but he had left his house ill, retired after early.

On June 10, 1861, Union forces under General Benjamin Butler converged on the Confederate outposts at Big and Little Bethel, Virginia, near Hampton Roads. In a poorly conceived and even more poorly executed attack, the 7th New York Infantry opened fire by accident on the gray-clad 3rd New York, causing numerous casualties and shattering any hope of surprise. The main attack on the entrenched Confederates failed miserably, with Union losses totaling seventy-nine versus only eight Confederate. Big Bethel was, arguably, the first battle of the Civil War.

> [Thursday, June 13, 1861] I have gotten the *New York Home Journal* to read paid the big sum of 11 cents for it. Awful price for a three-cent paper. These are war times we have to pay for what we get. The war has a terrible effect but it graces the latest screed of our people. Now a nation of soldiers all civilians but yesterday. My trade was dull today. The day hot. The governor of Missouri called out 50,000 troops a collision is now inevitable between Federal and State forces. Movements east are towards Harpers Ferry—I retired early, read some and calm, only a little trouble about some sheets.

On June 12, 1861, Governor Claiborne Jackson of Missouri issued a proclamation denouncing Federal government interference in the affairs of his state, and called for 50,000 volunteers to oppose "the military occupation of Missouri by Union troops." With this action the pro-southern governor essentially declared war against the Federal government—independent of the Confederacy.

> [Friday, June 14, 1861] Up bright and early as usual the day is hot and warm now business only moderate. More troops keep leaving and the city getting sparse of population consequently no consumers. I spent the greater part of my time reading. I managed to get along with my boarding house men now there's still a great opportunity for improvement. I see from the dispatches that Harpers Ferry is evacuated by the Confederate troops. I

stayed at house and retired early, I have some mosquitoes and bedbugs to trouble me now, no bar up yet.

[Saturday, June 15, 1861] The butchers made a great rush with their meats in the house. I am pretty busy most all day, ice sales improving. The Memphis Legion was out this eve in drill. Some boats came calling up answer us as far as Columbus Kentucky. Gov. Jackson of Missouri has called out 50,000 militia and commenced hostilities with the US—the *War Gazette* made its first appearance this Eve, a small affair. The CS government has assumed the mails and the Post Office Department in this state. I went down to the Main street house after closing up.

While most of the young men of Memphis volunteered for the Confederate army, the older men, and the stay-at-homes, organized for local defense. In a letter addressed to Lieutenant General Leonidas Polk dated August 6, 1861, the officers of the Memphis Legion (mostly prominent Memphis businessmen) explained that since the proclamation of war nearly 4,000 men from Memphis and vicinity had gone into the Confederate Armed forces, "leaving at home only the heads of families and business men who cannot go into regular service until compelled by dire necessity." Seven hundred of these men had formed a military organization called the Memphis Legion. "As originally intended our organization contemplated no other object than the protection of our families and our homes." However they offered to place the organization under General Polk's command, if the War Department would accept it on that basis, "to be detailed for duty mainly for the defense of Memphis and the immediate vicinity, with the understanding that when not on duty our members be allowed the privilege of attending to their ordinary business." A local lawyer, Leonidas V. Dixon (1816–78), commanded the Legion. This unit was possibly the forerunner of the 3rd, or Memphis, Battalion, raised in 1862 for local defense for one year.

[Sunday, June 16, 1861] George got out late this morning and I have been up ever since 5 o'ck. Working long as usual this is the best sale day in my house as yet. Several funerals have taken place military and firemen have turned out. I have been confined very steady for the last 3 weeks. This Sunday is passing off like any other day. The Negros turn out well to church up here, dressing in gay style with all their Sunday come to meeting clothes on with their beaux. I attend a lodge of services in honor of Charles Scott, the whole thing was a perfect success.

[Monday, June 17, 1861] This is a terrible cold day for the season of the year, my business is only moderate. There's nothing now worthy of mention thoughts now are for Peace—oh peace what a blessed boon it would be to our sorrows and afflictions. But there's no hope now but the discussion of the God of Battles, Hindman's regiment [2nd Arkansas Infantry] passed through today, on three sections for the porters of Arkansas. I went up and called at Mrs. Daniels had a pleasant chat, Vic is a fine lass.

Increasingly Gunther expresses longings for peace in his diary.

[Tuesday, June 18, 1861] Made an early start this morning. I layed down again several times snoozed gain till later in the morning. Ice sales no go again today. Mr. P makes his usual calls every a.m. This is really cooler weather than I expected south for this season. The mayor wishes all business houses to close at 4 o'ck. I had some customers—the first of the season but we are having some of the fruits and stock of all kinds, berries etc.—I retire early.

[Wednesday, June 19, 1861] Up as usual early and bright, the mornings are cool and pleasant. I am now getting used to being called up to help George out, but have always vowed to take up and snooze after. Nothing going on in the city, and apparently no business of any kind except printers and newspapers. I have finished my rounds, thus making small work of it. As usual I stayed at the house and go to bed early I am now going upon the mornings early to bed and early to rise.

[Thursday, June 20, 1861] This day is warmer again but cool and comfortable in my quarters. Ice business is increasing but nowhere apparently to last season. The only news I know and can glean from the city papers. W. H. Russell of the *London Times* is in the city, the papers are full of the encounter of heroes. I went down and called on Lloyd this Eve. Southern states are all vacating the commonwealth. The government subscription goes on very well. The nights are pleasant and cool and few mosquitoes.

William H. Russell, courtesy Library of Congress

Irish-born William Howard Russell (1820–1907) worked as the war correspondent for the *London Times*. He had won fame for his reporting of the Crimean War, and the *Times* hoped that Russell could repeat that journalistic coup by covering the American Civil War. One British soldier described Russell as "a vulgar low Irishman, [who] sings a good song, drinks anyone's brandy and water and smokes as many cigars as a Jolly Good Fellow. He is just the sort of chap to get information, particularly out of youngsters." Russell traveled throughout the South and the North, seemingly possessing a free pass to visit everything and talk to everyone. From his travels and gifted pen emerged a series of revealing dispatches on the war, and the classic book, *My Diary North and South* (1863). See, for example, above for the April 26 entry and Russell's comments on Confederate fortifications. Memphis did not impress Russell. "Of all the bad roads and dusty streets I have yet seen in the New World, where both prevail, North and South, those of Memphis are the worst."[5]

> [Friday, June 21] This is another fine day, I spent most of my leisure reading my *Eclectic* for this month. It is a fine number and nothing gives me more pleasure than perusal of its columns. This has been some small fighting in Missouri, General Lyon and the governor with the secessionists. No fight in the East yet but prospects for one are bright. It would be a great pleasure for me to get some news from home. Times here are getting worse and worse. All the batteries are finished for the Lincoln reception. I went down to Main street house in the Eve.

The fighting in Missouri referred to was a skirmish near Boonville on June 17. Union forces led by General Nathaniel Lyon had driven Governor Jackson and a small force of the pro-southern Missouri State Guard out of Jefferson City, the state capitol. Jackson ordered his few (500) ill-equipped guardsmen to make a stand at nearby Boonville, to buy time to rally recruits. Pursuing rapidly, Lyon's army (about 1,400 men) attacked and in a twenty-minute fight routed the guardsmen. Only a few men on either side were killed or wounded, but the small skirmish had enormous impact: the pro-southern state government administration had been driven from the state capitol, never to return, while the victorious Unionists seized control of the government and kept Missouri in the Union.

> [Saturday, June 22, 1861] This day is not only warm, but pronounced by everybody hot. Ice is selling good. The news from the seat of war is meager. A governor in western Virginia was elected. A state government is set up by the western Virginians themselves! I read my *Eclectic* most of the time. My thoughts are now directed for the future, in determination to save my money and set up shop for myself, this being a goal all my lifetime. It

Battle of Boonville, from Harper's Weekly, *July 13, 1861*

is preposterous in the extreme. George is considerable taken by Miss Arnold, poor fellow. I am afraid he will get taken in before he knows it.

On May 23, 1861, Virginia voters overwhelmingly approved the Ordinance of Secession. This vote led loyalists in the largely anti-secession Western Virginia to call a convention, which met at Wheeling on June 11, 1861. The delegates declared secession illegal and voted to reorganize the state government. On June 20, 1861, Marion County lawyer Francis Pierpont was elected governor of the loyal state government. This breakaway government declared a new state of "Kanawha" created, which was soon renamed "West Virginia" and admitted into the Union.

[Sunday, June 23, 1861] Sunday again, it appears hardly possible the week has so sped speedily past again, time flies certainly, before a man can realize, on how he has spent so much life's journey. I have been busy all day selling ice—no rest for the wicked now. But being necessity and no sin. I have not left the house today. But George has gone out riding with Miss Arnold—good boy. We had a fine shower this Eve, a perfect Godsend, I stayed at office all Eve.

[Monday, June 24, 1861] This is a very cool and pleasant day, not much sales of ice. The roads are very pleasant and no dust. I have finished my *Eclectic Magazine* now totally out of reading matter. Upon the state of the country nothing of any moment has taken place, some skirmishing in Missouri all the movements of troops are kept secret. Our city at present is very healthy, some 50 soldiers are now in the Mother's Home Hospital. I had the pleasure of attending the delectations of South Memphis Lodge. A magnificent hall and the whole passed off very pleasantly and a full turn out.

The *Memphis Appeal* of June 21, under the headline "The Southern Mother's Association," reported that the Southern Mother's Association had established a hospital on Second Street.

Gunther attended the meeting of the South Memphis Lodge No. 118, Free and Accepted Masons, chartered in 1845 when South Memphis was a separate city. Their new lodge room, at the corner of 2nd and Madison Streets, was dedicated in January 1861.

[Tuesday, June 25, 1861] We had quite a shower this Eve, the rain just poured down. Business is dull in our line and in general through the city, in fact shop might as well shut up. There are about 50 sick Arkansas soldiers at the S Mother's home commencing to get in the ranks. I occupy most of my leisure time writing, my room is very damp since I managed to get along very well with our unique room. I went downtown and bought me a few old *Eclectic*s to read.

[Wednesday, June 26, 1861] It cleared up again this a.m., nothing doing. No war news of any account but advances are being made. I expect to hear something every day, there must be a battle very soon. I had a *Scientific American* of the 15th inst., money is getting to be a very scarce article, precious—I am now having greens and all kinds of vegetables of dinner. I see some mule melons in the market. I went to SM [South Memphis] Lodge worked in the 2nd degree a pleasant meeting got caught in the rain coming home.

[Thursday, June 27, 1861] This day is only moderately hot, business is as usual. The election takes place today. Park was elected mayor a good change in the board. The war news is meager. And no new movements. We are now taking out ice from the city vault again—I've had some very fine tomatoes, the city is very quiet indeed—I went down to the Main street office in the Evening. I enjoyed my sleep some of the days and feel quite well.

In the election, wealthy Memphis merchant John Park (1813–97) was elected mayor, over three opponents. The Irish-born Park, a rabid Confederate, would remain mayor through 1866.

[Friday, June 28, 1861] As usual got up early, but also as usual managed to lay down again. The last few days we have had some showers in the Eve with slight thunder. From the seat of war nothing is heard both armies being very secret about their movements. Our city remains pretty quiet, except in case of murder is sometimes committed. The soldiers are mostly gone in camps. I stayed at house all Eve.

[Saturday, June 29, 1861] The weather continues remarkably cool for the season, much more so than I expected in the South. Oh how glad I would be to hear from home, my communications are cut off, and nothing is heard of much interest by us. I am daily and very steadily attending to my business, I bought me an old *Eclectic Magazine* for lost and ear for 10 cents apiece, cheap enough for I think and my cherished of reading—were it not for them what would I do to drive dull care away.

[Sunday, June 30, 1861] Oh lovely Sunday has come again, and with it past recollections of this glorious day as I used to spend at home at the church, the companion of a stroll with friends, pleasant indeed were they. But now what a change has come over my situation, work is now the order of the day and work it is—and a change will come some day, money is the article, I am going to save it. The rain came down again this Eve, concluded to remain at house and read with my eyelids about so I rolled over and went asleep.

July 1861

As the war in Virginia and Missouri heats up, Tennessee formally joins the Confederacy. The Memphis newspapers Gunther avidly pores over are filled with war news, some accurate, some wildly inaccurate. Troops fill the streets of Memphis, streets that heretofore had not heard the tramp of soldier's boots. Despite the warm weather, ice is not selling like it had in the past, as businesses, suffering from the partial shutdown of their northern trade, cut back on their orders. Gunther finds plenty of time to ruminate on the weather and politics.

> [Monday, July 1, 1861] There was a tremendous rain all day, but stopped this Eve and some. The weather is extremely cool for this season here. No sales here for ice such days. I spent most of my time reading the *Eclectic*, a great source of pleasure to me and very instructive. I peruse the morning *Appeal* with great avidity, it being the only paper except the *Argus*. I get to read. George is in a H_ll of a show all day, lateness, rain and mud all effect his mind. I visited Lloyd in the Eve and then returned in good season.

Charles Gunther spent much of his free time reading the local newspapers, avidly gleaning from them news of the war and of local events. For a city of 30,000 people, Memphis boasted several newspapers. The *Appeal* proudly proclaimed itself the leading Democratic Party newspaper of the southwest. When Union forces occupied Memphis in 1862, the publishers loaded the printing establishment onto railroad cars and for the next three years produced the *Appeal* in such places as Grenada, Mississippi, and Atlanta, Georgia, earning the nickname "The Moving *Appeal*."

Editor M. C. Galloway started the *Avalanche* in 1858 as a newspaper "southern in every sense of the word." J. H. MacMahon started the *Bulletin* in 1855 as a Whig/Unionist newspaper. It supported the Bell-Everett Constitutional Union ticket in 1860, but in late 1861 was forced to merge with the *Avalanche*. The *Argus* was started during the war by veteran editor J. M. Keating.

> [Tuesday, July 2, 1861] Oh this is a cold horrible day for this 2nd of this month, man fields comfortable with a coat on ice no go—a beautiful comet has made his appearance in the sky, the Sun shown all day, the roads are good again. The *Bulletin* has made its appearance as in the evening paper now. This was never as important I enjoy it my leisure time in reading the *Eclectic*. The *Bulletin* is out now as evening paper and promises well. I stayed at Main Street office all Eve and returned late.

> [Wednesday, July 3, 1861] This has been a very pleasant summer day, not hot at all—business is very dull. The city has a awful dead look, stores are shut up at dusk and nothing but a few restaurants are now open. There's something stirring times expecting in Virginia today or tomorrow. Colonel Thomas and other passengers captured the steamer *Nicholas* and three prizes in MD—we are having some trouble in east Tennessee—some of them want to set up shop for themselves, Brownlow, Johnson, etc. Etheridge others. Harry McCarthy is giving his drolleries at Odd Fellows Hall, I took a walk up the city in the Eve.

Emerson Etheridge (1818–1902), former Whig congressman; Andrew Johnson (1808–75), US Senator and future president of the United States; and William Gannaway Brownlow (1805–77), editor of the *Knoxville*

Whig, were leaders of the pro-Union faction that was especially numerous in East Tennessee.

Gunther refers to the bold capture of the steamship *Nicholas* in Chesapeake Bay by southern partisans under the command of Richard Thomas (1833–75), who had boarded the ship disguised as "Madam Zarvona," a woman! Union general John Dix described Thomas as "crack brained."

Harry Macarthy's ad in the *Memphis Appeal* of July 3 proclaimed: "The Arkansas Comedian, Vocalist, Banjoist, Dancer, the Author and the Man of Many Parts, will give his Personation Concerts/Every Night This Week,/At Odd-Fellows' Hall./Admission 50 cents. Servants and Children 25 cents." The July 9 *Appeal* reported Macarthy so popular, especially with his new song "Bonnie Blue Flag," that he had been held over another week. Irish-born Harry Macarthy (MacCarthy/McCarthy) (1804–74), songwriter and comedian, became a Southern favorite when he adapted an old Irish tune into "The Bonnie Blue Flag," the unofficial Confederate national anthem.

> [Thursday, July 4, 1861] No important news from the east. This is the glorious day of independence, and what a sight I see around me—this once happy country in a fratricidal war—in our armies momentarily I am expecting in expectation of a terrible battle, one year ago today I celebrate this day in a fine ride with Jonathan Schmale in the country, and indeed I enjoyed it—today I am in the sunny south, in the Confederate states, working as usual. The day has not been celebrated here as it ought to have been but passed off very cool loads of joy except a few fine firecrackers by the boys, what a change.

Gunther thought it odd, at the least, that the seceding South would celebrate the national independence day holiday. But not Southerners. As the *Memphis Appeal* explained on the 4th, "The Fourth of July is not a Yankee, but an American, institution, and it must be observed and perpetuated throughout the South."

[Friday, July 5, 1861] This is a warm day but not very hot. Ice sales are improving. There has been a fight near Martinsburg, Virginia the Confederates retreating, that is the report. There are no news of any importance. Congress is in session. Etheridge of this state is the clerk, military matters are about coming to a point. I wrote home today which they sent by express via Louisville, expense 30 cents. I visited the Leded Scott Lodge after had a dish of ice cream, but none fit to match up to Uncle John's.

The "fight near Martinsburg" was the engagement at Falling Waters, July 2, 1861. Three thousand Federal troops under General Robert Patterson pushed back a 380-man Confederate reconnaissance force under the soon-to-be-famous Stonewall Jackson. Patterson's casualties were around seventy-five, while the Confederates lost less than thirty.[6]

[Saturday, July 6, 1861] Up early as usual and to work. This is a pretty brisk day, and have been busy. The *Appeal* published Lincoln's message not much news today. I read considerable but I don't feel exactly well this Eve, pulled to hard on the ice this a.m. Beale Street is lively this Eve—I could not help notice the many beautiful ladies pass, this is an Eve-like house. This Eve is pleasant I went to bed early feeling very tired.

President Lincoln's July 4, 1861, message to Congress constituted Lincoln's first major public statement on the war. He blamed the South for starting the war and narrated the events that had taken place since Sumter.

[Sunday, July 7, 1861] Up as usual and at work—no rest for the wicked now, this has been a warm day, ice sales good. I stayed at house all day, read some. My mind is now very much occupied with the hope of promotion and for the future advancement pecuniarily, the start is all I am pushing for, and I am going to have it. I have not seen the inside of a church for some time, I took again both there is.

> [Monday, July 8, 1861] This is a very warm day, business brisk for the season. The war news is becoming interesting, a fight took place near Martinsburg, Virginia and the Federal troops were advancing. Things in the city look gloomy and hard, money is running very short, again many with small shops are closing up. I get along very well at my boarding house. I spent the Eve at Harry McCarthy's drolleries went in with George Wilson, I thought it was a poor affair myself, near where with Winchell.

The likeliest candidate for this George Wilson on the 1860 census of Memphis is a New York–born George Wilson, age 42, a prosperous grocer, whose store was located at the corner of Fourth and Union Streets.

> [Tuesday, July 9, 1861] I don't feel exactly right today, took some pills. Not much doing. The day is pleasant and not particularly warm, in fact quite cool for the season. I wrote letters to Melton the first letter mailed by me in the S.C. War news is unimportant today. Our city is quiet. The Holly Springs ladies gave a concert at the theater this Eve. I went to Main Street house and came home about ten, feeling better for a good sleep.

The *Appeal* reported, under the headline "Interesting Concert," that the "proficiency of the ladies of Holly Springs in 'the art divine' is no secret in Memphis…" The concert was held to benefit the soldiers of the 19th Mississippi Infantry, a Holly Springs-based unit, and drew a large crowd.

> [Wednesday, July 10, 1861] The weather continues cool + pleasant, ice no go. We have reports of the defeat of the Federals in MO by McCullough. I have my *Eclectic Mag.* most of the day. I have many things on my mind, but somehow or other I want time to fly—getting anxious to see a big fight—getting blood thirsty. I want to see an end to the troubles but prospects dubious. I spent the Eve walking with Mich Pyne + got in early.

[Thursday, July 11, 1861] I don't feel so well as I might today [illegible shorthand marks in text of diary]. Ice sales are very poor. I visited market this morning, there was a good display of vegetables but buyers scarce. Fruits of all kinds are never to be had, but too dear for the masses. The war news is messy. Major Polk is up for governor of this state. I took a stroll down to Lloyd's. There was a large fire on the levee Barnett's house and block was burnt. Got home early.

Nashville lawyer William Hawkins Polk (1815–62), brother of President Polk, was running for governor of Tennessee on a Unionist ticket, against the incumbent, Memphis resident Isham Green Harris (1818–97), described as "the most competent and skilful political leader in the history of Tennessee." Harris won the election overwhelmingly, and went on to serve as the Confederate governor of Tennessee and as US Senator postwar.

The *Appeal* of July 12 reported; "Fire—At two o'clock yesterday morning a vivid blaze broke from the premises at the corner of the alley on Water street, between Main and Washington streets, occupied by Mr. Thomas Barnett as a hotel." According to the newspaper, rumor had the estranged Mrs. Barnett starting the fire.

[Friday, July 12, 1861] The weather is exceedingly cool for this season and my black coat on the a.m. No business in my line, we got a feel of the fight in MO Sigel and Jackson. Major General Polk arrived and has now taken command of the army in this section. I am looking out for stirring events, sure. I spent the eve at a meeting of the South Memphis Lodge. The lodge is beautiful and now finished up in fine style. It is a pleasure to make a visit. My heart is with the craft doing and she is very well.

Leonidas Polk (1808–64) had perhaps the most unusual background of any high-ranking Civil War general. A graduate of West Point, Polk resigned from the army almost immediately after graduation and entered

Leonidas Polk, courtesy Library of Congress

the Episcopal ministry. He rose to Episcopal Bishop of the Southwest. In 1861 President Davis appointed Polk, his old friend and well-known public figure, as major general in command of "Department Number 2," which included Memphis and the Mississippi River defenses. Polk later rose to corps command. Polk, a very good bishop, proved to be a mediocre general. As General Porter Alexander put it, "The Lord had made him a splendid bishop & a great & good man. So all our pious people with one consent & with secret conviction that the Lord would surely favor a bishop turned in & made him a lieut. Gen., which the Lord had not." See Ezra Warner, *Generals in Gray* (Baton Rouge: LSU Press, 1959), 242–243; and E. Porter Alexander, *Fighting for the Confederacy* (Chapel Hill, U. of NC Press, 1989), 289.

At the battle of Carthage, Missouri, on July 5, 1861, the pro-Confederate Missouri State Guard, under Governor Jackson, defeated Union forces under the command of Colonel Franz Sigel. Sigel had tried to intercept the retreat southward of Jackson's forces, but Jackson's ill-equipped guardsmen routed Sigel's vastly outnumbered Unionists.[7]

The "battle in western VA" was the July 11, 1861, Battle of Rich Mountain. Union forces under General George B. McClellan attacked a smaller Confederate force under General Robert Garnett, defeating them and capturing a large number of prisoners. The victory brought McClellan national attention and eventual command of the Army of the Potomac. A few days later General Garnett was killed in a skirmish at Corrick's Ford during the retreat from this battle.

[Saturday, July 13, 1861] This is a fine day and very cool. Business is dull and nothing doing. This morning dispatches reported a battle in western VA McClellan and Wise. The Federals victorious. The city remains quiet, an election took place for the militia officers but it was totally disregarded—I am in good morale and quiet mind. Thinking of home sometimes and its pleasures to my lonesomeness at present but they soon vanish. Spent the eve at a meeting for the cotton loan. Speech by Walker Brooke.

The militia turnout in Memphis constantly disappointed Confederate officials. As one local newspaper observed, "The fact cannot be disguised that the militia service is somewhat obnoxious to our people, and they always respond to a call for its organization with reluctance." See "Organize! Drill," *Memphis Appeal*, November 21, 1861.

Walker Brooke (1813–69) was a former US senator from Mississippi and a Confederate congressman. He spoke at the Odd Fellows Hall on behalf of the Confederate loan.

[Sunday, July 14, 1861] I got up early but slept very sound. No mosquitoes to trouble one. This is a fine day. Tended my business all day, I have very little time myself to go out but make up spare time reading. The various church bells are all ringing and I would be glad to come if only I could, but this is our business season and we must make hay while the sun shines. I spent the eve taking a walk with Mich sat in our beautiful little park it is a delightful spot indeed.

Gunther often finds reasons NOT to attend church while in Memphis. It is possible that he refused to say the obligatory prayers for the Confederate cause.

[Monday, July 15, 1861] I don't feel just as well as I might, but I am happy to note that I am once again I believe relieved from my old complaint. Times in the city are dead and nothing doing. I visited market this morning bought me a few apples. Jim McCord is up to see me. He is going home sick. I find but little news in the papers. General Garnett has been killed in some fighting up in Western VA. I went to be very early, it is raining very hard—Geo. is sick.

[Tuesday, July 16, 1861] Oh, this is a horrid muddy, rainy day and awful at that. Jim McCord is up and starts for Peru this eve. I sent up affections to Hays. This is a very dull day, nothing doing—no fighting yet, except for reports from Western VA favorable to the Unionists. George is sick and crabbed all day. I read my *Eclectic* most of the time. I visited South Memphis Lodge and helped at a raising the night is damp and cloudy.

The newspapers promptly reported the Union advance into Virginia. The First Battle of Bull Run, or Manassas, was fought on July 21, 1861. A Union army under General Irwin McDowell attacked a Confederate defense force under General Pierre G. T. Beauregard, strung out along Bull Run (a northern Virginia watercourse). The attack met with initial success. However, Confederate reinforcements (including troops under General Joseph E. Johnston rushed in from the Shenandoah Valley) counterattacked and routed the Federals, who fled back to Washington. The equally green, equally exhausted, but victorious Confederates made only a feeble pursuit. Union losses were 2,896 out of an army of 35,000; the Confederates lost 1,982 out of 31,000. Not unexpectedly, Confederate morale soared after this victory.

[Wednesday, July 17, 1861] Still it rains and my house is very damp. Nothing doing at all. We have a report of the advance of the Federal troops at Fairfax Courthouse at 3 p.m. I had very quiet time all day, reading, my time passed very pleasantly. And nothing to distress my mind, and not homesick yet as I anticipated. I don't like the idea of waiting for my meals so long at my boarding house but still have to put up with it for the present.

[Thursday, July 18, 1861] I am glad it has cleared off again. It is now fine. Ice not much sale. I have been reading the *Eclectic* accordingly. There was a heavy skirmish at Manassas today the Federals retiring. Stirring news is now expected every day. I went down to the city this eve the band played at Odd Fellows Hall and there appears to be quite a stir in the works. I after had a good lounge with Lloyd and Mich and got home quite late.

[Friday, July 19, 1861] I feel well and slept all day. I was up from 3 ½ to various hours and stayed up all day. It is warm today and nothing new in the city. Same talk on the Federal retreat at Centreville. I read but little today I bought me a pair of pants today and mended another good one. I feel anxious for more news on the advance of the armies. I spent the day at room and retired to bed early after reading the NY news. There is a heavy rain all eve.

[Saturday, July 20, 1861] The day promises well and business is better, The street is lively, worked afternoon. I munched to the extent of a few apples, we have no further war news but tomorrow is the appointed day. I am getting tired and long for a more congenial occupation as some it is pleasurable and very cool for a summer's job. I cannot probably do better—except pay, and the making of money in war times is out of the question. I bought me an *Eclectic* for this month, and went through it for "moon lit."

[Sunday, July 21, 1861] I had a good sleep though I murdered some of those pestiferous insects called bedbugs, and I mean about to exterminate them. This is a very warm day as usual I worked hard. The sales being good. We were visited again with a shower this eve to the great mortification of George. I read the papers and Jeff Davis's message to Congress today at Richmond, we are in the midst of an awful volcano which may burst within the hour. The big battle of Manassas is expected to come off today.

Gayoso Hotel, 1887, courtesy Library of Congress

A Memphis landmark, the Gayoso Hotel was constructed in 1842 in a Greek Revival style intended to grace the downtown. Its nearly 300 rooms offered amenities not seen in other city hotels, such as indoor plumbing.

[Monday, July 22, 1861]

There was a heavy rain this morning again and no change of weather. Checked off this room and is now quite cold. My business is a very poor. I amuse myself by reading *Chambers Journal*. Received two extras of the great battle of Manassas Sunday. It was a terrible affair and the victory is claimed so far by both sides, it is hard telling who best. Our boys are very much excited. I went down the way and heard some speeches at the Gayoso by General Polk, Pillow and Governor Jackson of Missouri. The crowd was very enthusiastic over the war news.

A weekly 16-page magazine, *Chambers Journal of Popular Literature, Science, and Arts* started in 1832.

The *Memphis Bulletin* of July 23 reported that Governor Jackson, General Polk, General Pillow, and Dr. Joseph Nash McDowell (1803–68) of Saint Louis addressed the crowds at the Gayoso the night before. The Gayoso was Pillow's headquarters.

Politician-turned-general Gideon J. Pillow (1806–78) had commanded the Provisional Tennessee State Army until Tennessee joined the Confederacy. President Davis then put Pillow in command of Memphis and the Mississippi River defenses. There he clashed with his commander, General Polk, with his own subordinates, and with just about anyone else he came into contact with. Pillow's undoubted energy and organizational ability did not translate into battlefield success, and after an embarrassing performance at Fort Donelson in 1862, his military career essentially ended.

Gideon Pillow, courtesy Library of Congress

[Tuesday, July 23, 1861] This another cold day and nothing doing. The war news of the defeat of the Federals is confirmed. Johnston's coming turned the tide. Military spirit is increased. The people feel greatly rejoiced. I feel somewhat dull today. Visited the market this morning bought some fruit, the weather surprises everybody I never thought of such cold days in this month south. The crops are good and no person in want of provisions. Business in the city is dead, my only hope is peace and then all will be well. I spent the eve at Main Street House.

[Wednesday, July 24, 1861] No change in the weather no change in business everything quiet. The Memphis Battalion is out in drill, No later war news but all parties are preparing for another shake at it again around Washington. There was an enormous slaughter at the battle of Manassas, at lowest not less than 5,000 on all side according to all reports. I got a *Louisville Courier* with some particulars. I read my *Eclectic* all my leisure time. I went and heard Major Polk speak at Odd Fellows Hall. He is a candidate for governor. I was a little disappointed by his opinions and [shorthand marks in text].

The fact that these marks are in shorthand suggests that Gunther tried to hide his Union sentiments from anyone who read the diary. The *Appeal* of July 26 discusses Major Polk's views and proudly proclaims that it has endorsed Governor Harris.

[Thursday, July 25, 1861] I managed to get my usual sleep though up several times in the morning. I have not much to do, and am taking it easy. No news of importance. I feel the trouble somewhat our city is blockaded and an important military movement is on foot. Cairo I understand is the point. I found many business houses are closing up for want of business. I went down to Main Street house paid my money over on moss bed.

[Friday, July 26, 1861] The weather is getting warmer and an improvement in business. The city is quiet. I see an artillery company pass today. The roads are fine and everything looks fine and beautiful. The shrubbery gardens + C., the Park particularly so, the many fine showers fall at our hot days, have all lent their powers. I battle is reported at Harpers Ferry no confirmation as yet. I feel anxious to hear from home I went up to Main street house in the eve and supped in the _____.

[Saturday, July 27, 1861] The last of the month expeditions left today. There was many a tear shed at the departure to the source of strife. Today is hot and business is better as usual. Beale Street is lively. I read Breckinridge's speech in the senate on the unconstitutional acts of Lincoln. Our papers are filled with the details of the Manassas battle. It has created a great military enthusiasm among the southern people. I stayed near the house all eve and retired early feeling rather tired and another week has sped by with all the events of the revolution.

Former vice president, then US senator from neutral Kentucky, John C. Breckinridge (1821–75) delivered a widely publicized speech on July 16. Breckinridge denounced the Lincoln administration's acts as unconstitutional. Newspapers throughout the country ran the speech, which was later printed. Soon Union authorities issued warrants for Breckinridge's arrest. Breckinridge fled South to join the Confederacy. He ended the war as a Major General and Confederate Secretary of War.

> [Sunday, July 28, 1861] This is a very warm day and business in my line is brisk. Nothing to do but work accordingly. I have not seen the inside of a church for some time. Our city is getting thinned out and is looking very much like a deserted place than it did last fall. I have had no company at all today, and lonely is the hour but I managed to make time pass by reading. I bought a *Louisville Courier* and a *New York Ledger*. I spent the evening taking a walk through the park. And today an early hour for bed.

> [Monday, July 29, 1861] Got up several times during the hours 2 and 5. The night was warm, but slept well, with mosquitoes singing around my ear. The day opens with but little change of last week. There are yet a great many men in uniforms about the street. I see some Mississippi boys among them. I have read much and many accounts of the Manassas battle a perfect stampede of the Federals. I wrote a letter to Melton. I long for a letter from home. I heard a speech in the eve by Col. Payne at south Market he is running for the Confederate Congress he is the best speaker we heard in this city.

Memphis lawyer Robert Garnett Payne (1812–61) had been elected state senator in 1859. A fellow lawyer found Payne an "irrestiable" showman in front of juries. He lost his race for the Confederate Congress to David M. Currin.[8]

> [Tuesday, July 30, 1861] Tom goes out with George these few mornings. The day is quite warm business is moderate in my line,

> the consumers and money few—we were all enrolled in the militia. There's no new war movements. Polk and Pillow's troops are now at New Madrid, MO. It is now noticeable on the streets that the women predominate in the population now a days. I went down street in the eve had a talk in the Manse & Gould, got back pretty early after talking very fine. Glass of soda.

"Tom" is Thomas Williams, born circa 1835 in Pennsylvania, a LaSalle County ice worker in 1860 and a friend of Gunther's. "George" cannot be identified. Gunther tended to associate with fellow Northerners, and especially hometown buddies, while in Memphis.

> [Wednesday, July 31, 1861] This is another fine and warm day, business is dull generally. The steam fleet from Missouri got back and some military operations are looked for in Cairo directions. Not much news from the east. I see the Prince Napoleon and Clothilde have arrived in New York. McClellan is at the head of Lincoln's army and gives satisfaction much. Our troops are quiet in Richmond yet. I went downtown and heard Elder Graves preach on the war. I was disappointed in the man very much. A New Orleans company came in from mustering in the street.

Prince Jerome Napoleon Bonaparte, a cousin of French Emperor Napoleon III, and his wife Clothilde visited the United States in 1861. The prince eventually met with President Lincoln.

Virginia-born, Princeton-educated James Robinson Graves (1820–93), the editor of the Nashville religious newspaper *The Baptist*, moved to Memphis after the war, where he operated a Baptist book house.

August 1861

Ice sales decline even further in August. Avid for a second income stream, Gunther starts selling melons in the city's markets, but meets with little success. Although Memphis's once-bustling merchant houses are cutting back or shutting down, other businesses, mostly for war production, are increasing. To Memphisians the war seems like something one reads about in the newspaper but doesn't experience firsthand. The border slave state of Kentucky remains neutral, and as long as Kentucky is neutral, the Union army can hardly attack Tennessee or points further south.

However, nobody believes that Kentucky will remain neutral forever. The "neutrality" has been cooked up by the state's political leaders to paper over fundamental differences between pro- and anti-secession Kentuckians. The state government is itself split between a solidly pro-Union legislature and neutralist or pro-Southern governor. Ignoring the state's proclamation of neutrality, Confederate and Union authorities are recruiting Kentuckians to fight. And since the river route south to Memphis flows past the bluffs at Columbus, Kentucky, Memphis newspapers and, increasingly, local Confederate military leaders, are planning to safeguard Memphis by seizing those bluffs for the Confederacy. On the other side, President Abraham Lincoln recognized the importance of Kentucky when he declared "I hope to have God on my side, but I must have Kentucky." More tellingly, in a September 1861 letter Lincoln wrote, "I think to lose Kentucky is nearly the same as to lose the whole game.... We would as well consent to separation at once, including the surrender of the capital." Leaders who believe this will not allow Kentucky to remain neutral for long.

> [Thursday, August 1, 1861] George settled and is now adrift from our house. Tom taking charge of the wagon, George feels bad and don't like the idea of leaving at all. This is a hot day business pretty good. The election for governor takes place, two candidates, Harris and Polk, there appears to be very little animation and few voters. I feel very lonesome and forlorn somehow or other today. I read an old *Harper's Magazine* and took a stroll in the city this eve. The city is perfectly dead and no shops open except whisky and drug stores.

In the race for governor of Tennessee, the incumbent Isham Harris beat Major William Polk by a margin of more than 31,000—a landslide. The vote in Memphis was Harris 2,741, Polk 694 (*Augusta Chronicle*, August 6, 1861), the vote total representing a dramatic drop from June's secession vote.

> [Friday, August 2, 1861] Tom came around very early, but after, got a fine sleep again. This is a very warm day, ice sales good. I wrote a letter home, to be taken up by George. There's nothing of any import in the city, passports are required to travel nowadays or to leave the city. We are getting out some awful cakes of ice, perfect monsters. Have not seen Lloyd for some time. I spent the eve partly at Main Street and retired early.

> [Saturday, August 3, 1861] This is a very warm day and expressed by all persons, awful—I don't feel myself, very uncomfortable in my house. George and Henry left for Louisville this p.m. I was summoned for militia drill this eve did not go—business. South Market looked gaily with the feminine gender. Melons start coming in plenty, but high. I sent a letter and paper with George home. I had little affair de casse—Tom and I get out ice as usual. I stayed at the house all eve until late got me a pair of pantaloons--$5.50 a good bargain and made to order.

According to one newspaper account of Memphis, all male citizens age 16 to 60 had to drill three hours a day, using old and discarded US Army muskets. See "Reign of Terror in the South," *Portland Weekly Oregonian*, October 19, 1861.

> [Sunday, August 4, 1861] This is another very warm day, had a fine sleep last night. Up and early and the heavens such a business I have had this season. No religious ideas care to trouble me, and it has been so long since I have been in a church that most of the church religious ideas I had are getting in a dull state and need considerable furnishing up, but no prospects for some time. I stayed at house and retired early.

[Monday, August 5, 1861] This is another fine and warm day. Business is moderate comparatively compared to late yesterday. I am cool and serious, and militia calls etc. don't effect my state of mind. War news is getting extremely meager now-a-days. Missouri is getting to be the field of operations. Specie is getting to be very scarce and at high premium. Gold 15 cents I took a stroll down the city in the eve, but all is dead and nothing of any kind of business. Nights are pleasant.

[Tuesday, August 6, 1861] My early slumbers are not now interrupted by ice customers early in the morning have given them a better timing—this is another hot day, but my place is cold. I started in the watermelon today, sold two only for a start. All are hand for are concentrating at New Madrid, MO. It is expected that there will be a fight in that neighborhood. I stayed at Louis's all eve and retired early.

Gunther undoubtedly heard reports that local Confederate army leaders planned, since Kentucky remained neutral, to transfer their forces to Missouri, join Jeff Thompson's Missouri State Guardsmen and troops from Arkansas, to invade southeast Missouri.[9]

[Wednesday, August 7, 1861] I was woked by the catfish men, routing me out. Scarce times after Tom left. This is another fine and warm day. I bought some 3 melons today, again, range 15 cents, sales poor. I prepared me a good sign. Our city is full of army rumors. Columbus, KY is said to be taken. I went out for the first time to drill in the militia this eve. There was a poor turn out, and militia won't work well pressing men to take up arms but very poorly + no dependence can be put on them.

By state law, all white males between the ages of 18 and 45 were liable for duty in the state militia. However, Memphis was not the only city where those ordered to turn out, failed to turn out. Lack of arms discouraged many from even bothering. As one New Orleans lady wrote of a militia turnout there, "... how fine it would be if each man had a gun. They are very poorly armed."[10]

[Thursday, August 8, 1861] Up early this morning planted my watermelon standard above the walk and am now ready for action. This is a very warm day. It appeared like rain but cleared off. Mich Pyne and Tom Williams were both up boy we had several melons. There is nothing of any import for me to mention. Business is on a standstill, and no go. There is considerable excitement about town, by the pressing of numerous men to go in the army or work on the boats. I spent the eve at house and on my street above.

[Friday, August 9, 1861] We have had threatening rain for some day, but it appears to postpone its visit. My melon trade goes slow, but prospect good. Our papers have very little news of import. I am out of reading matter and feel slightly lonesome. There is some city gossip about the Gilbert and Shaw extortion case. We are shipping some ice, but not more than last season, if anything as much. I took a stroll up the city, had a talk with Nourse & Gould. We are having some fine over our militia, but the officers drill. Took a drink with the Capt. and returned home.

The *Richmond* (Virginia) *Dispatch* of August 27, 1861, gives the details of the Gilbert & Shaw case:

A scandal case. —A great scandal case has been going on before the Criminal Court at Memphis, for the past week. The *Appeal* gives the following outlines of it: Trial for Extortion.—At the Criminal Court yesterday afternoon, Chas. N. Martin and Ellen Shaw, wife of A. B. Shaw, were called for trial on the charge of "willfully and maliciously extorting from Dr. Samuel Gilbert five promissory notes, to the amount of ten thousand dollars, and his signature to a deed of trust upon real estate secure the same, by means of verbal threats upon his life." The *Appeal* of the 17th says the jury had not agreed upon a verdict.

The principals involved were wealthy merchant, former alderman Abel B. Shaw (1807-61), his wife Ellen McLean Shaw (1827-67), and Dr. Samuel Gilbert (1804-69), a Virginia-born Memphis physician."

> [Saturday, August 10, 1861] This is a warm day. Thunderclouds appear most every day but no rain. Business is poor, of the town I will say nothing, not enough doing to call it business—I got a fine load of melons from old Merril, cheap. I seen the city is full of all kinds of fruits, and melons are impressantly low. There are various rumors afloat that Genl. Lyon is taken, but it is all humbug—I stayed at house all eve and retired early.

> [Sunday, August 11, 1861] The holy Sabbath day has been inaugurated as usual by work. The day looks like rain. It did about eleven o'ck. The melon trade is pretty good—got a puff in the *Appeal*. I would hear the various church bells ring—reminds me of my church going days, but now it is work. There is a good time coming—I will make up in the winter season, I would like to hear from home. I stayed at house all eve and kept open late. Fell twice and laid myself down to sleep, soon to fall asleep.

The "puff" Gunther refers to is in the *Memphis Appeal* of August 11: "Fine Melons—A fine lot of choice melons will be found to-day at the Ice House of Bohlen, Wilson & Co., on Main street."

> [Monday, August 12, 1861] Got up early, there has been quite a shower today, something doing. I see no news from the seat of the war at present. The scandal case of Gilbert & Shaw is all the gossip. I went to a concert given by the ladies at the theater for

the benefit of southern mothers, there was a fine crowd out—the beauty and fashion of the city. It passed off very well, but still it might have been better. Too much sentimentality altogether. There was a fire as I returned. The night is cloudy and lightening.

[Tuesday, August 13, 1861] I sleep as long as possible this morning. This is an exceedingly cold day for the season, a coat is very comfortable. No trade at all. I finished my poem I think pretty good for a first attempt but for now. No war news and lying account best preparations for coming events re going on. City appears to be full of lawless characters, fights, murders and affairs appear all the go. Stayed at house in the eve.

As if to echo Gunther's worry about fights, the *Appeal* of Aug. 14th reported: "Unfeminine Women. —We cannot conjecture the cause, but the number of women arrested by our officers for fighting and other unfeminine proceedings has of late been unusually great."

[Wednesday, August 14, 1861] Cold morning and nothing doing. Tom brought me *Plutarch's Lives* so now I don't lack for reading. Our papers are full of reports of the Manassas fight, the federals are making big efforts the south is no idle, but moves right with great secrecy and nothing is known. General Polk is sending up all the forces he can to New Madrid, MO. MO is the field to which all eyes are turned at present. I stayed at house all eve not caring to go out self now-d-days I need to drill about one hour.

The historian Plutarch wrote his most famous work, *Lives of the Noble Greeks and Romans*, around the end of the first century A.D. *Plutarch's Lives*, as it is commonly called, remains a classic in literature and history.

[Thursday, August 15, 1861] There has been a severe fight at Springfield, MO. General Lyon killed. There is great excitement in the St. Louis MO. MO is no doubt all in a state of excitement

Battle of Wilson's Creek from Leslie's Illustrated, *courtesy Library of Congress*

and commotion there are now 3 divisions CS troops there. Extras have come out again. A humbug affair. Catch-penny. The weather is moderating, but still very cool—my melon sales go slow. I went down to Main Street house this eve, had a chat with the men, and discussed the possibility of St. Louis being taken.

The Battle of Wilson's Creek, near Springfield, Missouri, took place August 10, 1861. A 5,000-man Federal army under General Nathaniel Lyon (1818–61) attacked a much larger, but ill-equipped, force of Confederate soldiers and Missouri State Guardsmen commanded by General Ben McCulloch. The bloody battle, termed "the hardest four hours' fighting that up to that time had ever taken place on the American continent,"[11] resulted in the retreat of the Federal army and the death of General Lyon. Contrary to the hopes of many southerners, Saint Louis was never in danger of being captured by the Confederates.

[August 16, 1861] This is a bright sunshiny day, but still it is not warm for this season. The war news is all from MO. St. Louis has been put under martial law by Frémont, and things in the south west look squally. Sigel's command is reported safe. Nothing new in our city. After a few fights being the order of the day. Business on a stand still, ice moderate, some provisions are high. Coffee is very high—the stock is about out.

General Lyon at Wilson's Creek, from Harper's Weekly, Aug. 31, 1861

Gunther's worry about coffee doubtless derived from the *Appeal* article of the 16th: "Dear. —Drinking coffee has become transformed into a highly extravagant indulgence—the article is very scarce and very dear, and the New Orleans boats bring up but slender supplies; the whole stock in that city is sewed up in sixteen hundred sacks."

[Saturday, August 17, 1861] This is a day of sunshine and showers. Trade dull. Beale Street lovely this afternoon market. I have a short supply of melons, and none to be had this noon. Our papers chronicle the issue or proclamation rather by Lincoln shutting down all kinds of trade with the south, No war news. I am running short of melons can't get any. Market looks lively. I stayed at house all Eve and retired early.

On August 16, 1861, President Lincoln issued an order forbidding commercial intercourse between the north and the rebellious southern states.

[Sunday, August 18, 1861] I got up pretty early and at work again this Sunday, as many of my previous ones. Ice no go and melons to my great chagrin I ran out of at noon—the great demand for more. The Sunday *Appeal* is quite a respectable looking paper now. Our city is gone greatly a few fights on Beale Street. I went down town and stayed at Main Street and retired early.

[Monday, August 19, 1861] I feel very much disappointed in not getting no melons and a great demand for more. Nothing of any interest to mention in our city. Everything is quiet. I wrote a letter home. Home letters are examined by a committee before passing. Our streets look a little lively, carriages in passing but no business. I have commenced taking the *Argus*. It is a good paper for the price, 10 cents per week. I spent the eve at house and went up to my room after.

[Tuesday, August 20, 1861] This is a warm day and business is dull. I am all out of melons and feel bad at the idea of not having any. And call all the time. I'm now reading Plutarch with a great deal of interest. Beale Street looks gloomy and forsaken. Negros are plenty all over the street. There's some stir about Davis giving US citizens 4 days to leave or swear to the CS. I took a stroll down to the city. There is a floral concert at the theater by children.

[Wednesday, August 21, 1861] There has been but little of interest in the city. A boat was sunk in Commerce, CSA. An advance is expected on Washington but my opinion is contrary. I was disappointed in not getting any melons again. I am having some very unruly neighbors over Wilsons. I met a man at boarding house I see at West Point, Arkansas, Mich was up this eve to see a friend but was disappointed. I stayed at house all eve and retired early.

[Thursday, August 22, 1861] There has been numerous showers all day. It makes it pleasant and cool, no business doing. I read most of the day. I feel very lonesome this noon but have not yet the blues. The news from Washington is very meager, all being suppressed—I get the *New York News* most every day, but find little news for so much money—10 cents a copy. There is no life in the city after dark but all is quiet and all stores closed. I spent the eve at house and retired early.

[Friday, August 23, 1861] This is pleasant cool day, and not much doing—we have now full account of the Springfield fight—it was a hard one, General Lyon killed—there was a man shot by the Impressables—and the mayor has issued a card in regard to the matter. Everything is very quiet in the city and but few soldiers are to be seen. I am quite content. I would like to hear from home. I spent the eve at house and took a walk downtown south Mich and Rat.

[Saturday, August 24, 1861] This is a fine sunshiny day but cool. Beal Street this morning looks lively. I got in 150 melons today. I have a very large lot on hand. Prospects for sales are good. Times in the north scary and the arrest of southern women is a daily occurance. Kentucky must now come out on one side or the other, she cannot stay as she is much long on. I stayed at house until late and took a walk through the city.

[Sunday, August 25, 1861] I was up early this morning and ready for action. The day is pleasant, the church bells are sending forth their ringing peals and calling out those for worship, but I am as usual except a fresh boiled shirt at work. The ice trade is only moderate, but melon trade is good. I will make a great thing out of it today. The *Appeal* has a map of the seat of war in it and also Russell's letter on the Battle of Manassas. I stayed at home till late, Mich came up to see me. Lloyd has gone up to call on Savile—good day.

[Monday, August 26, 1861] It has rained incessantly all day the streets are muddy and nothing is doing—everybody remains indoors. There is no war news. The Federals are arresting any and every thing that is suspicious. Newspapers are suppressed and mobs are getting all peace papers north from all accounts. I took in just 20 cents from melons today. I wrote a letter home and send father 17 dollars—the last for probably some time as hopes for the future are gloomy indeed. Stayed at home all eve.

[Tuesday, August 27, 1861] There is no stop to the rain—and still it comes pouring down, no business. I see all letter communication is cut off now and so I was just in time for mine of yesterday how glad I am. I only hope father may get the money. I am reading Plutarch yet to pass time and desire much information. The concert for the benefit of the widows and orphans of soldiers was postponed on account of weather. Mich and Pat come up around me from bet—I had retired early after suing block.

[Wednesday, August 28, 1861] The day continues rainy and gloomy and nothing doing. New York news has been stopped and no friendly papers to the south allowed to come. There is a reported fight at Paducah, KY, but I think it is a mistake. The war news from the north is now all suppressed everything is kept very still. Troops keep coming up from below and going to Missouri and Virginia every nerve is now strained and such available men is off for the war in the cotton states. It is reported that the privateer *Jeff Davis* ran ashore on the Florida coast.

[Thursday, August 29, 1861] The weather is getting fine again and prospects for revival of trade. Our city papers have nothing in of any interest. The city remains quiet, some soldiers keep arriving from below. The river is yet up at a long stage of water. I am anxious to hear from home. Is now since last May last. I spent the eve taking a walk uptown and retired early. Went to the concert for the benefit of the widows and orphans. The performance was very good and a very large crowd was out.

Gunther was not alone in praising the concert. The *Appeal* of August 30 gushed:

> The Concert. —The theater was last night filled to overflowing. So immense was the audience that two-thirds of the parterre was filled with ladies. The appearance of the house thronged with fashionably dressed ladies, was imposing to a degree only those who saw it can appreciate. We regret that inability to be present, except during a short part of the evening, prevents our noticing the various portions of the performance. The audience appeared well pleased, and the various pieces were warmly applauded. We are greatly tempted to express our admiration of some of the pieces we heard, but to do so would be unjust to the rest. The program was a full one, and well varied with instrumental music and solos, duettes, quartettes, and choruses. We expect Messrs. Dr. Merritt, Dr. Shanks, and Col. Munford, the committee for the disposal of the funds, will have a substantial sum put into their hands for the patriotic and benevolent purpose for which the concert was given.

[Friday, August 30, 1861] I'm getting much more sleep nowadays then during the summer. Tom takes out but one load a day and demand in the morning is small, so of course, I make the best out of it. I got me a lot of fine cheap melons, stock on hand large. Beale Street remains quiet. Mich comes up in the eve. I took a stroll uptown in the eve, but make an early bed my practice since in the city.

[Saturday, August 31, 1861] We received the reports today that the Federals took Forts Hatteras and Clark NC with 500 prisoners. This is a warm fine day. The last day of summers has found, thus ends my first summer south being well and hearty, my situation being good, pleasant and cool, and warm, not hard, lonesome to be sure. But the times do not pass straight forward I bought me some fine apples today. Mich spent the eve at my house I retired early.

On August 28–29, a Union combined naval-army force under General Benjamin Butler and Flag Officer Silas Stringham attacked and overwhelmed two small Confederate forts at Hatteras Inlet, North Carolina, capturing 670 men. The defenders were badly outnumbered and outgunned, their cannon not having enough range to reach the bombarding Union vessels. This victory opened up the North Carolina inland waters to Union incursion.

Diary
September–December 1861

The diary makes clear that the local melon and ice trade were drying up. For Gunther, however, life is still pleasant, with theater trips most nights. It is unclear how he could still afford such entertaining diversions.

In the war news, Memphisians turn their eyes away from events in Virginia and Missouri. Events in Kentucky—their own back yard, so to speak—take center stage.

September 1861

[Sunday, September 1, 1861] I feel good this morning and ready for action. This is a fine warm day, the melon trade is good, sold some $19 worth. House had numerous complaints today. Some of my melons are very fine. The church bells are all ringing and numerous cortages pass my door from the country, with negro drivers all for church, Frémont yesterday issued a very strange proclamation putting the whole state of Missouri under martial law and freeing slaves etc. I took a good bath this eve and retired early.

[Monday, September 2, 1861] This is a fine warm day hot I must say. Ice business is good. I bought a lot of fine melons this noon.

Time appears to pass awful fast with me nowadays, and no diversity of business, but the same every day, makes me hardly notice the days that pass so fleetingly by. I read Plutarch at conswell throys. Tom and I have some fun and crack jokes with each other. He is loquacious and mirthful I spent the eve at home and retired early. Mich and Pat were up.

[Tuesday, September 3, 1861] This is a warm day September is trying to beat August for warm weather and so far has succeeded. No news to mention in our city. The papers are short up for news. Time passes as fast as ever, and no change in my state of affairs but read and time flies by, unmentioned. I spent the eve down in Main Street home. Jonathan Moss is unwell stayed rather late.

[Wednesday, September 4, 1861] I get in a lot more melons. I have now a large stock, reports east are the arrests of secessionists very numerous. Papers are saying more gloomy affairs in our city every day. The city is dull and prices for everything very high. Coffee and worse is from 40 to 60 cents a pound, no specie is the general complaint, nowadays. Gold 15 cents and silver 12 percent I stayed at house all eve, feeling rather dull and retired early for a good sleep.

The *Appeal* of September 4 printed a whole page on prices of various commodities. According to the Memphis Chamber of Commerce, coffee sold for 14-1/2 cents a pound in that city on March 1, and 40 cents (almost three times as much) on August 31, showing the effects of the war and the Union blockade.[1]

[Thursday, September 5, 1861] I am happy to note that up to the present time I have not had a sick day, or materially felt unwell, for so far my constitution has withstood a southern summer. We had a fine show last night. The gunboats have had some actions near Hickman, Kentucky skirmishes take place every day near

Washington. I got me a large lot of melons cheap today. Sales only moderate. I took a walk up towns this eve.

The September 5 *Appeal* reported on an engagement on the previous day, near Hickman, between a Confederate gunboat and land artillery, and "two of Lincoln's piratical craft," in which the "Hessians ... ingloriously fled up the river."

[Friday, September 6, 1861] The day has been pleasant. And mud drying up fast. We have stirring news from Hickman, Columbus which are or are about being occupied by the Confederates. Things are working down that was sure. Business is dull—there are many who are very seriously affected about the state of affairs, and the prospects of impressing or drafting of soldiers. I took a walk up town this eve and had a talk with George Coates.

On September 4, 1861, Confederate General Leonidas Polk violated the Kentucky Commonwealth's neutrality by ordering General Pillow to occupy Columbus. Polk ordered this action due to his belief that Union forces threatened to grab Columbus before he could. This action met with the approval of Memphis public (or at least, Memphis newspaper) opinion, as the newspapers had been urging such action for some weeks. While Polk's action might have been justified in the narrow sense of protecting the Mississippi River, in the larger picture Polk's advance destroyed the very Kentucky neutrality that had protected Tennessee up to then. In February 1862 Union forces advanced through Kentucky to capture Memphis and much of Tennessee.

While Gunther believed that business was "dull," the *Memphis Avalanche* proudly and patriotically claimed "the trade of that city has never been so prosperous at this season of the year as it is at present" (quoted in the *New Orleans Times-Picayune*, September 6, 1861). Best evidence suggests Gunther was correct, and the newspaper civic-boosting.

[Saturday, September 7, 1861] We are in the midst of military movements of which we know nothing. This has been a warm pleasant day, no business. I am active in my melon trade, no news from KY of any import, but her soil is occupied by CS troops. Beale Street as usual is lively this noon but privately everyone is on the move, some of our boys are sorely troubled at not being drafted—foolish to let come well or would. I must stand up to the rack.

[Sunday, September 8, 1861] Another bright Sabbath day rolls around. Pleasant sunshine and many peals of the church bells. I as usual will be at work. My individual melon trade is brisk—sold out large stock and cleared about $17 very good—will pay board. Most all of our boys were up from below. I was kept busy all day shut up early in the eve and went up to Main Street house. I am having some fierce times with our neighbors who think they are awfully sharp poor silly ladies—let them revel in their ignorance.

[Monday, September 9, 1861] Up early this morning and at market laying in a stock of melons sold 26 today. The weather is fine and warm. Nothing unusual today. No news from Cairo, Columbus and Hickman. Skirmishing with gunboats frequently takes place that's all, but sharp work is expected every day. I spent the eve by taking a short stroll and retired early tired. Am reading Plutarch yet—pesky mosquitoes are plenty in my room—perfect seasons.

[Tuesday, September 10, 1861] I must record the state of my mind in these times of war and destruction. I'm happy to note that I am happy of mind—nothing do I let trouble me, the coming events I await with a calm determinancy and an intent to make the best of the times, but come well or woe, so my mind has no trouble on these serious thoughts. We had a big fire. Pooley store, Cleaves & Vaden were burnt out this morning. Skirmish at Columbus gunboats. Took a walk up town. Stopped at Main Street house and spent home.

The "Pooley" whose business burned was that of wealthy Scots-born James Pooley (1825–65), who owned a jewelry store at 239 Main Street. The bookstore of Cleaves & Vaden was located next door at 241 Main. The *Appeal* of Sept. 11, under the headline "Fire on Main Street," reported that the fire broke out about 8:00 a.m. on the top of the Pooley store. "There was some talk of incendiarism, but probably on small foundation."

> [Wednesday, September 11, 1861] The air has been cooled, very much by a heavy shower, No trade agoin'—everything dull. There are concerts given every week by the ladies and gentlemen relief for the benefit of the soldiers, large turnout, considering. Melon trade moderate, I am having considerable fun with Tom, a mirthful genius—I enjoy good health and appetite excellent, board passably, very good for the price. Stayed home in the eve.

> [Thursday, September 12, 1861] This is a warm day, melon trade pretty good, our city is quiet and nothing doing—no movements in KY by our troops. The legislature has come out for Union, and exciting times are looked for in that direction. I am yet reading Plutarch. Seen Mich this eve. Took a walk uptown. Everything is calm and no stir in our streets in the eve, but stillness reigns supreme.

In contrast to Gunther's pessimistic view of the local market, the Memphis *Appeal* of September 12 bragged that "we are still doing more business in produce in Memphis than was done this time last year, when the St. Louis and Ohio boats were running."

> [Friday, September 13, 1861] I got a lot of melons, but all poor. Ice sales only moderate. There has been a heavy fighting in western Va, Rosecrans and Floyd—Floyd retired during the night. Ky is the point to which all eyes are turned. No reports from the east. All moves are secret, arrests are yet made all over the north. There was another alarm, no fire. I took a short walk up street. The Negroes have a big ball this eve all out in grand style a-la-mode.

On September 10, Union troops led by Brigadier General William S. Rosecrans engaged a Confederate force under General John B. Floyd at Carnifax Ferry, (West) Virginia. Although the Confederates repulsed the Union assault, they retreated across the Gauley River during the night, handing the Unionists the victory. The Confederate drive to regain control of the vital Kanawha River Valley failed, and as a result, the birth of West Virginia statehood proceeded without serious threat from the Confederates.

> [Saturday, September 14, 1861] This has been a very warm day. Ice business is better. No melons—can't get any—sold out. I feel a little lonesome all day by myself. Spent the greater part reading. I feel chagrined at my not having any melons—and plenty of calls, times are no better, and no prospect of any improvement. Tom is as gay as ever, and sings to the amusement of our neighboring ladies. I took a stroll uptown this eve. All quiet up town.

> [Sunday, September 15, 1861] This is a very warm day and business is lively for me. This is a quiet day, but many calls for melons, and to my great chagrin I have been unable to get any. I have had no visitors today. I have a quiet peace of mind and don't mind the war matters at all. Except for amusement, all the news with avidity. There's much of the brag game play and news lasts without regard to truth.

> [Monday, September 16, 1861] The month so far has outdone any for warm weather. The day has been fine. No war preparations of any extraordinary appearance take place, but shops of all kinds are so established in different parts of the city, where all kinds of accoutrements are being made and collections being made for the benefit of soldiers in various camps. All the wagons were put to my house so I have been quite busy all day getting the wagons loaded, and I retired early in the morning.

A typical notice of soldier's aid can be found in the September 15 *Appeal*:

> Military Aid Society. —We are requested by Mrs. E. H. Porter, president, and Miss L. W. Trout, secretary of the Military Aid Society, to ask all managers of auxiliary societies to report themselves on Monday evening at 8½ o'clock, at the headquarters in Adams' block, Second street, bringing with them all the work they have belonging to Col. Forrest, who is about to leave the city. The society earnestly calls upon the ladies of Memphis to assist them in sewing for destitute soldiers, as they have much work on hand and greatly need assistance.

The "Forrest" mentioned is future Lieutenant General Nathan Bedford Forrest.

> [Tuesday, September 17, 1861] We had a slight shower last night but the day is as good as ever as regards heat. No telegraphic news today. Railroad communication is yet open to Ky. The Ky legislature is strong Federal and their action is much lamented. I was up very early helping out the wagons. I took a stroll up town bought a *Louisville Courier*. The city looks very quiet. There is an amateur concert at the theater tonight. I feel quite tired and retired early. The nights are quite beautiful moonlight.

> [Wednesday, September 18, 1861] This is another very fine day. Business is moderate only. Very busy all day getting out ice for wagons. We have no news from Ky. Railroad shut down. All the troops in this neighborhood are ordered forward to Columbus, A. S. Johnston is now up there to lead them on. An engagement is now expected every day. I took a walk up town with Adams. Had some ice cream specials. The night is beautiful, moonlit and very pleasant to promenade.

President Davis placed his old friend, General Albert Sidney Johnston (1803–62), in command of the western Confederacy in September of 1861, superseding General Leonidas Polk, who expressed relief that the veteran

Albert Sidney Johnston, courtesy Library of Congress

Johnston could take his place. A brevet general in the prewar regular army, Johnston had perhaps the most outstanding credentials of any of the old army officers who resigned to join the Confederacy. As Davis observed, "If Sidney Johnston is not a general ... we have no general." While commanding the Confederate army at the Battle of Shiloh, Johnston was shot and bled to death, becoming the highest-ranking officer to be killed during the war. According to the *Appeal* of September 13, Johnston's appointment "will give the most universal satisfaction throughout the Southwest ..."

> [Thursday, September 19, 1861] No news at all by telegraph from the north. Confederate troops occupy Ky at Bowling Green. The city is quiet as usual, nothing new on Beale Street. We have been very busy on the little vault all day. Melons are very high now. I went up town this eve. Had a spat with Mrs. Gazools. But let her shout. Very maniacal. I have concluded to have nothing to do with them.

The "Mrs. Gazools" referred to here is a member of the family of John B. Gazzollo, residing at 226 Main Street.

> [Friday, September 20, 1861] This has been a warm day, not much business doing and plenty work. Mich is getting his hand in at the work. We have no late news. Ky is now supposed to be in a perfect blaze. There is a feeling of gladness that she had to come out of her neutral state, which she held so long. The ice is being taken out of ice house very fast. I was very annoyed by

being routed out of bed scarce times. I went up to the city this eve and returned early.

[Saturday, September 21, 1861] There has been a great change in the weather, cold wind all day. The news today in Ky the legislature comes down on the invasion of here territory by the south favors the Federals strongly. No fight within a few days. The [Louisville] *Courier* is suppressed and [Ex-Governor] Morehead sent to Fort Lafayette. Must be suppressed. I went in the melon trade again today, Beale Street market is lively. Everything at extortionate prices. I took a walk up street and retired early. Mike goes to bed at 7 o'ck.

[Sunday, September 22, 1861] After quite a cold night this is a warm day again. I got a lot of melons from the river but I was quite disappointed at sales today and am determined to quit the business for the season. I bought me some shirts and boots on Friday made a bargain. I have had but little company and poor sales for ice. I have not been in a church for months, we have no news coming today from the north. I went up early and went to bed for a fine sleep.

[Monday, September 23, 1861] I did not get up for the wagons, got up late. There was a fog and the air chilly, but got warm this noon. No business doing at all, bought me another shirt this day. Everything is quiet in the city. The *Argus* has raised the price 5 cents. We had a fine large melon sent home to H. Neff. I took a stroll up the street this eve, and stopped at Main St. House. See Miller down from the boats, walked home as usual with the old gent himself.

H. Neff's boarding house was located at the corner of Poplar and Front Row.

[Tuesday, September 24, 1861] I was roused this morning by the drivers and my last night's does of pills gave me some trouble. I feel better for it. There's no news, no dispatches from the east. Northern news is out of the question. There appears to be a

> feeling of fear for the Lincolnites coming here, a fine company of "a" came up from Louisiana. For all I can see, Lee, Floyd and Wise have fell back in West Va. The federalists are pressing them heavily. I spent the eve at the theater. The tableaux vivo a perfect success a large crowd and General Jeff Thompson is being one of the lions of the Eve.

Again, the *Appeal* (September 25) agreed with Gunther on the tableau:
> The Tableaux Vivants. —The entertainment last night, given for the benefit of the soldiers was decidedly *the* one of the season, excelling anything of the kind that we have yet seen, and drawing one of the largest and most brilliant audiences ever congregated in the theater. So crowded was the house, that many of the ladies were forced to sit in the galleries.

The profit was $400. General Jeff Thompson related a humorous story on the tableau in his *Reminiscences,* 95.

> [Wednesday, September 25, 1861] I had a good sleep last night, though the drivers annoyed me as much as possible. This is a cold day although the sun shines warm this noon. Our city is very quiet and the papers have but little to say. All kinds of woolen goods are getting to be a scarce article and are being bought up for the soldiers. Socks 75 cents per pair, Jim is sick. We made a start on the lower tier of my house. Went to be very early and helped Mich to get a block of ice out at 1 o'ck.

> [Thursday, September 26, 1861] This is an extraordinary cold chilly day, and there was quite a requisition for winter clothing. I pitched in, bought me a lot of things in the clothing line. There is nothing new in the city, all looks gloomy and H of ell. Ice sales are playing out, I fear there is a terrible winter coming on us and if the blockade is not opened there will be much suffering. I went down the city, see Jim at Main Street is better—retired early.

Siege of Lexington, from Frank Leslie's The Soldier in our Civil War *(1893)*

[Friday, September 27, 1861] This has been a terrible cold day and cloudy some, my business has stopped, We had an extra of Mulligan's capture at Lexington, Missouri. There is a warm time in Ky and a fearful civil war is now commencing. It is hard telling how we all are coming to, news with us is meager, All avenues from the north are closed. I made some more fur purchases in the woolen line. I was presented with a free ticket and went to the theater "German" and was well pleased.

From September 18 to 20, Union forces under Colonel James Mulligan withstood a siege from a much larger force of pro-southern Missouri State Guardsmen under General Sterling Price, only surrendering when Price's men used hemp bales as mobile earthworks to advance upon the Union lines. About 3,000 Union soldiers were taken prisoner and paroled.

Gunther probably attended a show at Memphis's German Gymnastic Society Hall, at 3rd Street near Gayoso. Perhaps due to German pride, he rated this performance better than most of the theater shows he attended while in Memphis.

> [Saturday, September 28, 1861] I was not forced out of bed this 2 o'ck and the drivers are got off safe—+ I heartily glad of it. The sun shines genial warm again + the day is very pleasant although no ice sales. The streets look lively, crinoline predominates largely. 30,000 more men are called for from this state by A. S. Johnston now commander of this department for some time. I stayed at house all eve and retired early, it is not over safe now a days To be out much at night.

> [Sunday, September 29, 1861] This is a cold and very unpleasant day. There is nothing of any interest particular to mention. Gen Buckner of Ky had destroyed a Lincoln camp at Owen, War news is meager, and news not to be had—A Northern paper is a prize to our press for items, + but few appear to get through. This has been a very quiet day with me. I put on my grays for the first time, fit well and I am now satisfied. I remained at house + went to bed very early.

An advance force of the Confederate army, under General Simon B. Buckner, pushed north from Bowling Green, Kentucky, and destroyed a Unionist recruiting camp at Hopkinsville.

> [Monday, September 30, 1861] The nights remain very cool—but the sun helps the day and gets quite warm. Ice business is getting low and not much doing. I pass time reading old *Eclectic Mags* my house is getting empty slowly. Jim is yet quite sick. Market this morning was lively but everything is high. I see Lane from Columbus. The army is all there yet. I took a walk up town there stillness reigns supreme except a few hacks on the streets. Had a discussion with Gozooles again, war is all the topic now a days.

October 1861

Business is slow in October for Gunther. Nobody much has need for ice, and no shipments of ice are coming in from the North. He finds plenty of time to chat with customers, attend the theater, read the newspapers, and generally mark time until, as Dickens's Mr. Micawber would put it, "something turns up." By midmonth the Bohlens send the underemployed Gunther out to collect debts owed them in west Tennessee and north Mississippi.

> [Tuesday, October 1, 1861] I got up this morning + helped the boys out with the ice. We have but 2 wagons today on the want. I have been very lonesome to day, had a little fun with a few customers. Dye shops are all very busy now dying cloth for use. Quinby + Robinson Foundry burnt last night, loss heavy. News, Buckner dispersed the Hopkinsville Federalists the capture of arms + cannon. Beal Street is lively in the Eve. I stopped at Adams + had a pleasant chat and retired early.

The *Memphis Appeal* of October 1 described the loss, which partially destroyed the foundry that produced so much for the army:

> Fire Last Night. —A fire broke out last night, at half-past eight o'clock, in the engine room, which is entirely of brick, of Messrs. Quinby & Robinson, machinists and founders, on Poplar street, below Front Row. The flames could readily have been got under, but there was no water at hand. The steam fire engine succeeded at last in getting a stream from a pond at a considerable distance, near the navy yard. Notwithstanding every effort, the delay in getting water proved fatal to the building.

Prior to the war, the "Western Foundry" of William T. Quinby and William A. Robinson manufactured steam engines and iron castings. With Tennessee's secession, the foundry converted to war production, manufacturing 77 cannon for the Confederate army. Just before the fall of Memphis in 1862, Quinby and Robinson transferred their machinery and operations to Georgia.

[Wednesday, October 2, 1861] Up as usual and down again for a nap this morning—rain again. The *Appeal* came out in new dress this AM + looks well. No news of any account, all quiet, military duty is now strictly performed by all in Louisiana and New Orleans. Our city militia is called out for muster. Times in Missouri are very warm, + a continual skirmishing is kept up. I spent the Eve at the theater, ended with a Festival at Odd Fellows Hall, did not go to the festival, concert poor.

The October 2 *Appeal* bragged about its new look:

> New Dress of the *Appeal*. As will readily be observed by our constant readers, the *Appeal* appears this morning in a full dress of new type. Its typographical execution is now quite as good, perhaps, as that of any other journal in the South, being quite an improvement on what it has been for several months past. The impression will become even more distinct than at present in the course of a few days time.

The same newspaper spoke of the concert Gunther skipped that evening:

> The Entertainment—The Supper. —The young gentlemen who do not take crinoline to the entertainment at the theater to-night, and to that *recherche*, which has cost fair ladies so much thought and toil, must not be surprised if they find themselves sent to Coventry [i.e., dumped by their girlfriends] before the week is out. Every effort has been made to get up something, both at the theater and Odd Fellows' Hall, which will contribute to the amusement and enjoyment of the public.

[Thursday, October 3, 1861] This is a pleasant warm day. Ice business is reviving again, we have but little news from the north+ what we have is old, but new to us. The city is quiet, there are some few troops encamped without the city, it is reported that Mason Hill has been taken by the federals. + a fight in W.Va. All quiet at Columbus. I took a stroll up town, and had another set to with Gozooles, I find it very unpleasant to have any conversation at all.

[Friday, October 4, 1861] I am raised from my morning slumbers by the knocking at my door for ice by the niggers so up I get rather late however make up for lost sleep at night by the wagons. Business is pretty good. The warm weather for several days has started things again. There, we had a great excitement + all the soldiers were out. It was reported that the gun boats were coming—such a time—all humbug. I stayed around Beal Street that eve + retired early. Ice is going out of my house very fast.

[Saturday, October 5, 1861] It was reported this morning that Lee had beat Rosecrans in W.Va. badly—only report. The federal fleet was coming up the Miss. River at Orleans. The Federals were at Falls Church + something of a stirring nature the event of a great battle is looked for. Corry & Co. have raised ice at 2 cents and o day I have sold some for the same for the first time, it is a big price—but can't be helped. I went up town in the eve, and had a chat, returned early.

Corry & Co. competed with Bohlen & Wilson for the ice trade, using the steamboat *Winchester* to deliver its ice from the north.

Wartime newspapers often printed wildly inaccurate rumors, such as the one above about Robert E. Lee's Confederates defeating William Rosecrans's Union army. This is probably a garbled report of a skirmish at Greenbriar River on the October 3. Some would observe that newspapers have not become any more accurate in the 150 years since the war!

[Sunday, October 6, 1861] I got up this morning about 3 a.m. + helped the boys out. Tom Williams made a mean bragging assault on me, but I put him to reason. This is a moderate fine day. No news of any importance from Richmond, or papers publish old things from all appearances to fill up—news so scarce. Mich was up this eve—There is but little sale for ice to day. There is something up up above—as all the cars + engines were ordered up from here. I went up to Main Street House this eve.

[Monday, October 7, 1861] No military news today. The city is very quiet. Such things as a fight & C, why, are only slight unfriendly affairs + can not be recorded when so numerous, the death of one is soon forgot + passed over, such things happen now every week. It is pleasant and cool to day. The Market stalls were sold at auction today. I have very sore lips. The last of the ice was taken out this house by the way—gone this a.m. I had easy times all day.

[Tuesday, October 8, 1861] I got up rather late and waited in vain for Mr. B—but did not come lost my breakfast in consequence. I have very sore lips + it gives me much trouble. There was a gun boat fight at Columbus to day. Everything is quiet in the city. The militia is now being put in active drill. There was an alarm of fire but it was false. No ice sales. I went up town this Eve, all looks very quiet, + Main Street deserted.

The *Memphis Avalanche* of October 9 carried a long account of the action at Columbus, where some Federal gunboats engaged the Confederate riverfront batteries. The long-range cannonading caused little damage to either side. One interesting sidenote of this affair—the newspaper reported that the Confederate cannon were either too short-range to hit the gunboats, or so large that the artillerists, distrusting their gunpowder, thought it unsafe to fire the cannon. One wonders if the reporter gave a thought to the fact that the enemy would read this article and discover the weakness.

[Wednesday, October 9, 1861] I took an early breakfast. I did not feel first rate took some pills. We have some late news, but nothing of any importance. I was on Market St. looked very dead. Our militia laws all about being enforced + various calls are made to turn out, but few turn out. It is not very agreeable. I went up to Main Street. The river is rising, there were great floods in Western Va. The men have gone up to the *Capitol.*

[Thursday, October 10, 1861] This is a fine day. I feel quite lone some + out of some reading matter. There was an attack made by the C troops on Wilson's Zouaves at Pensacola, report 40 killed + wounded. No news from Richmond for several days. We are continually having changes in the small establishment on Beal Street. I am selling but little ice, about played out, my life troubles me much. Spent the eve with Adams + retired very early, it is quite cool.

Gunther notes accounts of the Battle of Santa Rosa Island, near Pensacola, Florida. On October 9, Confederate forces under General Richard Anderson made a nighttime landing and attack on the camp of Colonel William Wilson's 6th New York Zouaves. The Confederates burned the camp, but retired when Union reinforcements arrived.

"Mrs. Markham" (the pen name for Elizabeth Penrose) wrote the popular *A History of England* in 1829.

[Friday, October 11, 1861] My paper this morning is sorry for news, + no reports. This has been a very cool day. I read Markham's *English History* to pass time. Mr. B. [Bohlen] was around this morning. Things look truly gloomy, and the general impression is that direful times are before us. Cold appears to bring things to a person's mind + the circumstances by which we are surrounded. I went up town in the eve + saw Loyd at the lower house.

[Saturday, October 12, 1861] This is quite a cool morning but the sun shines warm again through the day. Business is dull and ice

> nearly played out, we have news of an engagement to day at the N Orleans Passes by the Fleet + Batteries. I am in a bad fix, raw sore lips and a cold. Universal hard times are now all the complaint. Our troops are all at Columbus yet + no news from the Potomac. I went up to Angerona Lodge this eve worked in the 3rd + retired immediately after.

On the morning of October 12 a ramshackle Confederate river defense fleet under Commodore George Hollins, including the CSS *Manassas*, attacked Union warships at Head of Passes in the Mississippi River, driving their opponents out of the river and back into the Gulf of Mexico.

> [Sunday, October 13, 1861] No further news from Orleans, + little from any where else. This is a very fine day + quite warm. I as usual am at work + cleaned the whole institution completely by 4 o'ck, so ends my Beal Street residence since last May. Lonesome—but an easy job, so I am going up to report to headquarters I went up this Eve, but prospects for the winter look gloomy. I spent the eve at house + had a talk with the old gentlemen.

With the company's Beale Street ice house cleaned out of ice, Gunther moved to the river landing office. With city work becoming scarce, Bohlen sends Gunther out to collect some debts owed by merchants in the surrounding areas.

> [Monday, October 14, 1861] I moved my things up from the Beal Street house to the River home. I spent the greater part of the day at the lower house with Loyd, Mich + Mr. B—had a fall out I am sorry for it. M is a good fellow. Times look hard although paper money is not so very scarce the house is shipping all useful material. I stayed with Loyd all eve + got my instructions for my morning trip on a collecting tour.

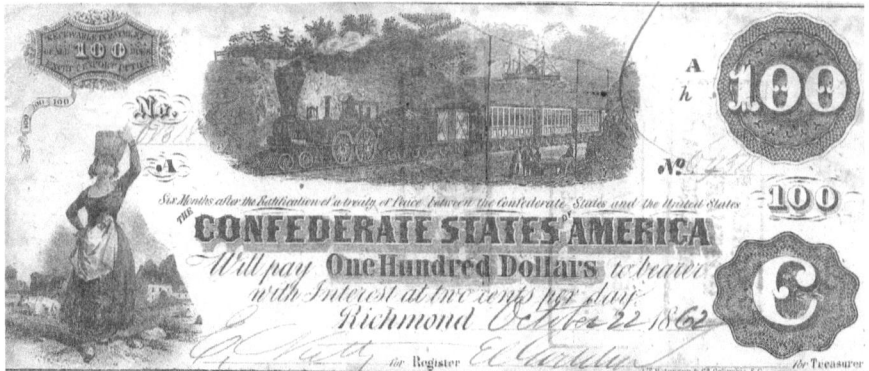

Confederate bill (from author's collection)

[Tuesday, October 15, 1861] I got up this a.m at 5 o'ck + took the M[emphis] & Charleston RR for Tuscumbia, Ala, arrived at 3 ½ + took branch road for Florence 20 minutes after arrived at 5 ½ crossed the Tenn River there. F is a small place + looks rather seedy. Did up all my business before supper and took to bed early. This section of the country is very fine and healthy country to live in well settled and very pleasant and good people. The courts are in the hands of the few.

[Wednesday, October 16, 1861] Tuscumbia. I got in from Florence this morning at 5 o'ck and am compelled to stay over here all day, as there is but one train running a day. I managed to collect one bill. The balance of the day I sat around the hotel. There is a camp of soldiers around here about 600. This is a beautiful country around here, but the place looks very seedy indeed, and has gone backwards for some years. I took to bed early this eve, my fair will do, but have seen better for the money.

[Thursday, October 17, 1861] I got [up] this morning at 5 and waited for the train which was delayed until 8 ½ to the chagrin of many fellow travelers got into conversation with several and took cars for Corinth Miss after breakfast, the cars are full—and many soldiers among them. We had a good time coming down,

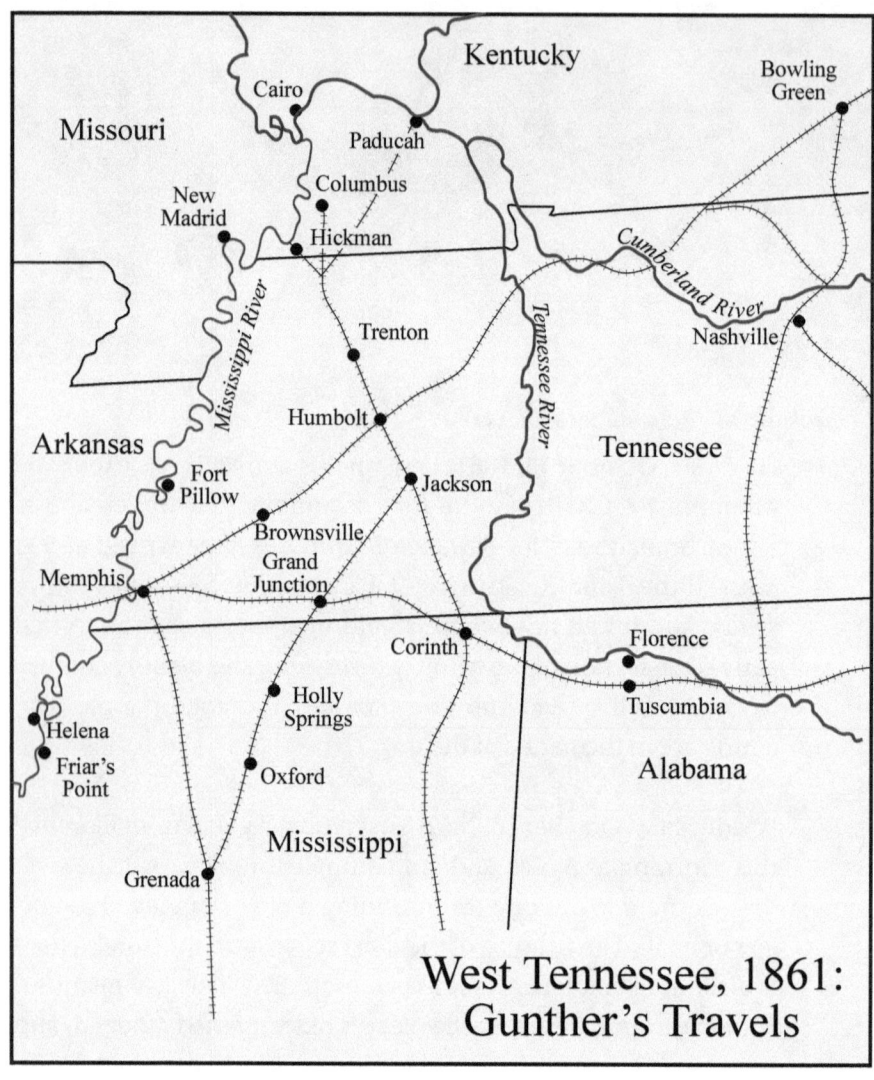

went out a collecting but did not succeed in anyone all very poor debts. C is a small place + looks hard. I went to a concert in the eve for the benefit of soldiers.

The strategically vital railroad junction town of Corinth, Mississippi, did not impress English correspondent William Howard Russell:

> Here is Corinth, which consists of a wooden grog-shop and three log shanties; the acropolis is represented by a grocery store, of which the proprietors, no doubt, have gone to the wars, as their names were suspiciously Milesian [Irish], and the doors and windows were fastened.[2]

Undoubtedly Russell exaggerated, playing to the anti-American prejudices of his British readership. By Mississippi standards, Corinth could be considered a new boomtown, with 2,800 residents (only a few less than Jackson, the state capital), a college, many fine homes, and the landmark Tishomingo Hotel. In 1862 the Union and Confederate armies fought several battles to control the town.

> [Friday, October 18, 1861] I took breakfast and got off for Grand Junction at 8 o'ck. I saw Terry's Texas Reg there a hard looking set + I think will fight well. Took cars for Winona down the Miss Central. The day is cold and rains heavily this eve. Road all day and arrived at W at 6 ½ and took a poor supper and transacted my business and after waiting for cars till 12 p.m. got aboard for Oxford. This is a gloomy place and I make haste for a better point.

The small village of Grand Junction, Tennessee, is located at the junction of the Memphis & Charleston and Mississippi Central Railroads. In an October 6 letter to his father, Benjamin Burke of Terry's regiment described the area around Grand Junction as a "rather poor country, mostly piny woods and settlements not very thick."

"Terry's Texas Reg." was Colonel Benjamin F. Terry's 8th Texas Cavalry, the famous "Terry's Texas Rangers." Colonel Terry was killed in December (see Gunther's diary for December 18). Most of the regiment had already reached Nashville from the south, so Gunther must have met some of the trailing detachments.[3]

> [Saturday, October 19, 1861] Arrived at Oxford this morning at 5 after laying around on the seats and no rest. After breakfast see Reynolds finished business and set around the town the balance

> of the day. O is a fine looking little town + appears though some business may be done here. I am very well satisfied with Hotel. I loafed around the greater part of eve, the town is very quiet and so taking a bed early a not very daring nature.

The home of the University of Mississippi, Oxford was (and is) considered one of the most elegant and cultured cities in Mississippi. Holly Springs was the site of the famous 1862 Confederate raid that destroyed General Ulysses Grant's supply base there, halting Grant's first advance upon Vicksburg.

> [Sunday, October 20, 1861] Was started up at 5 o'ck + took cars for Holly Springs where we arrived at about 6 ½ o'ck. The morning is beautiful, the cotton looks fine, finished my business + continued on for the Junction, finished business there + put through for La Grange put up at the Galt House. Went to Episcopal church in the morning—a very small congregation out after dinner looked around and went to the Presbyterian Church in the eve + soon took bed at Hotel a very good one.

The 1860–61 *Tennessee State Gazetteer and Business Directory* described LaGrange as "an important post village of Fayette County," incorporated in 1831.[4]

> [Monday, October 21, 1861] Did my business this morning and took cars for Junction. See Mr. McCraw and put off for home. The road is dusty and traveling is not very pleasant, our cars are half filled with soldiers going to various camps and homes, railroad business looks brisk and are making money. Arrived at 1 o'ck reported at headquarters all right—spent the balance of the day at the lower house and took a walk on river in the Eve.

> [Tuesday, October 22, 1861] I got up this morning rather late march on Beale for breakfast. I stayed around the house on river

the greater part of the day. The levee is full of boats. See *Alice Dean*, sugar is coming up plenty and are getting cheap, now our city is astir what is left. I took the M & O for Paris this noon, collecting again. Traveled all afternoon until 12-1/2 p.m. The night is cold took hack for hotel and got a middling good bed.

[Wednesday, October 23, 1861] Paris, Tenn. I am at the Conway House, a good man, but can't keep hotel, paid my bill and left for the Youell House, much better. Looked around all day. Paris is a pretty good little town with a square and a large courthouse in the center numerous brick buildings are upon the streets. We have a report of a big battle at Harpers Ferry the Federals badly beaten and Colonel Baker killed—of Oregon, More enemy report are in circulation here of the Federals at Mayfield, Ky. burning the town.

Paris, Tennessee, on the Mobile & Ohio Railroad, was established in 1823. According to the *1860–61 State Gazetteer*, it "contains a court house, jail, academy, and various professions and trades."[5]

The Battle of Ball's Bluff took place October 21, 1861, between Union forces led by Colonel Edward Baker, and Confederate forces under the nominal command of General Nathan G. "Shanks" Evans. The inexpertly led Union troops crossed the Potomac River and climbed the bluff, only to be driven back into the river by a Confederate attack. Union losses totaled almost 1,000. Baker, the US senator from Oregon, remains to this day the only sitting US senator to be killed in battle.

[Thursday, October 24, 1861] Roused out and took hack for the cars at 2 o'ck. Cars behind time but came at least, slept some coming down and got out at Humboldt on my way to Trenton. This Humboldt is a miserable place for a man to spend a day, the whole place consisting of nothing but a hotel and a few shanties, there are some soldiers here on their way to camp. The day is warm, but was quite cold this morning. I took cars for Trenton

Ball's Bluff, courtesy Library of Congress

at 8-1/2 and arrive at 9-/14, the cars are full put up at the Union Hall Pierce and Board Poor House.

The *1860–61 State Gazetteer* described Paris as "a flourishing and prominent post village," with a population of 2,000, and a "place of considerable business." The town featured the "Union Hall Hotel, Seay & Goodloe, proprietors," and the "Gibson House, Pearce & Bro., props."[6]

With about 200 inhabitants and one hotel (the Osborne House), Humboldt fit Gunther's description as a "miserable place for a man to spend a day." Neither this part of Tennessee nor the railroad impressed William Howard Russell.

> The portion of Tennessee through which the rail runs is exceedingly uninteresting, and looks unhealthy ... The twists and curves of the rail, through cane brakes and swamps exceeded in that respect any other line I have ever travelled on; but the vertical irregularities of the rail were still greater, and the engine bounded as if it were at sea.[7]

[Friday, October 25, 1861] Trenton, Tenn. Got up this morning after a good sleep at 6-1/2 o'ck. Had breakfast—poor—have sat around until 9 o'ck. Started out on my business, with no success, the money's good, but exhaust an error. Trenton is a very seedy looking, old place and everything appears to go in the small fisted way, there are now some 27 companies of soldiers below the town in camp, whisky is selling at 35 cents per quart here, the products of the farm are cheap. I sat around the most of the day and got a good bed in the eve.

[Saturday, October 26, 1861] Trenton. Was roused out of the cars at 4 o'ck., train on time. The cars as usual full, principally soldiers, took breakfast at Humboldt, and arrived at Brownsville at 9 o'ck., made one collection point. B is a pretty sprightly looking place, though old, with a poor courthouse the architectural beauties are few, all the buildings are old and homely built, the few residences, put up at the Exchange Hotel, as usual expect to loaf all day. The weather is fine.

Brownsville, the county seat of Haywood County, was (perhaps inevitably) described in the *1860–61 State Gazetteer* as "a place of considerable trade."[8]

[Sunday, October 27, 1861] Brownsville. I got up at 6-1/2, took a hasty breakfast and left on the cars for Memphis, same I arrived at 9-1/2. The day is pleasant, and the city is very quiet. I went up and reported at headquarters, affairs all right, and becomes unsatisfactory. I am now without any thing more to do, but something turns up in a few days.

[Monday, October 28, 1861] I am now stopping with Lloyd at the lower house. Mr. Bohlen and I sell out today. I am now adrift but prospects good, I hope. Done very well this summer. And if it were not for this cursed war I could be in clover and just doing what would please me. Times in the city are gloomy. Army supplies are being fitted out here and hundreds of women all now sewing for the military. The nights are still and quiet.

[Tuesday, October 29, 1861] The weather continues warm and pleasant, but cool nights. We have several frosts and the foliage is beginning to get variegated in autumnal hues. The river business is brisking up a little by the arrival of plenty of sugar on the levee. We get but little army news and no movements appear to take place in VA, we are expecting a big fight every day in Va. Mo. and Ky. There are still accounts of the Leesburg fight coming in. I went up to Beal Street house in the Eve.

[Wednesday, October 30, 1861] It is reported that the Federals are advancing in Ky., we get considerable news in the *Appeal*. The *Appeal* is now my standard of news, and all my reliance is placed in it. Of course I believe what I think right – but humbug is all the go, an end to this war is all the wish, and none more so than myself, everything is high and still going up. Mr. Bohlen went down to Vicksburg on the *Natchez*, she is a magnificent boat—a floating palace. There was a regiment the 13th Ar. went up on the *Hill* for Columbus, spent the eve up town and retired early.

[Thursday, October 31, 1861] I feel myself though a medical process and am taking a bottle of Bull's Sarsaparilla for the blood. I feel all right and this present disease and fever. We here had a terrible fire today, missed my dinner, the half square on the corner of Madison and Main burnt down and also Lizzie White's. There is great excitement among many of the people. It is supposed to be incendiary, and northerners are getting Hell. The city has now many fire notches over the streets and looks bad. I went up on Beal Street in the Eve. There is some sort of theater at Odd Fellows Hall.

Under the headline "Two Great Fires!" the *Appeal* of Nov. 1 reported on the fire, which destroyed stores, government warehouses and "Lizzie Whitehouse's house of ill fame."

Advertisements for Dr. John Bull's sarsaparilla, "The Great Kentucky Southern Remedy," promised relief from "scrofula, or the King's Disease," cancer, syphilis, liver disease, and almost any other ailment known to man. Bull advertised himself as the "King of Pain." See the ad in the *Columbia Daily South Carolinian*, September 21, 1853, for the full list. It appears Gunther suffered from recurring bouts of malaria.

November 1861
Increasingly, the Confederacy (and Memphis) tighten up their internal security. Northerners residing in Memphis feared being hauled, on mere suspicion, before the Safety Committee, or harassed by self-appointed vigilantes (see August 3, 1861, note). Throughout the South, cities wouldn't allow people to leave town unless they had a pass signed by the local Safety Committee or local military authority. Travel to the North required a special passport, as if to a foreign country—which, by November, the North was. The person traveling north had to swear not to reveal any information about the Confederate defenses and also swear not to bear arms against the Confederacy. The city of Memphis proved especially strict on monitoring travel. The city was not only a major hub of transportation for soldiers and war materials, but the bustling river port was also home to thousands of people born or raised in the northern states, some of whom (such as the Bohlens) have been residents for years, and others (such as Gunther) who have been stranded by the outbreak of the war.

According to one newspaper account of a civilian who escaped north, Memphis started issuing passes on June 1, 1861. By late July, Confederate General Leonidas Polk appointed Memphis alderman Samuel T. Morgan (1825–67) as the army's agent to issue passports to persons leaving Memphis (*Memphis Appeal*, July 27, 1861). Army officers rode each train headed north, clothed with authority "to demand and examine the passport of all passengers not officers or soldiers, and to remove from the cars all who fail to present proper passports" (Special Order No. 81, Central Army of Kentucky, printed in the *Memphis Appeal* January 12, 1862).

Historian Mark Neely points out that the whole pass system constituted what was for the time a shocking violation of civilian civil rights.

> [Friday, November 1, 1861] It rained hard all day, and is miserably cold and disagreeable. We are doing nothing in the business line. I am stopping with Lloyd and commenced boarding this morning at the Green Tree House, a pretty good place, but it all goes too much on the great principle to please me. The late fires are all the topic, no late war news, it is reported the Federal fleet sailed south. I was up on Beale Street a while this eve, but I came down early, it is a dangerous walk to come alone at night on this levee.

John Ringold's "Green Tree House" was located at 358 Front Street.

> [Saturday, November 2, 1861] It was clear this morning again, and the sun dried up the mud finally. The levee is full of boats, but no freight except sugar. No Richmond news yet. Our city is quiet and nothing doing. I was at the lower house all day. It is reported that Frémont is falling back again, but little ice selling. There is a great quantity of sugar on the levee, flour is very high and advancing. Jeff Thompson is in the city yet. I stayed at house all eve and retired very early.

Missouri State Guard general Meriwether Jeff Thompson (1826–76) regularly visited Memphis to plead for supplies and to confer with the Confederate high command.

> [Sunday, November 3, 1861] I spent this day as many of my others and former Sundays since I have been away from home, doing nothing but staying around the house, no church is thought of by me, but to pass the Sunday the best I can and to kill time. We are now anxiously awaiting events of the future. I am now in waiting for events and no prospect of any business for me yet.

[Monday, November 4, 1861] I am hanging on, killing time and staying at Lloyds. We have nothing of any interest. Our city is quiet, and nothing to disturb the quiet time of our way at the river house. The levee is full of boats, but little freight except sugar and molasses which is plenty and now getting very cheap. Lloyd and I went to the theater this eve. The Inkermann Zouaves performed, all French a very poor performance in my opinion and greatly disappointed.

The November 1 *Appeal* advertised the "world renowned" "Zouaves of Inkerman," who were to appear "in their grand military spectacle in five and seven Acts Tableaux. The Camp of Hell! or, Abd-El-Kader!" at the New Memphis Theater. By November 9, if the *Appeal* is to be believed, the Zouaves had completely changed their act.

[Tuesday, November 5, 1861] The joke of the day appear to be the Zouaves—a universal expressed opinion that it was a great humbug. The weather continues very fine and not uncomfortable to sit out on an evening. I notice numerous flocks of wild ducks making their way southward, which the blockade did not stop. I went up to the German Theater in the eve. I was well pleased and the performance was good, a full house see Adams, got home late.

[Wednesday, November 6, 1861] The first election for president and vice president of the C.S. takes place today, voted for Jeff Davis and Alec Stephens, my first vote in the south. The city is very quiet and the weather sometimes fine. We get but little news from the Potomac. The fleet is expected to make an attack every day upon some southern city. Spent the eve taking a walk with Carr. Stopped in the senate a minute.

[Thursday, November 7, 1861] There are various reports afloat of a fight at Columbus. The fleet is now off Savannah, GA, No news from the Potomac and it is hard telling how things stand –no reports from Ky., the troops yet remain where they did. We expect to hear momentarily from Price and Frémont in Mo., speculation appears all the go, and everything is now at an exorbitant price in the city, coffee 75 cents salt $7 per sack, flour 18 per barrel. Spent the eve at levee with Loyd.

Gunther here refers to the Battle of Belmont, which was fought on November 7. Union forces attacked the Confederate camp at Belmont, across the river from Columbus, and achieved an initial success, until Confederate reinforcements crossed the river and drove Grant back. The battle is considered either a draw or a Confederate victory. Generals Leonidas Polk and Gideon Pillow led the Confederate forces, which included several units raised in Memphis such as the 2nd, 15th, and 154th Tennessee Infantry. Both sides lost about 600 men out of 3,000 engaged.

[Friday, November 8, 1861] We have accounts of a big battle at Columbus today, on the Mo. Side, There must have been a severe fight and many killed and wounded. There is much excitement in the city, and many rumors flying, but it is hard telling how it is. Reed and Ferris had a fight this evening. Larkin made an assault on me at upper house but got off uninjured. We are in a great state of ferment in the city to learn to who is hurt and further news.

[Saturday, November 9, 1861] No reports from Columbus, but the excitement and sorrow for the dead is great. Many people may be seen around the levee and bluffs watching for the appearance of a steamer from above, many rumors are flying, and it is hard to tell what is true. Most of the stores are closed and business is almost suspended. Savannah is reported taken by the Federals and severe losses on the Confederate side. Nothing in the city to note, evenings pleasant.

Battle of Belmont, from Leslie's Famous Leaders and Battle Scenes of the Civil War *(1896)*

[Sunday, November 10, 1861] I spent the day at Lower house most of the time. There is no news of any importance. Savannah is reported saved—though Port Royal is taken. The bluffs above were occupied by many people—ladies and gents all watching for the arrival of a steamer of Columbus with the wounded. There is great excitement among many people in regard to their friends. I stayed with Lloyd all eve.

Gunther echoes the *Appeal* of November 10, which observed:
> The City Yesterday. There was much gloom and anxiety in the city yesterday, and hundreds of hearts were aching in painful suspense to know the fate of loved friends, who were in the battle near Columbus. It was expected that the steamboat *Kentucky*, which was due the previous day, had been detained to bring down a portion of the wounded, and that she would arrive in the course of the day. From morning into night, crowds, a large portion of which were ladies, waited in sad expectation at the landing, straining their eyes for long, weary hours,

to catch a sight of the expected boat; but the boat did not come.

[Monday, November 11, 1861] The boats got down last night, brought 150 wounded down. Our city is cast in great gloom for the wounded soldiers and dead. Overton Hotel is used for a hospital, numerous reports are in circulation, and no truth is in them. No news from Ky. Mo. or from the Potomac. There is not much doing among the businesses. Speculation is about played out. But high prices are all the go, for everything. Theater or concert every evening.

[Tuesday, November 12, 1861] Stirring news from east Tn., insurrection and bridge burning is in opposition, and trouble is feared. A very bad explosion took place Columbus, killing 7 persons. Mr. Bohlen and Wilson got back from White River. The weather is fine and pleasant, the levee looks lively for the times. We are having some fun with Andy Kriel our house looks like a regular headquarters for river boys. Stayed at house all eve.

Defying the rest of the state, mountainous East Tennessee seethed with "disloyal" (or loyal, depending on one's point of view) sentiments. On the night of November 8, 1861, East Tennessee Unionists burned or attempted to burn numerous bridges along the vital East Tennessee and Virginia Railroad. Panicked Confederate commanders such as Colonel William B. Wood in Knoxville felt that "the whole country is now in a state of rebellion" (against the Confederacy). Swift Confederate reaction included flooding the area with more troops and arresting suspected Unionists.

The explosion of the large cannon "Lady Polk" on November 11 killed her gun crew and several nearby officers. General Polk, who was nearby, escaped death, but was so stunned by the blast that he had to temporarily turn over command of the garrison to General Pillow.

[Wednesday, November 13, 1861] We managed to get up at about 6-1/2 o'ck. The weather is pleasant. I see Brack and engaged to go to work for him at Columbus, could not get ready in time, had to get a passport, very particular—no news from any quarter, but expect to hear some at any moment. I am yet boarding at the Green Tree House, raised on us one dollar per week and half day board. Mr. W left for Vicksburg this morning. I stayed at house all eve, had some fun with Andy and retired early.

"Brack" may be J. Brock, listed in the 1861 Chamber of Commerce as a Baker & Flour Dealer, 8 Howard's Row, or J. C. Brack (died 1862; same as J. Brock?). The 1860 census of Memphis turns up a Julius Brock (Brach), a twenty-four-year-old Baden-born merchant. These are probably three listings for the same man.

[Thursday, November 14, 1861] I was around with Brack all morning and got ready for a trip up to Columbus. I started at 2 o'ck and arrived Columbus at 4 this morning, after much difficulty going through the lines. Met Bean, was very glad to see him, and he to see me. Had a good time of it and talked over old matters at LaSalle. The cars are full of passengers, passports are all the go and none pass without."

"Bean" is Chauncey Bean (1818–1914), a wholesale grocer who lived in Ottawa, Illinois in 1860.

In 1860 Columbus was a busy port city on the Mississippi River, with a population of 1,000. At the outbreak of the war both sides recognized the enormous importance of Columbus as a place to block the Mississippi River. Columbus is situated near the highest bluffs (180 feet) on the Mississippi River north of Memphis. As the terminus of the Mobile & Ohio Railroad, the Confederacy could easily ship troops and cannon to fortify those bluffs.

[Friday, November 15, 1861] I took a short nap from 4 to 7 at the Buchanan House on a very hard bed. The night is very cold and

Columbus, Kentucky, 1862, from Harper's Weekly, *March 29, 1862*

I feel some north of Memphis. I attended to some of my business and went out visiting to the different camps with some of the boys, who were glad to see me, Dominch, Hamm and others, took supper with them and stayed in camp all night, we serenaded some of the neighboring regiments and had a fine time in the evening and took a soldier's bed in the evening, after eating some coarse fare.

The Confederate army camps at Columbus, like almost everything else in America, failed to impress Englishman William Howard Russell:

> There is no appearance of military order or discipline about the camps, though they were guarded by sentries and cannon, and implements of war and soldiers' accoutrements were abundant. Some of the sentinels carried their firelocks under their arms like umbrellas, others carried the butt over their shoulder and the muzzle downwards ... whilst sybarites less ingenious, had simply deposited their muskets against the trees, and were lying down reading newspapers.[9]

[Saturday, November 16, 1861] The reveille was called at early dawn, we all got up and after had a very good breakfast. Hamm giving us his best. I attended my business, and walk over the town. It is a lively scene—the many soldiers and tented field, horses, big cannon and etc. a flag of truce boat came down and our officers met them in the river, went up and took supper with the boys in the Arkansas regiment (Tappins) and went to the station house in the eve at 7 in order to pass the guard house before 9, an attack is expected at any time.

Colonel James Camp Tappan's 13th Arkansas Infantry formed part of the Columbus garrison.

[Sunday, November 17, 1861] Humboldt. Just my luck. Left Columbus at 1 o'ck and arrived here at 5. I intend to loaf the whole day at this miserable little one house place, but made the best out of it, many passengers are in the same fix. No news except a reported Federal victory up Pikeville Ky. An attack upon Columbus is expected at any time, and all the talk is of fights and expected movements. Came across Jennings from Van Buren, Ar, was glad to see him. I spent part of the eve with him, also Bean on the cars.

Also known as the Battle of Ivy Mountain, Kentucky, the November 8–9, 1861, engagement saw General William "Bull" Nelson's larger Union force drive back a Confederate force under Colonel John S. Williams.

[Monday, November 18, 1861] The weather is fine and pleasant and no business doing. I am as usual stopping with Lloyd—we are having some fun with Andy Kriel. It is reported that Mason and Slidell have been captured upon the high seas. There are many rumors and reports about many things going on above here, but no truth in them. Spent the eve at home.

Gunther refers here to the Mason-Slidell affair. James Mason and John Slidell, two Confederate diplomats removed illegally from the British mail

Slidell and Mason, courtesy Library of Congress

packet *Trent* by Captain Charles Wilkes on November 8, 1861, started an international diplomatic nightmare for the Lincoln administration as these envoys were bound on their way to Great Britain and France to seek diplomatic recognition for the new Confederate States of America. Their seizure sparked an immediate outcry from the British public for the North's violation of British neutrality rights. After weeks of war talk, inflamed emotions, parliamentary threats, and diplomatic exchanges, the Lincoln administration released the envoys and disavowed Captain Wilkes's actions, probably forestalling an imminent British recognition of the Confederacy.

[Tuesday, November 19, 1861] The weather continues very fine. We are all excitement and many rumors continue to fly about. There is much discussion about Mason and Slidell affair. Times are getting very hard in our city. Militia gossip is all the talk and many are getting scared and afraid to go about. We stayed at house all eve and go to be early.

[Wednesday, November 20, 1861] Everybody is admiring this beautiful weather, warm and so genial. No fights reported for a few days past, reports—east all quiet. The uprising in E. Tenn. is being suppressed by a strong military force. We are going to have a strong militia muster in a few days. No war news at present. The Federal prisoners have been removed to a slave mart. We went to a negro concert a poor affair + quite disappointed in the performance.

[Thursday, November 21, 1861] I am very much pleased with the Commercial Hotel board and am enjoying the times first rate, though troubled some on account of the present state of affairs. Specie is very scarce, selling at 28%, all provisions are very high. Our lives is very quiet, some 4 companies of cavalry came up from LA fine looking men, Lloyd, Andy + my self took a walk up in the city in the Eve called around on some friends.

The Commercial Hotel was at the corner of Jefferson and Front Streets.

[Friday, November 22, 1861] The weather is getting colder and winter is slowly approaching. We have considerable excitement about the militia and our office is full of boys all talking and discussing the subject. Times are getting very hard in the city, and nothing but war is the excitement. Andy and I took a walk up town in the Eve. The city is very quiet in the evenings and no shops open except saloons.

Brigadier General James A. Carnes of the 23rd Brigade, Tennessee Militia, issued General Order No. 1 on November 22. This order required local militia captains to furnish a list of their men subject to militia duty. On November 27 the men were to report for duty, with one-half of them being detailed to active service. As can be seen, Charles Gunther took a job on a riverboat the day he was to report for duty. This was not a coincidence. The newspapers reported "much complaint as to the mode of selecting" those detailed. See *Memphis Appeal*, November 23, 1861; *New Orleans Daily True Delta*, November 29, 1861.

[Saturday, November 23, 1861] Our Federal prisoners are all now in the Slave mart, and a guard is watching over them every day. We have no news of any importance. The bombardment of Fort Pickens is going on a few days past, but no assault, nothing new from the camps, all quiet, but preparations are going on all the time, a few gunboats have gone up the River, the *Tuscarora* has been burnt down the river. We stayed at office all eve, talking and having some fun with the boys.

The Confederate gunboat *Tuscarora*, a side-wheel river steamer, accidently burned that day (November 23) near Helena, Arkansas.

On November 22 and 23 Union naval vessels, assisted by the cannon at Union-held Fort Pickens, bombarded Confederate forts at Pensacola, Florida. Although the bombardment severely damaged the Confederate forts, the Union forces never tried to take the town.

> [Sunday, November 24, 1861] Another Sunday has come and passed like all my former ones for some time past, no church going at present, but drilling in the militia is the order of the day. Lloyd + I drilled all morning got my dinner late, but a fine one, all the luxuries of the season. The bombardment of Pensacola has suspended for the present. We are all excitement about the militia business, and detailing has commenced. Stayed at office all eve.

> [Monday, November 25, 1861] Business opens very poorly this morning, but few boats are at the Levee, but some laid up ones are coming out. Freight is scarce, the embargo above is now open, no news from any of the camps. The Federals have fallen back in Missouri, and great preparations are making for a descent down to this city, but equal ones to meet them. Militia creates a great fluttering among the boys, and loafers will soon be scarce around here. Andy + I stayed at the house all eve. There is a concert this eve at the Theatre for the wounded soldiers.

> [Tuesday, November 26, 1861] We get up morning about 6 o'ck, the nights are getting cold. Levee business is slow but little ice is going out. We are having lots of fun over the militia excitement and the boys, money is getting to be very scarce in our city + no specie to be had, no news from the camps. I am in a quandary what I shall do—leave I can't, but my hope now is a government boat with Harmstad. After supper I stayed at office, + retired early.

[Wednesday, November 27, 1861] Lloyd is in a regular fever heat upon the militia question, as well as many more who are in the same fix. There was a heavy rain last night, but cleared off today. I + others had some fun with Andy + others by marching up to his shop. I shipped this Eve upon the *Rose Douglas*, as steward, what another change in my life all at once but who cares, these are war times so let her rip, a good way of backing out of the militia question.

Charles Gunther here ties his fate to that of the steamer *Rose Douglas*. Described by one newspaper as having "superior officers and excellent accommodations," (*Weekly Arkansas Gazette,* June 1, 1861), the *Douglas* (aka *Douglass*) regularly plied the Arkansas and Mississippi Rivers, carrying passengers, freight, and the mails. In September 1860 it snagged and sank, but was raised. As the war started the vessel added another service—transporting troops and war supplies as needed. In August 1861 General Polk seized the *Douglas* and other vessels tied up in Memphis for transporting troops from Memphis to New Madrid ("Interesting from the South," *Daily National Intelligencer,* August 17, 1861). Her skipper was James L. Maginnis ("McGinnis," 1825–73), an old steamboat hand. According to his death notice (in the *Cincinnati Daily Gazette,* November 10, 1873), the Maryland-born Maginnis "was familiar with the Mississippi, Ohio, and Arkansas [Rivers] for many years as master, owner, and pilot.... A man of fine natural abilities, and one of the most agreeable men it is possible to find." The steamer was named after Rose Douglas, sister of William F. Douglas (1832–79), a newspaper editor in Pine Bluff and major of the 6th Arkansas Infantry.

[Thursday, November 28, 1861] We got off late last night and went along very well during the night, I got up at 5-1/2 o'ck, got my boys to work cleaning up, and had a good breakfast at 7-1/2. We are getting along finely + I must say, my new occupation is not unpleasant to me. Am learning all the time and am wearing off awkwardness. We past [*sic*] Fort Pillow at noon it looks very formidable, we going ahead at my—this eve and I know not.

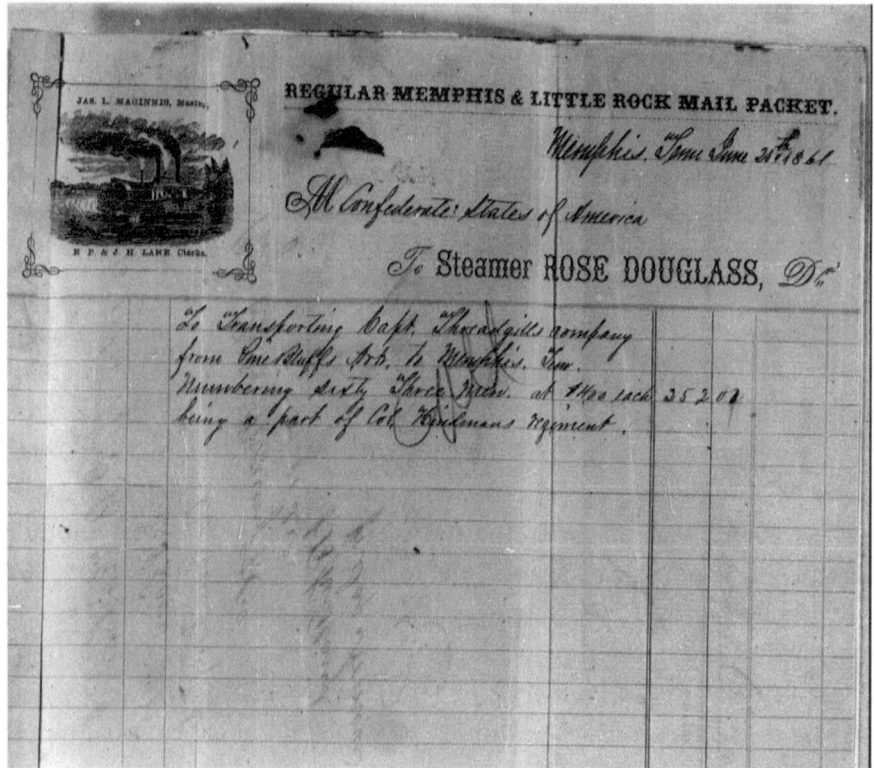

The Rose Douglas, *image on company stationary, from the Confederate vessel papers, National Archives Microfilm M909, Rose Douglas, page 11*

[Friday, November 29, 1861] Steamer *Rose Douglass*. We are making slow progress upstream layed up all night. The weather is exceedingly bad and very unpleasant. Our passengers appear to be very well satisfied and I in my own vocation am getting along very well + getting my hand in the business. There is nothing of any interest to note along the river, all looks bleak. I sat up pretty late talking with the passengers.

[Saturday, November 30, 1861] We still get along slowly, some of our rough passengers are having good times + a – for eating. The weather continues not very pleasant + the guards are more or less wet. I see but little money among my passengers, who amuse themselves playing cards. I am enjoying the trip, but not so well if I had more stories to help to manage things spent the setting around the cabin.

December 1861

The New Orleans that Charles Gunther visited in December was the largest city in the Confederacy, a bustling prewar river port whose commerce was slowly being strangled by the Union blockade. That summer William Howard Russell visited New Orleans, and marveled.

> The streets are badly paved as are those of most of the American cities, if not of all of those I have ever been in, but in other respects they are more worthy of a great city than are those of New York. There is an air thoroughly French about the people—cafes, restaurants, billiard-rooms abound, with oyster and lager-bier saloons interspersed. The shops are all *magazins*, the people in the street all speaking French, particularly the negroes, who are going out shopping with their masters and mistresses, exceedingly well dressed, noisy, and not unhappy looking. The extent of the drive gave an imposing idea about the size of New Orleans—the richness of some of the shops, the vehicles on the streets, and the multitude of well-dressed people on the pavements, an impression of its wealth and the comfort of its inhabitants.[10]

[Sunday, December 1, 1861] We got in Columbus last night, our cabin being crowded with men + soldiers. We are all glad we made port. The sheets are exceedingly muddy and traveling rough. There are many soldiers on the street + the military spectacle is fine. All is hustle, bustle, carts + wagons. The fleet under Comm. Hollins went up stream expecting to meet the gun boats of Lincoln. We left for Memphis at 1 o'ck after seeing but little of the place + every thing closed.

[Monday, December 2, 1861] Hickman + New Madrid are poor little one horse places. The day was very cold, with a small storm it felt like a real northerner + I longed to get from the south. I had a real romantic excursion for stores with Mills, + got back at 12 o'ck. We are taking up freight + a lot of hogs, pork is a scarce article + miles high. I see lots of wild geese, cranes, + ducks. We are out of oil, and I am in a great stew to get to Memphis.

[Tuesday, December 3, 1861] I am having a good time reading some St. Louis papers of the 29th ult. a great curiosity with me. I soon read all the advertisements + commercial affairs particularly. The day is cold and weather is moderating. We have – passengers on board first from the upper country. We are not making much headway down our wheel is not in good condition. We made Memphis this eve at 6 o'ck. I went up town but returned early.

[Wednesday, December 4, 1861] I got up early + had a late breakfast. The weather is pleasant. Memphis looks lively + I was glad to get back again. I went around to see all the boys, nothing new. The militia excitement has died out. Andy is yet alive + in good spirits, times in the city look hard. I see the celebrated gunboat *Manassas*, she looks very formidable indeed + perfect turtle. I sent a letter up home by a gentleman, spent the eve at Ice House with Lloyd.

CSS *Manassas*—aka, the "Turtle." Converted from the river towboat *Enoch Train* and covered with iron, the curious-looking vessel had been designed as a ram. However, its slow speed and lack of firepower rendered it ineffective. The ship was sunk during the naval engagement below New Orleans in April 1862.

[Thursday, December 5, 1861] We are up for New Orleans, and I am very glad of it, just suits me. I brought in my stores for the

CSS Manassas, from Scharf, History of the Confederate States Navy *(1887)*

boat, walked all over the city, see some of the Yankee prisoners in the slave mart, no war news at all, some small affairs on the coasts. Drew $5 from Mr. Bohlen. I see the floating dock battery, it looks formidable, but my opinion is that it will be no account too *much exposed* to the enemies fire. We left for up the River a few miles + then returned on our way South.

The "floating battery" had been fashioned from New Orleans's "Pelican" floating dry dock. As Gunther suspected, the battery proved nearly useless.

[Friday, December 6, 1861] I woke up this morning going down. I got some two new boys + it makes quite a difference in my business affairs, work appears simple + not so much attention is required by me for my niggers. Stores are high. Butter 45 + 50 c, eggs 35c per doz Coffee 80 c per lb flour 12 c/lb. There is nothing along the river of note + looks monotonous. We passed Helena Ark at 10-1/2 + arrived at Napoleon at 8 o'ck bought some eggs at 35c retired early.

At 80 cents per pound, coffee was five times the March price of coffee in Memphis.

[Saturday, December 7, 1861] We laid up all last night at Napoleon + started down stream at 5. The weather is fine + pleasant, warm, comfortable sitting out of doors. Vegetation along the banks of the River retains it verdancy but some difference is perceptible between here and Memphis. We are getting along very well, but the weather at night is some foggy. We took on some wood and in the eve we went up to the woodman's house, had a fine time 3 young ladies. I lectured one all eve, we got to the boat at 2-1/2 o'ck + off for Dixie.

[Sunday, December 8, 1861] We are getting along fine we stopped at Lake Providence, bought a few stores, we all going down finely. Made Vicksburg at 2 o'ck, passed along without stopping. She looks natural. The scenery is not very interesting some few fine plantations that is all. I am reading Dickens, *Tale of Two Cities* I like it. We have no amusement on the boat, all is quiet, no life. I retired early in the eve, prospects are for a fog tonight + a laying up of the boat.

[Monday, December 9, 1861] We passed Natchez last night + layed up for a fog. The scenery is fine in some parts, fine plantations and green woods. It looks more like Spring to me than anything else. We made good headway, nothing of any interest on the boat, the day passing as usual. The meals are very good, + I am finding my passing is much better than on my first trip. The night is warm, fine moonlight, but a fog is coming up, retired early.

In his *Life on the Mississippi*, Mark Twain described the river town of Natchez:

> Famous Natchez-under-the-hill has not changed notably in twenty years; in outward aspect—judging by the descriptions of the ancient procession of foreign tourists—it has not changed in sixty; for it is still small,

Natchez, from Mark Twain, Life on the Mississippi *(1883)*

straggling, and shabby. It had a desperate reputation, morally, in the old keel-boating and early steamboating times—plenty of drinking, carousing, fisticuffing, and killing there, among the riff-raff of the river, in those days. But Natchez-on-top-of-the-hill is attractive; has always been attractive. Even Mrs. Trollope (1827) had to confess its charms.

[Tuesday, December 10, 1861] Woke up this morning + found I was not running but layed up again, and I have time on again. We layed below Baton Rouge some two miles. The scenery is beautiful everything is green, fine plantations, fine summer days, all truly Southern. The green sugar cane looks very much like the corn fields of Illinois, a little more pea green that is all. The residences are very fine, with some beautiful orange groves + tropical plants. The night is fine.

Baton Rouge in 1862, from Guernsey, Harper's Pictorial History *(1894)*

[Wednesday, December 11, 1861] We laid up again last night, we had quite a load of sugar + molasses which we got today Eve. Mr. Miner + ladies are on board, no meat for dinner, so we went in on Joe's turkeys. The day is beautiful + warm. The scenery along the River is one continuous line of fine plantations sugar houses + beautiful groves of oranges. We made Orleans this Eve about 3 o'ck. The city looks dull + quiet on the landing. Stayed on boat all Eve.

In commerce, in wealth, and in size, no other city in the Confederacy compared with New Orleans. With 160,000 inhabitants, its population exceeded that of the state of Florida and was four times larger than Richmond, the Confederate capitol. Cotton exports had fueled its prewar growth. In 1860, cotton exports from the "Crescent City" accounted for more wealth than the exports of the rest of the South combined. The leading southern city, New Orleans was in many respects the least "southern" southern city, with its large immigrant and northern-born population.

The Mississippi River trade, and the cotton trade in particular, tied New Orleans and Memphis together. The Union blockade of the river above Memphis and below New Orleans slowly strangled the commerce of both cities. The normal shipments of flour from the north almost ceased; dockhands, often immigrants, found themselves idle. The New Orleans Gunther observes is far removed from its usually bustling character.

New Orleans levee, 1860, from Leslie's Illustrated, *April 14, 1860*

[Thursday, December 12, 1861] Up bright + early visited both St. Mary's + French markets. The markets are very good + plenty of everything. Everything on the boat passes off quietly. I was out over the city. I am a little disappointed in N.O., the streets are very narrow, old style houses + roof windows. There are but few ships in port + all layed up, some steamers on the Levee. Sugar trade is all that is going. Visited St. Charles Hotel in the Eve + returned early to boat.

William Howard Russell found the Saint Charles
> an enormous establishment, of the American type, with a Southern character about it. A number of gentlemen were seated in the hall, and front of the office, with their legs up against the wall, and on the backs of chairs, smoking, spitting, and reading the papers. Officers crowded the bar. The bustle and noise of the place would make it anything but an agreeable residence for one fond of quiet; but this hotel is famous for its difficulties.

The job of steward or purser was to handle the boat's finances and to purchase supplies, including food for the voyage.

St. Charles Hotel and New Orleans Custom House, from Harpers Weekly, *February 16, 1861*

[Friday, December 13, 1861] The weather is delightful + everything looks like summers North. Green sod + all the shrubbery in full leaves flowers blooming + oranges hang on all the orange trees. Everything gives such a fine picturesque tropical appearance. I run over all the markets today again, bought my meats + vegetables. Omnibuses and street cars fare 5c, running in all directions. Oysters are plenty + cheap, had a fine lot with Joe. Went to German Theatre in the Eve very good play Kabale + Liebe, Schiller.

The play *Kabale und Liebe* [*Intrigue and Love*], by Friedrich Schiller, explores and critiques absolutism and hypocrisy.

[Saturday, December 14, 1861] The weather is fine + pleasant. We are yet laying high + dry on the dock. Everything passed off quietly. Thos Elton +I went out to Lake Ponchartrain on the R.R. The country back of the city is all swamp, but everything green like summer. The Lake is beautiful + the house + garden around the depot are neat, the shrubbery is beautiful, got back to Algiers at 6 o'ck. Things all right on boat.

[Sunday, December 15, 1861] This is a fine day again. Algiers is quiet, except all the French are out drilling + no work being done on the boat. This does not appear much like Sunday to me. The various church bells in N.O. + Algiers are filling the air with their chimes. I see a beautiful large elk in a garden. Chas. And I took a walk + I inspected the gun boats finishing. No news of any importance. Spent the eve on boat.

The *New Orleans Daily True Delta* of December 15, under "Steamboat and River News," announced that the "reliable packet *Rose Douglas*, Captain J. D. Maginnis, leaves for White River Monday evening at 5 o'clock, from foot of Bienville street." As it turned out, they missed their Monday evening departure. Newspapers such as the *Delta* ran regular

advertisements announcing steamboat departures, such as the December 14 ad to left:

[Monday, December 16, 1861] There is some hope yet of getting off these docks tonight. I was over in the city today, walking all over it, seeing the Elephant. I am very much disappointed in my expectations, the streets very narrow + very poorly built up. I passed a cemetery, all persons being buried above ground, the tombs looking very picturesque. I spend the Eve on boat, not going off in the Evening on this side. Ferrying across the River only one picayune.

The ferry cost one picayune—an old Spanish coin worth about 6-1/2 cents.

[Tuesday, December 17, 1861] We are all glad to get off these docs again, arrived at old landing again at 12:00 + loading in freight as fast as possible. I was out through the city all day on business. The city is very dull + everything is quiet. The Custom House building is all occupied with government works, cannon etc. being turned out every day. There is much rejoicing at the news from the North and the Mason excitement in England + the probability of a rupture with England. Was around town with Hughes.

[Wednesday, December 18, 1861] N.O. Up bright + early + off to market at 4 o'ck. I have been very busy all day laying in stores + walking my legs off. We work under the disadvantage of the stores closing at 3 o'ck. Everybody has to drill + muster. No news of importance. Col. Terry of Texas was killed in a skirmish in Ky. The armies occupy their old position yet. Great expectations are felt from England. I was running until 7 o'ck. up town buying some few things yet.

With Gunther and the *Rose Douglas* departing New Orleans, it is worthwhile to imagine their departure as Mark Twain described similar departures:

> It was always the custom for the boats to leave New Orleans between four and five o'clock in the afternoon. From three o'clock onward they would be burning rosin and pitch pine (the sign of preparation), and so one had the picturesque spectacle of a rank, some two or three miles long, of tall, ascending columns of coal-black smoke; a colonnade which supported a sable roof of the same smoke blended together and spreading abroad over the city. Every outward-bound boat had its flag flying at the jack-staff, and sometimes a duplicate on the verge staff astern. Two or three miles of mates were commanding and swearing with more than usual emphasis; countless processions of freight barrels and boxes were spinning athwart the levee and flying aboard the stage-planks, belated passengers were dodging and skipping among these frantic things, hoping to reach the forecastle companion way alive, but having their doubts about it; women with reticules and bandboxes were trying to keep up with husbands freighted with carpet-sacks and crying babies, and making a failure of it by losing their heads in the whirl and roar and general distraction; drays and baggage-vans were clattering hither and thither in a wild hurry, every now and then getting blocked and jammed together, and then during ten seconds one could not see them for the profanity, except vaguely and dimly; every windlass connected with every forehatch, from one end of that long array of steamboats to the other, was keeping up a deafening whiz and whir, lowering freight into the hold, and the half-naked crews of perspiring negroes that worked them were roaring such songs as 'De Las' Sack! De Las' Sack!'—inspired to unimaginable exaltation by the chaos of turmoil and racket that was driving

everybody else mad. By this time the hurricane and boiler decks of the steamers would be packed and black with passengers. The 'last bells' would begin to clang, all down the line, and then the powwow seemed to double; in a moment or two the final warning came—a simultaneous din of Chinese gongs, with the cry, 'All dat ain't goin', please to git asho'!'—and behold, the powwow quadrupled! People came swarming ashore, overturning excited stragglers that were trying to swarm aboard. One more moment later a long array of stage-planks was being hauled in, each with its customary latest passenger clinging to the end of it with teeth, nails, and everything else, and the customary latest procrastinator making a wild spring shoreward over his head.[12]

Colonel Benjamin Franklin Terry (1821–61) of the 8th Texas Cavalry was killed in a skirmish at Woodsonville, Kentucky, on December 17. Gunther had met this unit on October 18 in Grand Junction.[13]

[Thursday, December 19, 1861] I found myself this morning going up the Miss again. The weather is fine and pleasant. The sugar mills along the river are all in full blast, the cane looking beautiful pea green. Passed several boats going down. Feel fine + all right today, my oranges for the trip will be very pleasant. We are going along very finely this Eve, but a prospect for a fog. Spent the Eve sitting around doing nothing + retired early. Now at Baton Rouge.

[Friday, December 20, 1861] We had to lay up again last night for a fog, going along finely again this a.m. Passed Baton Rouge at 10 o'ck. The place looks fine + like the appearance of it. The State House is a beautiful building + also the Asylum. We are yet in the Sugar Region, beautiful plantations. Nothing of any interest today. We all making slow time, am anxious to get some news.

[Saturday, December 21, 1861] I had a fine sleep + running all night. Everything passes all right. We are in the Cotton region again, the scenery is monotonous + not interesting. I finished Dickens' *Two Cities*. Joe + I had some fun. The *Quitman* passed us going up. We made Natchez at 8 o'ck. I did not go up town the night being quite dark. I read a late *Memphis Avalanche* of the 19th.

[Sunday, December 22, 1861] We were going all night. The day is cold + cloudy. This appears little to me like a Sunday + I am passing the day like the others. We passed Rodney + Grand Gulf small one horse places, strong head wind. My sugar cane + oranges are a luxury now. I am thankful for my excellent health + long as we near Christmas to be at home. I know my mother feels for me, but it is all in a life time.

[Monday, December 23, 1861] The weather has changed quite cold this a.m. We are making good time upstream, passed Vicksburgh [sic] before daylight, the sun is shining, but not warm. There is nothing of any interest to note. The river is monotonous, passed several boats downward bound. Our passengers appear to be very well satisfied, made New Providence at 8 o'ck. We expect to stop at our wood yard, but no go. Stayed up late.

[Tuesday, December 24, 1861] I am trying to have my breakfast earlier than common. The weather is clear but a cold wind prevails + a fire is very comfortable. We had some fun, shooting at Swans + Pelicans + had an exciting race with the *Morrison*, got ahead. Passed the *Turtle* [CSS *Manassas*] downward bound. An odd looking thing. Christmas is coming, but I have no feeling as usual. My book only tells me so. The scenery is monotonous today stayed up pretty late.

Described as a "first class, fast running and magnificent passenger packet" (*New Orleans Times Picayune* December 6, 1861), the steamboat

William M. Morrison ran between New Orleans and Memphis. A 662-ton sidewheel steamer, the *Morrison* was built in 1856 in Cincinnati and was burned by her crew when New Orleans fell in 1862. In 1857 and 1858 Samuel Clemens (Mark Twain) served as a pilot aboard the *Morrison*.

> [Wednesday, December 25, 1861] Up bright + early, but a dull Christmas. Made Napoleon at 10 o'ck. The place looks forsaken + numerous persons are all on a big drunk. Bought some stores, and left for White River with a few passengers on board + loaded down to the guards. Nothing more than an ordinary dinner nothing to be had. I had many thoughts of home + mother. See late papers + some fighting is imminent. C.S. defeat near Manassas. We had some fine egg nog + retired early.

> [Thursday, December 26, 1861] Christmas is passed + it is hard for me to realize that this is a holiday week, nothing but business is the go, we are making good progress up White River + have some pleasant passengers. Judge Ringo + family. Time flies along + I am anxious to hear some news of some kind. The weather is chilly, + the things along the river have a country aspect. We had some music by Jack + I got to be late, laid up until moon rise.

Daniel Ringo (1803–73), a distinguished lawyer, was the judge of the US District Court in Arkansas when that state seceded, and after held the same position under the Confederate government.

> [Friday, December 27, 1861] White River. The fresh air or wind rather bites a man's nose this morning. The sun shone pleasantly at noon passed Aberdeen, Clarendon + DeValls Bluff all looked miserable + seedy + no stir whatsoever in the streets. I ran very short of meat, but got a little. Some of our passengers got off a D. Bluffs. There is nothing of any interest to note, the scenery being nothing but mud banks + cane brakes. Laid up tonight again 30 miles this side of Des Arc.

De Valls Bluff is located in Prairie County along the White River, about halfway between Clarendon and Des Arc. At the beginning of the Civil War, the area was simply a settlement with a store, a house, and a boat landing. De Valls Bluff would often be used as a port to unload goods bound for Little Rock in instances when the Arkansas River was too low to navigate. After realizing the importance the town played, Union forces heavily fortified the port at De Valls Bluff until the end of the war.

In peacetime most steamers abandoned the White River trade during the summer, as the water levels became too low to navigate safely.

> [Saturday, December 28, 1861] Up bright + early it is quite cold, but got warm again at noon. We arrived at Des Arc at 10 o'ck., there were many at the levee to see us, a boat here is not an everyday thing, got some late news. The Federals within 30 miles of Bowling Green, no fights otherwise. I was very busy all day, laying in stores. Everything is dead, no business, many stores closed up. Left this Eve for up the river. Nothing worthy of note.

> [Sunday, December 29, 1861] White River. I found myself upward bound this morning, made Augusta at 10. There is nothing to indicate that this is a Sabbath to me, consequently my reverential feelings are at a low ebb. Business + travel is all the go. Everything is very quiet on board the boat, a few passengers, all the Villagers pour down to see us off + learn the news. At W__ we ran until dark + laid up for the night the water being very shallow.

> [Monday, December 30, 1861] We are making time for Jacksonport arrived at 10 oc. The place looks like all Arkansas towns, "pretty hard." Saw a big fight, one man shoot another + a general time of it. Bought plenty of stores cheap comparatively for the country. Business has dried up in this section, some few soldiers here. Have put off lots of sugar + molasses. Also boat laid up on the other side of the river for the night.

Jacksonport, Arkansas, located at the confluence of the White River and the Black River, was a small but important steamboat stop during the Civil War as well as a transportation hub for Confederate forces.

> [Tuesday, December 31, 1861] The last day of this unhappy year has come so soon + it is hard for me to realize how I managed to get along so well. Today find myself steaming down White River on the *Rose Douglas* for N.O. A steward, what a change, but who cares for that! Any way to get along these times, war times, indeed—I cast many reflections back upon home + the good old folks there, how I would enjoy it to be with them. We laid up for the night at Augusta a one horse place. The evening being pleasant.
>
> In summing up the last year's doings of my humble self I can not help reflecting on this past unhappy year. We, a once happy, united people but a year ago are now severed + in areas deadly foes, one section against another. Oh how I long for that peace to come which is so often spoken of, but I fear in the far distance, from my observations + knowledge the soon expected peace is but a phantom in the eyes of the many.
>
> I have made a great trip of it this year, seen much, travelled in most southern states from Tenn. to La. And feel though I had done my share of rambling + yet be employed continually + saving up something for a rainy day. Times at present are very dull + everything for the present is at a standstill, specie is out of the question + paper money all the go. The armies confront each other upon the banks of the Potomac, Kentucky, + all along on the coast, + stirring times are momentarily expected. The Mason + Slidell affair turns out to be humbug at least as far as England is concerned. While writing this I am upon the old *Rose Douglas* steaming down the White River for N.O. The way is pleasant, + I have nothing to cause me any uneasiness of mind, but go along with the tide of public events + wait for "something to turn up," + watch the events of this war with deep feelings and anxiety, but let nothing disturb the equanimity of my temper, + sail on upon this tempestuous sea of life.

Diary January–April 1862

It was a mild 30 degrees with a gentle breeze out of the north when Charles F. Gunther, the purser aboard the steam packet *Rose Douglas*, helped to guide his ship southeast toward the Crescent City of New Orleans. The year 1862 was opening with the fond hopes and dreams of avoiding the terrors of the new Civil War and yet simultaneously showing a profit hauling crops of southern rice and cotton, soldiers, and life's myriad necessities to the small river towns along the Mississippi, Arkansas, and White Rivers. Small towns like Des Arc, the county seat of Prairie County, Arkansas, were to be among his first stops. Little did he know at the time that just six months later, on June 17, 1862, this small town and the surrounding countryside would become the site of the Battle of Saint Charles, where a Confederate shell would penetrate the hull of the Union ship *Mound City*, killing 129 of her crew.

But those events were still six months in the future when the steamer's crew celebrated the New Year with the popping of a bottle of imported champagne.

January 1862

[Wednesday, January 1, 1862] A happy New Year I might say, but far from it, my conscience tells me otherwise but I must make the best of it. We are N.O. [New Orleans] bound and making slow progress for the Crescent City. There is nothing of any interest transpiring. We had a good dinner. Joe & I bursting the champaign. A great many passengers. I have many thoughts that carry me from hence, but space will not permit me to note them. Layed all night at Augusta.

[January 2, 1862] New Year has passed again & I on the two last found myself on the steamers of Ark. [Arkansas] but one far different from the other. Today we reached Des Arc. Everything is quiet & the long expected fights have not taken place yet. We are getting blood thirsty & anxious for our brother men to pitch in & kill one another. There is nothing of any interest on the river except a few child farolas we see fly. Layed at St. Charles all night.

Saint Charles in 1862 was a small, sleepy river town of only 261 people, a town where rivermen bedded down at night, took on a few provisions, exchanged much sought-after war news (hopefully of Confederate victories), picked up a precious newspaper, and perhaps boarded a few passengers or cargo from a local farmer.

After a night's rest, Gunther and the *Rose Douglas* would cast off and head for De Valls Bluff, another small port town of just 186 residents. De Valls Bluff, however, held the greatest strategic value of any town in eastern Arkansas. It was here, with the town's one store, one dwelling, and a rickety boat landing, that, when the Arkansas River was low, transports that could not reach Little Rock but that could navigate the White River would transfer soldiers and war material and supplies to either Memphis or Little Rock. After the Union forces seized De Valls Bluff in January of 1863, Confederate forces were forced to rely on bushwackers to make several attempts to disrupt Union boat traffic on the White River and retake this important post. Their most successful attempt to reopen this port was achieved on June 24, 1864, when Confederate General Joe Shelby's troops sank the Union ship *Queen City*. As spectacular as the lone action was, Union forces held De Valls Bluff until the end of the war.

De Valls Bluff, from Leslie's Illustrated Magazine, *February 26, 1864*

[January 3, 1862] Started early. Made good progress. Reached Devalls Bluff & took on a large lot of hay at St. Charles & Prairie Ldg. We have as passengers Maj. Harris, Col. Price & others of Mo. on their way to Richmond. We are all anxious to get into the Old Father of Waters again 'the Miss.' Arrived at Napoleon at 11-1/2. It makes me feel as though I were upon the true element again. Laying up at night. Played out.

The two military passengers purser Gunther welcomed aboard were probably Colonel Edwin W. Price (1834–1908) and Major Thomas A. Harris (1826–96) of Missouri. They accompanied the *Rose Douglas* down river to Eunice, Louisiana, and further to New Orleans, to catch transportation to Virginia.

An obvious topic of conversation in the evenings aboard the steamer was the latest war news. Sitting around the steamer stove at night the newspaper was devoured, news discussed as to its veracity, and exaggerated accounts of Confederate victories, impending victories, or Union routs eagerly expanded upon.

[January 4, 1862] Layed up again this morning—heavy fog—& rain all day, one of those miserable, disagreeable blue days.

> Passed the Str. *Jno. Walsh* upward bound. Made one landing at Eunice, Louisiana. A stove feels very agreeable. See Memphis paper 2d. Says Mason & Slidell are given up. Read Lincoln's message this eve. We ran all night. Rasd. [raised] a good time with our passengers in the Eve.

Eunice, Louisiana, is located in Acadia, Evangeline, and Saint Landry parishes. It was founded as a port town by lawman and pioneer land developer C. C. Duson, and named by Duson for his wife. Charles Gunther and his passengers "raised their good time" to the strains of Cajun banjos, singing and dancing to traditional Cajun strains as they discussed the lovely simplicity of this peaceful area disturbed by the anger and sectional hatred then engulfing their nation.

> [January 5, 1862] Sunday again and it is almost impossible for me to comprehend it—no change. The same return of business & our good progress down makes all go pleasant & easy. To kill time I am reading the *Naval Officer* by Maryatt. We passed Vicksburgh at 2-1/2 oc'k, made a short stop. Everything very quiet.

Frequently Charles Gunther refers to books he is reading. An avid absorber of the literature of the day, he thrilled in popular current novels, particularly British, involving naval accounts. *The Naval Officer: or, Scenes and Adventures in the Life of Frank Mildmay*, was a three-volume novel written in 1829. Typical of the adventure novels Gunther enjoyed, this book was a thrilling narrative of naval escapades, compiled mostly from the author's personal experience, in which the characters seemed real, the exploits unlimited and rewarding, and the financial success immediate and substantial. Such an enterprising hero would foreshadow Gunther's future success as a candy magnate in postwar Chicago.

> [January 6, 1862] On waking up this morning I found myself 40 miles south of Natchez going along finely. We got into the

Sugar Country again & the verdent appearance of the landscape brings back fall recollections. We arrived at Baton Rough [Rouge] at 5-1/2 fondly should I have stopped to see Mrs. Kearnes but no stop. All go's pleasant & nothing to mar the pleasure of the trip.

[January 7, 1862] We made good time last night & made the stock Ldg. of N. Orleans at 8. Shortly before we had a sad accident befall us. One of the deck hands fell overboard & was lost. It cast a gloom over the whole boat. I & others got off & inspected the new gunboats building. The boat layed over at Algiers. I had to go over in the rain. Layed there all night.

Charles Gunther was an inquisitive entrepreneur with a thirst for knowledge whose curiosity led to his exploration of new inventions such as new naval devices suited to shipbuilding and sailing, food preparation tips, and medical cures. It was this adventurous spirit that led him to inspect the new gunboat.

Algiers is a neighborhood within New Orleans on the west bank of the Mississippi River, originally known as Slaughterhouse Point. This area of New Orleans became a holding area for newly arrived African slaves and the location of a powder house for gunpowder and weapons storage. By the first quarter of the nineteenth century shipbuilding gained prominence in the city, which, along with New Orleans's growth as a major railroad center for freight and rolling stock, eventually served Confederate needs. Gunther would stay in New Orleans through January 15, enjoying the Crescent City's night life, visiting the French market and local attractions, conversing with friends, and generally "living it up" as a diversion to the tedium of river life.

[January 8, 1862] The weather cloudy. This is a grand gailey day. The celebration of the battle of N.O. [New Orleans]. The military were out in large force & reviewed by Gens. Lovell & others. Canal

Aerial view of New Orleans, 1862, from Harper's Pictorial History of the Great Rebellion *(1894)*

Street was full of ladies. The troops looked very well & made a credible appearance. Negro companies were a curiosity. I spent the Eve taking a walk up the city & to the St. Charles [Hotel]. The rotunda is full of people.

[January 9, 1862] Up bright & early to market. The city is very dull & nothing going on. I visited the small museum on St. Charles St. Joe & I took a walk over the city this noon. Oysters & oranges are plenty & cheap. We are living good. The new gun boat above us is some attraction. Spent the Eve calling on McGee. The city is dull of nights.

It is unclear which of the many people named McGee/Magee then living in New Orleans Gunther calls on this week. The best bet is the firm of James Magee & Co., commission merchants and ship owners.

[January 10, 1862] The weather continues warm & pleasant. Nothing of any interest in the city. Some few war reports but no fights & prospects are poor for any at present. I am enjoying my city stay some & am continually running my legs off over the city's hard pavements. Called on McGee.

While Gunther describes a lull in military activity, his curiosity constantly sought news of war activity. During his stay in New Orleans, the commander of Confederate troops was General Mansfield Lovell, a West Pointer from the Class of 1842. As commander of the defenses of New Orleans, he spurred the creation of the Confederate River Defense Fleet, a part of which was the new gunboat that was such a curiosity to Gunther. In consequence of his later loss of New Orleans he was never given another Civil War command, although he was cleared of wrongdoing by a court martial.

[January 11, 1862] I am up & early to market laying in stock. The markets are dull & not much doing. The greatest nuisance in the city is the circulating medium representing money, nothing but small tickets. The streets are pretty lively but no trade. It is reported a ship run the blockade to this port. Spent the day on the boat & calling on McGee.

[January 12, 1862] This is a beautiful fine summer day. We might say, the shining warm & a coat is uncomfortable. I visited the Cathedral & after a sermon by Dr. Palmer of the Pres. Church, after dinner, Charley Hazelton & I took an excursion down to the barracks & lower end of the city, intend to go to the battle ground. The road's bad. Spent balance of day at boat & McGee.

Attending sermons was one of Charles Gunther's favorite Sunday pastimes. Dr. Benjamin Palmer was a famed orator and Presbyterian theologian who, as pastor of the First Presbyterian Church of New Orleans, became a leading Louisiana voice for secession. Charles Gunther, obviously pro-southern in his leanings, enjoyed this fiery orator who

Benjamin M. Palmer, from Jewett's Crescent City Illustrated *(1873)*

was already gaining fame for his famous Thanksgiving sermon shortly after Lincoln's election. It was then that he vigorously defended slavery, called on Louisiana to join the Confederacy, and devoted himself to bringing Christian messages to Confederate soldiers both in New Orleans and surrounding areas. He spent the rest of his life as an unreconstructed Confederate, dying at his pastoral post in 1902 at the age of eighty-four.

Not all of Charles Gunther's time in New Orleans was sightseeing and frivolity. He was also in charge of procuring needed supplies for the *Rose Douglas* and struggled to find a variety of foodstuffs in the French Market, a six-block, open-air, hustle-and-bustle spectacle of barter on the riverside of the lower French Market. Home to a magnificent array of fruits and vegetables, this was America's oldest continually operating market, having been founded in 1791 as a Native American trading post.

Even though wartime supplies of fresh produce were sharply curtailed by the blockade and foraging of both Union and Confederate troops, a sufficient variety of provisions could still be found at this time. Today, the Farmer's Market, still in operation, hosts the Creole Tomato Festival and the famous Boo Carré Halloween and harvest festival—a vestige of the gay life and good times of antebellum New Orleans.

[January 13, 1862] I was up bright & early as usual. Visited the French Market. It is very foggy all morning & some rain. The streets are lively. We are receiving freights & sure for a good cargo. I run all day over the city & when night comes my feet feel very sore & a bed is found a great luxury & the greatest of all—rest. Took a ride in the eve down Esplanade.

[January 14, 1862] I got up early, having much to do today. The streets are muddy. The day is unpleasant, a drizzling rain. It is reported Galveston being taken. No fight yet & prospects no better. See Gen. Lovell today. Had some fine oysters. The streets look very gloomy & forsaken in the Eve. Had some fun at McGees—in the Eve.

Charles Gunther joined hundreds of other tourists in the evening hours enjoying the sights and sounds of New Orleans. The Union occupation was not yet a reality, and touring of the city was a popular pastime. His ride down Esplanade Avenue was such an enjoyable respite. Esplanade runs from the Mississippi River to the intersection with Carrollton Avenue just past Bayou Saint John. Esplanade was an important portage route for trade between the Bayou, Lake Ponchartrain, and the Mississippi River—an aspect Gunther would likely have explored not just for pleasure, but for an understanding of this route for trade purposes. The avenue, from the French Quarter to Faubourg Marigny and Faubourg Saint John, was lined with homes evidencing the finest architectural styles of the nineteenth century.

[January 15, 1862] We intended going out last Eve, but could not on account of fog. Well to day. We got off for once again. I am glad of it, as I am getting tired of it. We have a fine cargo. This is a disagreeable stormy day with rain. Got me a fine lot of oranges & fine reading for this trip so time will pass very pleasantly this trip. But few passengers. Retired early this Eve.

[January 16, 1862] We stopped last night taking in 50 bbds. sugar & are going along finely, but rather slow. There is nothing of note today. The weather is moderate & warm. Everything quiet onboard. We are still in the Sugar Country yet. I amused myself reading the *Eclectic Mag.* Felt sleepy & turned in bunk early.

[January 17, 1862] Took in more sugar last night. Our guards are completely in the water. Passed Baton Rouge at day light, & are going along slowly. Several boats passed us. The day has been quiet & warm. I am enjoying myself—feasting on oysters, oranges & sugar cane, reading &c. Was offered a situation by Barker of Saint Charles, but will not pay.

While Charles Gunther relates the tedious shipboard duties of the day, he and his crew are constantly on the lookout for news of the war, a diversion with which to entertain the passengers, a practical joke at the expense of naive foreigners, or some gastronomic indulgence. But war news was the substance of late night discussions, the meat of loud exchanges between opposing hopes and expectations, and the intelligence by which they could guide their purchases and routes. Word was to shortly arrive that Simon Cameron resigned as Lincoln's secretary of war amidst a vast corruption scandal, which only reinforced Southern views of Yankee morality. Cameron was then shipped off by Lincoln as minister to Russia, a post he held for just a year but which removed him from the swirling investigations in Washington.

The "Barker of St. Charles" referred to was Virginia-born John Butler Barker (1812–67), a Saint Charles, Arkansas, merchant.

[January 18, 1862] The days are perceptibly getting longer & I manage to get up much earlier. We get along very well, & had considerable excitement by the reports of rats leaving the boat. Our Englishmen & others are in a great stew about it. Life preservers are in requisition. Read the greater part of the day & Eve. Some sport with passengers at the Englishmen's expense & rats.

[January 19, 1862] The rat story is the story of the boat & many a joke is got off upon it, not sunk yet. Sunday again. I am sorry to say the surroundings are such that all religious thoughts & feelings are missing & the day passes like all others,—quiet with the usual monotonous scenery of the river. Arrived at Vicksburg at 8. News: Cameron resigned & a fight in Ky.

Simon Cameron, courtesy Library of Congress

The battle in Kentucky that Gunther refers to was the Battle of Mill Springs (also known as Fishing Creek), fought near Nancy, Kentucky, on January 19, 1862. It concluded an early Confederate offensive campaign for Eastern Kentucky and stands as the first significant Union victory of the war. The main units involved for the Union were the 2nd Minnesota and 10th Indiana and, for the Confederates, the 15th Mississippi and 20th Tennessee.

Confederate general Felix Zollicoffer was killed leading his troops here. These are the exciting bits of war news that would have been pored over aboard the *Rose Douglas* late into the night.

> [January 20, 1862] The weather continues fine & pleasant. We are making progress slowly. Layed up this noon in a big storm. Everything passes quietly. My thoughts wander homewards & too my folks & Oh what would I not give to get a letter from home. Read the greater part of the day & Eve.

Charles Gunther, though not in the Confederate Army, suffered the same pangs of separation from family and home as those often noted by military men as he made a living ferrying Confederate troops, supplies, and

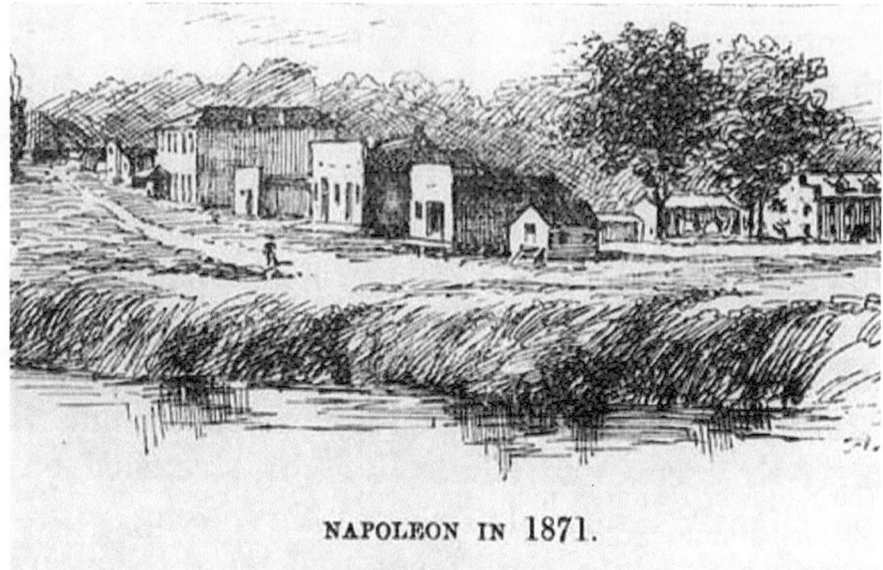

Napoleon, Arkansas, in 1871, from Twain's Life on the Mississippi

goods up and down the Mississippi and its tributaries from New Orleans to Memphis and Little Rock. The boredom on board ship paralleled the monotony and routine in the hundreds of army camps while in winter quarters or waiting to be called into action. Reading, writing letters home, visiting friends in river towns, and engaging in endless conversations with passengers and crew provided some relief from the tedium and uncertainty of a nation at war.

One of the small towns Gunther visited on his trips was Napoleon, Arkansas, a thriving port town in 1862. Later Napoleon was abandoned when the Mississippi River burst through its levee, devastating the small town.

> [January 21, 1862] Up as usual this morning & through the usual routine of my business. We are making slow progress for Napoleon. The time however passes very quietly & pleasantly. Oranges, sugar cane to eat when wanting refreshments. The weather is unpleasant. Read all day—spare time & keep good hours.

[January 22, 1862] We are yet far from Napoleon & going slow. I am running out of stores & am anxious to get up. The day is unpleasant & cold but not enough to freeze. We are having good times. Plenty of oranges, cane &c. Arrived at Napoleon at 8. Layed in stores & off for White River. Took Gen. Pike & staff on.

As Gunther continued his journey north on the Mississippi, the Confederacy utilized his steam packet to ferry General Albert Pike and his staff north. Albert Pike, a brigadier general since November 22, 1861, was in command of the Indian territories. Here, with General Ben McCulloch, he trained three regiments of Indian cavalry as part of his Confederate force. In March 1862 he led his Indians in the Confederate defeat at Pea Ridge. He resigned from the army on July 12, 1862, after a lengthy dispute regarding charges of mishandling money and material, insubordination and treason—charges later dropped. Gunther delighted in having notable Confederate personages on board, always breaking out the brandy, engaging in late night conversations, gathering the most recent war news (however embellished), and breaking the monotony of the Mississippi and White River scenery, which amounted to forested lands, muddy, marshy inlets, and mosquitoes in thick swarms of biblical proportion.

[January 23, 1862] We have Pike's staff & large amount of specie on board, & things were pretty lively last night, until morning brandy had to take it. We are going up White River finely. Sent a letter up to Lloyd. Nothing of any interest to day. Spent the greater part of Eve. reading.

It is interesting to note Gunther's mention of a "large amount of specie" on board, as one of the charges against Pike in his subsequent court martial related to mishandling money. While this was probably of little note to Gunther that evening, where revelry was the order of the day, it raises interesting questions of Pike's innocence. Nevertheless, Gunther was tasked this trip with merely transporting Pike and his staff up the White River, a 722-mile-long river that flows through Arkansas and Missouri in

Albert Pike, courtesy Library of Congress

a southward course. On entering the Mississippi River Delta Region near Batesville, Arkansas, it becomes navigable to shallow-draft vessels, like the *Rose Douglas*.

This trip would allow General Pike and his staff to rejoin their troops in Arkansas to begin training their Indian cavalry. Here again Charles Gunther is viewing important war developments from a front-row seat without personally engaging in combat.

[January 24, 1862] We left St. Charles this Eve after stopping some time, & are now going along slow & quiet again. The company on board is agreeable & pleasant. The Gen. & staff taking all things as they come. Stopped at Adams Bluff for the night. Had fun & music by Jack. A. [Adams] Bluff is a very small place about 2 shops & 5 houses.

Adams Bluff is in Arkansas County, on the White River.

[January 25, 1862] Off bright & early this morning, a fine pleasant sunshiney day. Joe & I bought a pet deer. Passed Aberdeen & Clarendon without stopping, reached Duvalls [De Valls] Bluff at 4 ock. Stopped all night. The Gen. & staff staying all night. The Eve passed pleasantly.

[January 26, 1862] We got the Gen. & staff an early breakfast. We reached Des Arc at 12. The day is fine & many persons on the levee. Heard the news of Zollicoffer's defeat & death. Causes considerable gloom. Remained all night. Gallagher & Tefenon got off here. Some sport with Gallagher. Rained tonight.

The *Rose Douglas* is passing a series of small river towns on its trip northward. Augusta, Arkansas, located in Woodruff County, to this day only boasts 2,665 residents. Jacksonport, Arkansas, located at the confluence of the White River and Black River, was a small but important steamboat stop during the Civil War, as well as a transportation hub for Confederate forces. It is probably here in Jacksonport that Gunther first heard rumors of the Union forces advancing upon General Sterling Price in southwest Missouri. It no doubt made Gunther more cautious in revealing who was on board and where they were traveling, as enemy spies were a constant threat to military secrecy.

[January 27, 1862] Off again at daylight. The day is pleasant & warm. Reached Augusta at 4. Our crew is getting very slim. Lane is sick. Read the greater part of the day. Nothing of any interest going on. Stopped at a wood for the night.

"Lane" is either John Howard Lane (usually "Howard" in this diary; see May 25 entry) or his brother, college-educated Edward Payson Lane (1833–69), clerks on the *Rose Douglas*. The two were sons of Ebenezer Lane, who headed the Lane Theological Seminary in Ohio.

[January 28, 1862] We are off at an early hour. The weather is getting colder. Nothing of any interest. The same monotonous scenery all along White River. Canebrakes passed Grand Glaze & reached Jacksonport in the Eve. Layed all night. The place is very quiet indeed a one horse place any how.

[January 29, 1862] O what a cold disagreeable day this is. Enough to give every body the blues. I was out running through the mud buying stores & stayed on boat the balance of the day. Several

Steamer Price, *courtesy Library of Congress*

small boats here. The Feds reported after *Price*. This place looks dull & not much doing.

Frequently while sailing the Mississippi and White Rivers, Gunther is delighted to see other river traffic: steam packets like the *Rose Douglas*, flatboats, skiffs, and every other imaginable type of river craft. Races with other steam packets, exchanges with old salts about river dangers and escapades, and the trading of information and passengers became a welcome break to the monotony of river work. Such was his excitement when the *General Price*, a wooden sidewheel steamboat built in 1856 in Cincinnati, made its appearance ahead of his vessel. The *Rose Douglas* raced the other ship.

The *General Price* would gain fame during the war when, upon being taken into Confederate service, she was renamed from her former identity (the *Laurent Millaudon*), converted into a ram, and assigned to defensive actions around Fort Pillow and Memphis, Tennessee. While enjoying her race now with the *Rose Douglas,* she was sunk on June 6, 1862, by Union naval forces under Flag Officer C. H. Davis. On June 16 of the same year she was raised, sent to Cairo, Illinois, and forced into Union service.

> [January 30, 1862] This is another cold disagreeable day. See a little ice, something new for me. My thoughts are all for N.O. now. I am anxious to get back. We left this Eve & reached the Glaze & took on a lot of cattle for N.O. Layed here all night. We are all anxious to hear some news. The Str. *Gen. Price* is ahead of us.

> [January 31, 1862] We are off again this morning & after the *Price.* Going along slowly. All passed quietly. Made Augusta at 4. We are running short of meat, but did not stop. A very unpleasant thing to run out of anything. Stopped in the woods for the night.

As January ended aboard the *Rose Douglas,* Gunther's thoughts drifted back to New Orleans, home, his folks, and a speedy end to that horrible Civil War. Like his Confederate military counterparts, he dreamed of home and thought the war would be over by now. The reality was slowly setting in that this conflict would not end quickly, that the monotony and shortages of the war would mount, that casualties would soar, that river traffic would include armed warships, and that life on the Mississippi would never be the same again.

February 1862

February opened with a chill in the wind, not only regarding the weather but the prospects of seeing the war drag on for three more long years. Trips up the Mississippi became more dangerous. Gunther's parents expressed the concern of so many relatives during this time that traveling anywhere in the war zone (which virtually meant the entire Confederacy) was becoming more hazardous. Ships were frequently half empty, goods scarce, the weather miserable, and separations from loved ones more extended.

[February 1, 1862] February here again. How fast time is passing. Hardly know it. My folks I fear are much troubled about me. My only wish now is an end to this war. How happy we might be. We reached Des Arc at 4 & stayed but a few minutes & made Devalls Bluff by night, making a run of 140 miles in this river from sun to sun.

[February 2, 1862] Were it not for the name of such a day, my surroundings would not tell me it is Sabbath. No reverential feelings perceptible with any of the crew. Steaming down White River & Making the best out of our time. See a lot of wild turkeys. The weather is chilly & cloudy.

The year 1862 saw the Mississippi River Valley experience a cold, rainy, chilly first quarter. The Mississippi and its tributaries frequently overflowed their banks, soil erosion occurred along the banks, and riverboating became monotonous and unfullfilling. What little news the *Rose Douglas* could gather from its frequent port calls was also depressing. Rumors of the fall of Forts Henry and Donelson were finally confirmed to the dismay of river traffic, as all this foreshadowed increased Union presence on the river, heightened military operations, and more dangerous times for supply ships that also ferried troops and war material.

[February 3, 1862] We made St. Charles & layed there all last night taking on a lot of hoop poles. This is a very rainy disagreeable day. Got away by noon. The river is rising fast. We layed at Prairie Ldg. Played some chequers & came out champion of the boat.

[February 4, 1862]. We steamed down at daylight. The river is overflowing the banks backwater from the Mississippi. Glad to get to Napoleon at 11 o'ck. Layed in stores & feel all right now. Cook left us. Put Dave in the kitchen. Retired early in the Eve.

[February 5, 1862]. We wooded last night at our old friend at Providence. Today we made a good run. We passed Vicksburgh

& Natchez in the Eve. The weather continues changeable rain & wind. Everything quiet. Some music in the Eve by Tuss & Sack. Returned in good season.

[February 6, 1862] I was roused from my bed last night by our boat running into the bank—nobody hurt. Another accident the Eve. The cilender [*sic*] head blowing out, with a loud report. Compelled to run with one engine alone. Passed Baton Rouge at 2 o'ck & got along very well. This Eve. read until bed time.

Upon recovering from the blown cylinder, running aground, and navigating through a storm with one engine, the *Rose Douglas* is finally arriving back home to New Orleans. Here the crew confirms the loss of Forts Henry and Donelson. This February 6, 1862, battle became the first significant Union victory in the Western Theater and also the first for new Brigadier General Ulysses S. Grant. Effective naval fire by Cmdr. Andrew Foote's gunboats, the poor situation of the forts as rising river water nearly overran them, and fully staffed units from the Union army forced Confederate generals Lloyd Tilghman and Simon Bolivar Buckner to surrender these forts, opening up the Kentucky/Tennessee section of the Mississippi River to Union control and naval superiority. The worry on the faces of the crew of Gunther's ship was apparent. They not only knew the importance of these ports to the South, but also realized the increasing difficulty this loss would impose on their shipment of troops and supplies north on the Mississippi to assist the Confederacy in Little Rock and Memphis.

[February 7, 1862] We were delayed all last night by our accident. Am anxious to get to N.O. The weather is fine. The coast along looks beautiful. Green like summer. A heavy storm came up and were compelled to lay up for the night. A terrible time. But got started after night again.

[February 8, 1862). We made the stock landing by 7 o'ck. & I started for market. Had a terrible time finding boat again at lower landing. Got a late dinner. This is a very unpleasant rainy day. News. Feds captured Fort Henry & Tennessee Bridge. See my numerous friends & feel at home again.

[February 9, 1862] Another very unpleasant and rainy day. Makes all things look gloomy & very quiet. Passed the greater part of the day running around with Dave Hughes through the city. Stayed until Eve. down at Lafayette & stopped at Gilsons for the night.

When in the Port of New Orleans, Charles Gunther, his crew, and friends typified sailors of today. They toured the city sights, visited friends, drank at the local bars, bought items of necessity, ate a good meal, and enjoyed the available nightlife. The French Quarter, or Vieux Carré, was the ideal spot to find all of these pleasures and more. Situated adjacent to the Mississippi River, this paradise of sensuality and history provided the tourist with all the temptations and diversion necessary to relieve the boredom of the river life. The French Market, continuously operating since the 1700s, supplied the crew with foods, vegetables, fruits, and necessities until the next voyage brought them back. City Park, a 1,300-acre public park established in the mid-1800s on land fronting Metairie Road, was a bucolic retreat from the Quarter's hustle and bustle and provided lanes where sailors could enjoy the beauty of nature and the solitude to dream about loved ones back home.

[February 10, 1862] The weather has cleared up finely, a clear sun shiny day. Sold my lot of broom. Cleared $50 on them. Bought me some clothing & a fob chain. Feel all right & enjoy good health. Ran over the city considerable through the day. Called on McGee in the Eve.

[February 11, 1862] Got up pretty early this morning. Went to market. The city is pretty lively, & the military is continually drilling. News—Feds have taken Roanoke Island & meeting with success, causes much excitement & casts a general gloom over faces. The Str. *Price* went up this Eve in our trade. Up town in the Eve.

[February 12, 1862] I stopped up on French Street. Got up early. Had a late breakfast & go to market at 9 o'ck. The markets are all dull & but little life among the people. The free market is a great institution. The federals are moving on Tenn. River. There is nothing but war gossip talked about. Spent the Eve at M [McGee?].

War news was quickly turning from bad to worse in the Western theater. Forts Henry and Donelson had fallen, Federal gunboats roamed the Tennessee River, and Union transports were ferrying troops to pursue General Sterling Price and isolate his army from those east of the Mississippi. New gunboats continually appeared on the river, Union plans to seize New Orleans and control the mouth of the Mississippi were in the air, Vicksburg was rumored to be the next target, and control of Arkansas was seriously threatened. Grant was preparing to execute a modified "Anaconda" plan to cut the Confederacy in half along the Mississippi River. Amid all of this impending doom, Gunther and his crew tried to absorb every newspaper, rumor, bit of intelligence, and gossip in order to assess their futures on the Father of Waters.

[February 13, 1862] The weather continues fine & very pleasant. I did considerable walking over the city today. My feet are very sore. Feel unwell this Eve. Joe & I went to the German Theatre (*das Kathchen von Heilbronn*). Very good. Met some of the boys & play a game of ten pins. Got back back [sic] to the boat late.

[February 14, 1862] The report is that Bowling Green was evacuated & the Feds are after *Price*. Stirring times these. There was a severe storm last night. Joe & I went up over the city this morning. We also went out to City Park & Bayou. See several new gunboats. Spent the Eve up at M—S. Had a pleasant time.

> [February 15, 1862] This is a fine day. The news is interesting, fighting still going on at Fort Donelson. The city is quiet otherwise. Numerous regiments have left here for Mobile. An attack is apprehended by Butler. I had to leave this Eve on business to Baton Rouge on the *Eliza G.*

The Battle of Fort Donelson took place between February 11–16, 1862. After opening an avenue of escape, Confederate General John B. Floyd erred in ordering a retreat to entrenched positions. There General U. S. Grant, aided by naval bombardments from Commodore Foote's fleet, forced Confederate General Simon Bolivar Buckner to surrender the fort, opening the Cumberland River to Union troops for their invasion of the South and giving them a vital water supply avenue for troop support. It was not long before Grant would design the plan to besiege Vicksburg and sever the Confederacy in two, isolating the trans-Mississippi forces in Texas, Arkansas, and Missouri from the rest of the Confederacy.

When this news reached the crew of the *Rose Douglas*, it was evident that their time in gay New Orleans was tempered by the setback suffered by Confederate forces. Nevertheless, the crew began another trek upriver, anxious to hear further news of a hoped-for Confederate upset, and an assurance that the folks back home were safe from invading Yankees.

> [February 16, 1862] We are making but very slow progress up the river today. The *E. G.* is a very slow old tub. I sleep the greater part of the day. Am anxious to see the news, & my very thoughts are frequently turned to those who I love best at home. Retired early.

> [February 17, 1862] We had laid up in a fog this A.M. This is a very unpleasant rainy day. Made Sugar Pile by 9-1/2 o'ck. We got off again & I got to Baton Rouge at 4-1/2. Made enquiries about Kearns but learned he had left. Remained but a short time & got on the *Anna Perret* for N.O. again.

*Ulysses S. Grant, 1822–85,
courtesy Library of Congress*

Andrew H. Foote, 1806–63, Harper's
Weekly, *February 22, 1862*

*John B. Floyd, 1806–63,
courtesy Library of Congress*

*Simon B. Buckner 1823–1914, courtesy
Library of Congress*

> [February 18, 1862] We were delayed last night [a]gain by the fog. Made but 67 miles. Got a long very well today. Reached stock landing at 12-1/2 amidst a tremendous rain. Exciting news. Fort Donelson taken & Nashville in danger—great excitement & gloom among the people. Spent the Eve up at M—s.

Although news of the fall of Fort Donelson had previously been told through news reports to the crew, Gunther and his shipmates would frequently seek additional verification. Some of this concern emanated from their hopes that the bad news was incorrect or at least exaggerated, some stemmed from a distrust of rumors from those perceived as pro-Union, and some resulted from a denial of facts. Yet, eventually the facts asserted themselves, gloom set in, and Gunther expressed this sense of overriding uncertainty by suggesting he felt insecure about his money (Confederate currency) and would invest in a pin (probably gold) which was always an historical reserve in hard economic times.

> [February 19, 1862] Made preparation to lay in my stores. Bought all morning. The streets are muddy & a continuous rain & wind. Ran of the city considerable today—feel insecure in my money. Resolved to invest in a good pin. Spent the Eve up at Mrs. O.

> [February 20, 1862] We have fine weather for once again & the streets are drying up fast. There is considerable crinoline out on Canal Street. News. Davis send succor to Nashville & says hold it. We got off for good this Even. Bot [bought] me a lot of oranges for the trip & feel glad to get off.

New Orleans was more than a port stop for supplies. For Gunther and his crew the city not only held markets to buy goods, historical places to visit, and friends to drop in on; it held crinoline (girls in billowing dresses that obviously were a delight to the visiting sailors). Much of this girl-watching and night life occurred on Canal Street, a major thoroughfare forming the upriver boundary of the French Quarter and the historic dividing line between the older French and Spanish Quarters from the newly settled American neighborhood. For more than a hundred years Canal Street was the main shopping and entertainment focus of New Orleans, anchoring such historic stores as D. H. Holmes, Maison Blanche, and Godchaux's. It was an exciting place to visit and the hub for war news, fashion, and relief from the drudgery of the river.

> [February 21, 1862] We had a very exciting race last night with the *Trent*. Was up until 12 o'ck. We came out victorious. All pleased. This is a fine warm day & are going up finely bound for Arkansas River. We have many anticipations of war news from all quarters & are fully anxious to hear it. Retired early.

> [February 22, 1862] We had some bad weather today, & cleared off again. Fine in the Eve. We made slow progress up stream. Passed Donaldsonville & Plaquemine. Took on a lot of sugar for Ark. The scenery is very picturesque & spring is at hand. All looks beautiful green.

The temporary arrival of springlike weather conditions not only raised the spirits of the crew of the *Rose Douglas* but also provided for a more pleasant river journey, as sailors were able to sit on the deck enjoying the sights, play games outside, fish from the decks, and sing to the stars at night. Both of the areas, Donaldsonville and Plaquemine, Louisiana, saw themselves affected by the war. Donaldsonville was the parish seat of Ascension parish, named after Barthelemy Lafon's benefactor William Donaldson. It was Lafon, the architect, who laid out the city plans and saw his city become the Louisiana capitol in 1830. By this summer of 1862 however, Donaldsonville was being bombarded by Union troops, was burned almost to the ground by Admiral Farragut, and saw most of its hotels, warehouses, and neighboring plantations devastated. While Plaquemine received less damage during the war, the growth it experienced following its incorporation in 1838 was substantially slowed as the robust river traffic slowed and the massive plantations faced runaway slaves, pillaging, and seizure of crops. The war had come home to the river folk.

> [February 23, 1862] What a beautiful warm, sunny day. The sun shines so genial. We passed Red River & Fort Adams at noon. Will make Natchez tonight. There are no signs of this being Sunday, & of course but little thought off by the crew. The same routine is gone through as daily.

> [February 24, 1862] We have loved up again last night. The river is high & plenty of drift wood is running. I am reading for amusement some old *Atlantic Monthlies*. I have some fine hopes & many are my thoughts of the future. Spring is really making its appearance & birds singing gayley as spring.

Purser Gunther did not confine himself to newspapers detailing depressing war news. He was a voracious reader, an educated and urbane consumer of literature, and a consummate seeker of the best that authors, essayists, and poets of the era had to offer. One of his favorite magazines was the *Atlantic Monthly*. Founded in 1857 by James Russell Lowell, Oliver Wendell Holmes, Ralph Waldo Emerson, Henry Wadsworth Longfellow, and others, it proudly billed itself as a magazine of "literature, politics, science, and the arts." Its mission statement reflected the breadth of Gunther's interests and his commitment to the magazine's mission of standing up for "freedom, national progress and honor." These were values that led Gunther to support the Southern Confederacy and its ideals, politics, and philosophy. He gleaned his ideas from the writings of not only the founders of the magazine but also from eminent national and international political scientists, historians, writers, and scientists. In fact, another of Gunther's favorite publications was the *Westminster Review*, a quarterly British publication of philosophical radicals. Many of its articles by such notables as John Stuart Mill and Robert Chambers dealt with free thought, reform movements, and the "Law of Progress." How much more eclectic and passionate about literary diversity could one get in the 1860s South?

[February 25, 1862] This is a lovely day. Perfect Spring. We are running along slowly, stemming a heavy current. Layed up at a wood pile. See a Vicksburgh paper, and glad to see some late news but nothing of any importance, but things look gloomy, & every body feels so. A storm came up at night.

[February 26, 1862] Here we are layed up half the day in a fog. 20 miles to Vicksburgh. Drift running heavily. Everybody is killing time the best they know how. Read some myself. Anxious to get to V. My mind is continuely reverting to the war. We made V. by 3 o'ck. Got some meats. News, Feds at Nash[ville].

Vicksburg was not only an important river port stop for the *Rose Douglas*, but was also a strategic river control point for the Confederacy. The only city on the map in Warren County in 1862, it is located 234 miles north of New Orleans on the Mississippi and Yazoo Rivers. In 1863, after an extensive siege campaign, Vicksburg was to fall to General U. S. Grant. Having been starved during the forty-seven-day siege, the residents subsisted by living in caves, eating horses and rats, and cringing in terror as shells pounded their lovely city. Its strategic location on a high bluff overlooking the Mississippi was vital for Grant's control of the Mississippi and its extensive riverboat trade. When Vicksburg fell, all river traffic was subject to Union control, seizure, confiscation, and impoundment. This quite probably was the result of the Union blockade on shipping, the use of the Mississippi exclusively for Union military maneuvers, and the conversion of many of the steam packets for Federal purposes. But for now the *Rose Douglas* continued its trips up and down the Mississippi, supplying goods and services to the area's people and soldiers and allowing the crew to take one last look at the beauty of the countryside, the plantations, and the stately antebellum mansions.

[February 27, 1862] We laid up all night at wood yard & took an early start. This is a fine pleasant day. The river is high. The

Vicksburg, from Harper's Weekly *August 2, 1862*

plantations look fine & crops are being put in. Passed L. [Lake] Providence at 4. Was disappointed at not stopping at wood yard. Running tonight.

[February 28, 1862] Made an early start this A.M. The weather is fine & traveling is pleasant. There was nothing of any interest to note. The Miss. River plantations look much finer since we can see them better from the high water. Read all day *Westminster Review* of an old day, better than nothing & interesting.

March 1862

As March opened, the South and its supporters began to question their faith in a quick Southern victory. Men began to enlist who otherwise would have avoided military service, the war news contained few bright spots for those living in the Western theater, and Ulysses S. Grant was doggedly pursuing his goal of Vicksburg and his own reputation as a fighting general. Charles Gunther observed all of these events first hand and saw the effects of the war as he traveled up and down the Mississippi, Arkansas, and White Rivers. What he saw frightened him and dampened the spirits of his crew.

[March 1, 1862] 40 miles from Napoleon this A.M. Glad of it. This has been a long & tedious trip, 9 days out of port today. Arrived at N. all right & started for Arkansas River in the afternoon. Quite a change from the Miss. Got some late news—the Federals reported marching on Columbus. We laid for the night at wood yard.

[March 2, 1862). We made an early start and got along finely. Had a race with the *Era No.7* & came out victorious. We have but 5 passengers all told. There is much feeling in regard to matters. Many are mustering to take the field. No visible sign of Sabbath to me & all goes as usual.

From his diary entries this month, Gunther clearly felt the impact of reduced passenger traffic, the dark feelings of foreboding among the people, and the beginning stirrings of a life on the river that was to drastically change—and change soon. He would discover further evidence of this in Pine Bluff, Arkansas, his next port of call. Pine Bluff, the largest city and county seat of Jefferson County, was prospering in 1862, with its wealth built on local cotton production. Plantations in this area were massive, utilizing large gangs of slave labor. Thus, when the town fell to Union forces under General Frederick Steele in 1863, slaves became contrabands of war, plantations were deserted, and the economy crumbled. Instead of healthy, vibrant plantations dotting the countryside, it became filled with refugee camps and a haven for Negro escapees. Such would be the condition of this port town for the rest of the war. Although Confederate General J. S. Marmaduke tried to expel the Union army in a skirmish on October 25, 1863, he was repulsed and no further sustained effort was successful. Another port city had fallen and another rumor of Union encroachment was validated.

[March 3, 1862] We layed up last night at Rob Roy. Old Johnson was aboard. We had some fun & Jack picked on the banjo for us. This is a very cold, windy, disagreeable day, & very hard steaming. We were unable to make Pine Bluff today, but laid up a short distance this side. Bars are very hard to get over.

[March 4, 1862] Up bright & early. Made an early start & reached Pine Bluff at 9 o'ck. The town is lively. Lots of soldiers going to the war. I see more drinking men today than in 3 months before. Met Holland & had a good time. Went to an amateur theatre (Rob McClare). A full house. They did very well considering.

"Holland" is Edward C. Holland of Pine Bluff, who enlisted in the Confederate army in 1862 and was detailed to the quartermaster department as a telegrapher.

Fort Smith, Arkansas, was to become the next target of Union advances. Rumors that Union troops were approaching Fort Smith left the crew of the *Rose Douglas* to ponder the possibility of another Union advance. Fort Smith had been held by Confederate forces since the beginning of the war, and they would be successful in maintaining their control until September 1, 1863, when Federal troops under General Steele captured the town. Union troops were to remain in control until the end of the war, using Fort Smith as a haven for runaway slaves, orphans, Southern Unionists, and victims from the guerrilla wars raging throughout the Arkansas border towns.

> [March 5, 1862] We left the Bluff at 6 & are now only drawing 28 inches water. Getting up fast. News. This A.M. the Feds within 20 miles of F. Smith. This is a fair day, but strong head wind. But very few passengers & all is quiet. Spend the Eve having some music & playing a few games at cards.

> [March 6, 1862] We started this morning all full of glee in sure expectation of getting to the Rock this A.M. But we were all doomed to disappointment. Fouch Bar & head winds keep us working all day. 8 miles from the Rock run out of stores. Went out this Eve to a farm house, got some turkeys & chickens.

> [March 7, 1862] Fouch Bar, near Rock. I see the second look of snowy day this winter, & quite cold. This is a pleasant sunshiny day. Had quite a time on the river in the yawl, after a lost turkey. All in expectation of seeing the Rock this morning sure, but no go. Took out a lot of freight & sparred over rolled barrels all day. Everybody pitching in. Feel very tired this Eve.

"Fouch Bar" is where the Bayou Fouch River flows into the Arkansas River, just below Little Rock.

From Pine Bluff and up to Little Rock, Charles Gunther and his crew were becoming sadly aware of several new results of the Union occupation of the Mississippi's banks. Food shortages were becoming more pronounced, livestock was disappearing due to scavenging, news reports were drying up due to decreased ability to get newspapers, passenger travel slackened off, and prices soared on what little produce and livestock remained with local farmers. This was coupled with a sharp decline in the convertibility of Confederate currency and the refusal by many merchants and farmers to accept anything but specie or Union greenbacks. What news did reach the crew of the *Rose Douglas* was disheartening and fueled their feeling of the futility of their runs to and from New Orleans. The seeds of malaise were slowly setting in.

> [March 8, 1862] We made an early start for the Rock. Reached there at 10 o'ck. Feel quite sore from my exercise y-day [yesterday]. Am very glad we made port. Run entirely out of provisions, & had hard times picking up things from farmers at exorbitant prices. The Rock looks natural but things have all dryed up. Can't get any news. Columbus reported evacuated. Had boots mended.

> [March 9, 1862] I got all my stores on boat, & got off for the mouth at 9 o'ck., but unfortunately a strong wind layed us up at Fouch Bar again for the balance of the day. A heavy rain came up in the Eve. We have but 4 passengers, all very quiet on board. Read some & retired early. The Sabbath out of the question.

As can be seen from the following receipts (from the Confederate vessel papers), the *Rose Douglas* hauled army supplies as well as civilian cargo during its trips on the Arkansas River.

During this part of Gunther's journey and after the surrender of Forts Henry and Donelson and the evacuation of Columbus, General P. G. T. Beauregard, the Confederate commander of the Army of the

From Confederate vessel papers, Rose Douglas, *page 3*

Mississippi, chose Island No. 10 as his new strongest point for the defense of the Mississippi River. Nearby Island No. 10 was New Madrid, Missouri, a vulnerable point of the defense where Union General John Pope began his siege of the city on March 3, 1862. By March 14, the Confederate defenders had deserted New Madrid. Later they were cut off by Pope's army, forcing Confederate General William Mackall to surrender Island No. 10 on April 8, 1862. Again the Mississippi River trade was slowly being strangled by advancing Union forces, making Gunther's river expeditions more dangerous, more prone to seizure, and more threatening for passenger traffic, all elements in the reduction of revenue from these trips and the increased alarm among both passengers and crew for their own safety. This in turn aggravated the loss of passengers, hampered the provisioning of the *Rose Douglas*, and reduced the profitability of the shipping business.

From Confederate vessel papers, Rose Douglas, *page 5*

[March 10, 1862] We got up early & are making good time down. Reached Pine Bluff at 4 o'ck. & got below some 12 miles. We have on board a lot of recruits for Memphis, a terrible wild & rough set, & will be glad when they get off. There is plenty of card playing this Eve.

> [March 11, 1862] All is lively on board this morning, & are making a tremendous big run. Ark. River is high & back water of the Miss. has run up some 60 miles. We reached Napoleon at 7. All glad of it, & are feeling anxious to hear the news, but no news. Boats most all stopped. The Fed at Point Pleasant & New Madrid.
>
> [March 12, 1862] Am very anxious to get rid of my rough passengers but they hang to the boat like leeches & particularly my table. I bought all my stores, got a lot of passengers again for back trip. The Str. *Acacia* came down from White River full of passengers. No news.

The danger facing Mississippi River steamers became painfully evident from a headline in the *New York Times* datelined August 27, 1862, which reported the loss of the steamer *Acacia* and the drowning of over thirty passengers. Among the losses was Mrs. Robert Dale Owen and the wife of Captain Richardson of the 53rd Ohio Regiment, U.S.A. War was coming home to the Mississippi River. In reared its head again when Charles Gunther heard rumors the next day of the death of General Ben McCulloch (McCullough). This rumor was in fact true. As General McCulloch was directing the right wing of his command at the Battle of Elkhorn Tavern on March 7, 1862, he was shot in the chest by a Union sharpshooter, killed almost instantly. Death seemed to now permeate every week of travel, either in passenger mishaps, engagements where the participants knew Gunther or his crew, or where travel or river traffic was further disrupted. War was quickly becoming the "hell" General Sherman would refer to later in the conflict. The peaceful days of plying the river with only cares of avoiding driftwood and mosquitoes were over. New hazards had appeared, new dangers were evident, and nerves were increasingly frayed.

> [March 13, 1862] I am busy running around this morning. We have a report of a big fight on the 7th. McCullough & others killed, but no reliance is placed upon it. We got off this Eve, with

a full trip & cabin full of passengers. Everything is lively on board, & glad to get off. I retired pretty early.

[March 14, 1862] This is a terrible rainy day—disagreeable. We go along slowly, having many landings to make. A passenger off the *Cotton Plant* gave me a Memphis paper of the 12. The late fight confirmed, and cast a great gloom over the people on the river. Things look hard. Martial law in Memphis. Wrote a letter to Mr. Bohlen yesterday. Eve.

For the first time in his diary Gunther speaks of the imposition of martial law in Memphis. The free traversing of the Mississippi, Arkansas, and White Rivers was becoming more restricted and more subject to Union military dictates. This not only lessened the freedom the river steamers enjoyed to transport passengers and military recruits, as well as goods and food products vital to the maintenance of an army, but psychologically cornered the river crews into increasing melancholy and a sense of impending disaster. The war was not going well for Southern forces in the Western Theater, and each day this apprehension is evident in Gunther's diary entries.

[March 15, 1862] This is a very unpleasant rainy morning. We are steaming up slowly, having too many landings to make. We have but few passengers on board. We reached Pine Bluff at 8 o'ck., & left again at 9. No news. Telegraph played out. This is a fine Eve for running.

[March 16, 1862] This is a very fine & pleasant day. We are getting along finely, but many landings to make. There is nothing of any note today. Many wild fowls are out on the Sand Beach sunning themselves. We reached Little Rock this Eve. I went up town to hear the news, but none. Retired early.

While the war news continued to depress the hopes of Gunther and his crew, he discusses the transportation of new Southern recruits—an "ungentlemanly group" of ruffians who do not inspire Gunther's confidence in their ability to repel the Union invaders. It likewise demonstrates that more and more frequently the Southern Confederacy is scraping the bottom of the barrel in enlisting new recruits. This shortage of high quality enlistees and those with prior military or militia experience is a problem that is going to plague the South throughout the war. Most of these new soldiers are farm boys, many younger than eighteen years of age, who have never fired more than a squirrel gun or shot a deer for supper. They would need to be trained in the obeying of military commands, discipline, and strategy in an extremely short time if they were to become effective in halting the Union advance.

> [March 17, 1862] We learn this A.M. that New Madrid is evacuated. No news from above. The town is lively with soldiers who are going to various forts. Got all my stores. We left this Eve. at 4 o'clock. We have on board a lot of soldiers, terrible rough ungentlemanly set. Trouble this trip sure. Also a lot of lady passengers.

> [March 18, 1862] I am glad we are going to Memphis. This suits me. We had but little rest last night for the noise. We reached Pine Bluff at 8-1/2 o'ck. A lot of cavalry there. Some head wind, but are making good time down—We laid up at the Post tonight. There is a storm.

> [March 19, 1862] We are having a fine pleasant day, quite warm. We reached Napoleon at 9 o'ck. We are just full of passengers. We got some off the *Ashley* this A.M. Island No. 10 is given up. We are going up the Miss. finally. Met two boats *Acacia* & *Kennett*. All quiet this Eve.

While Gunther and his crew can still obtain sufficient food and fuel for their steamer, specie is becoming increasingly scarce, further putting a stranglehold on commercial activity. The Confederacy, despite controlling the mints at New Orleans, Charlotte, North Carolina, and Dahlonega, Georgia, never had sufficient specie to mint coins for general circulation during the war. The inability of the Confederacy to obtain sufficient specie was further compounded by the hoarding of coins and massive bank failures immediately after secession. Paper currency instead was issued in massive quantities (with estimates as high as $2 billion) in denominations from $1000 to 50¢. As the war news became more disheartening for the Confederacy, inflation increasingly weakened the paper currency, drove prices out of reach of the ordinary citizen, and depleted the Confederate treasury. By March 1862, the Confederate treasury held less than $85,000 in gold and $36,000 in silver. Gunther and his crew increasingly became victims of this soaring inflation, as did virtually all workers, farmers, and homeowners in the South.

> [March 20, 1862] I am getting awfully tired of my crowd and am getting rather impatient to get to Memphis. We had a fine favorable wind all day. Arrived at Memphis this Eve. Things look awfully gloomy & dead. The yellow flag floats over the Overton Hospital. See Lloyd this Eve. Was glad to see all here yet. Hard times sure.

> [March 21, 1862] I went up town today. Things look really like war times over the city. Many stores are closed up. City under martial law. NO specie to be seen, and great doubts about C.[Confederate] notes. Everything is being removed from the city, & looks very much like giving up things here. Spent the Eve. with Lloyd.

Gunther notes further signs of the war-torn city of Memphis and the surrounding countryside. Yellow fever and epidemics are rampant, stores are closed, Confederate notes are not readily accepted in payment for goods and services, and a depressing gloominess hangs over both the city and the countryside. Refugees are beginning to flee the cities and go to stay with relatives in areas of the South where the war has yet to come. Every day seems to bring new word of cities being besieged, the countryside being stripped of goods, and the spirits of the people being tested by signs of defeat, loss, and death at their very doorstep.

> [March 22, 1862] We expected to leave today, but did not get off. Glad of it. still fighting at No. 10 & the Feds reported near Savannah. News is very hard to get, & it is hard telling what takes place. A fight expected at Corinth. There are a lot of boats at Levee. All impressed into service. Was up over the city this A.M. Spent the Eve at boat with R.

The March 22 *Appeal* contains an ad in its "Steamboat Column": "For Arkansas Run—This Day, 22nd Inst. *Rose Douglass*, Capt. Macginis. This splendid passenger steamer will leave as above at 5 p.m. Larry Harmstad, Agent." Philadelphia-born Lawrence Harmstad (Harmstead) (1830–82) acted as Memphis agent for several steamboats. Well-respected at the time, Harmstad fled Memphis soon after the war to avoid his many creditors. According to the local newspapers, "wine, women, and cards" proved Harmstad's downfall.

> [March 23, 1862] A Memphis Sunday at the present time is indeed one of the quiet ones. Everything looks lost & forsaken. But few people on the streets. I stayed at the Ice House most of the day. No news of any kind. No telegraphic news coming through. Times look hard. Weather is very cold.

> [March 24, 1862] We expected to leave today, but did not get off. Our boat is full of passengers, & it keeps us pretty busy. I had considerable business to attend too, see Mr. Bohlen again—all right with me. No news from above M[emphis]. Papers are issued on color paper & half sheets.

Charles Gunther ruminates again about the increasing shortages at the ports of call. Newspapers are printed on half sheets on anything available (including wallpaper in Vicksburg); the government is impressing ships for military purposes, reducing capitalistic adventures; and war news is increasingly unreliable from all sources. A state of confusion, uncertainty, and paranoia begins gripping inhabitants along the Mississippi. Every battle fought seems to further constrict the chances of the Confederacy ever gaining its freedom. Gunther's news of the Battle of New Bern only increases this pall of impending disaster. The main battle of New Bern was fought March 14, 1862, as part of General Ambrose Burnside's incursion into North Carolina. General Burnside managed to break the Confederate lines under CSA General Lawrence O. B. Branch, rout the ill-trained North Carolina recruits, and hold the town until the end of the war.

> [March 25, 1862] Off for Arkansas River this morning full of passengers. This is a fine day. There are a good many boats at levee detained by the government. Particulars of the New Bern fight. C[Confederacy) badly beaten. We are going along finely, considerable fun & music this Eve. Our whole cabin is covered with beds.

> [March 26, 1862—Napoleon] I had a pretty good sleep last night & up bright & early. The weather is fine. More passengers, crowded now, keeps me very busy, & provisions hard to get. No news. The Miss. River is very high. The whole country looks drowned out. We had a pretty lively time this Eve & plenty of music. Cabin is all covered.

> [March 27, 1862] We laid up below the Post for the night. Am getting awfully anxious to get up. Tormented to death with my crowd but still all goes on galley [gaily] considering. Had some fun with my lady passengers. Provisions running out again. That is hell. More music in the Eve.

The last week of March saw Charles Gunther and his crew trying to break the monotony of the trip, the river hazards of low water and sandbars, and the lack of available provisions with nightly entertainment of music, singing, dancing, and lively conversation. This helped to mask their fears of the nonexistent war news, the rowdy soldiers whom they had to prevent from causing trouble on board, and the somber mood of the crew when they could see the signs of loss and looming disaster all around them. While spring was slowly coming to the Mississippi Valley, the eternal hope that normally accompanies the milder weather was somehow missing. No news was not good news, as the last information they received had been of more losses, more shortages, and more Federal depredations.

> [March 28, 1862] This is a pretty fine day, & cool. We have many landings to make & we get along slowly. Our boat is full of Dr.'s. We arrived at Pine Bluff at 4. Run all over the city for meats & had a hard time of it. Got off again at 5. Lost many of our passengers. Am glad of it. Some more fun this Eve.

> [March 29, 1862] The weather is getting quite warm but not many indications of spring from the appearance of the landscape. The river is falling & our progress is slow. Feel very anxious to hear some news. Our passengers are a very clever set of men, some 6 ladies also. Had plenty of fun all Eve. Music, singing, &c.

> [March 30, 1862] This is a fine pleasant day. We got on Fouch Bar this morning & no go. Went up to the Rock a foot. Got me some meats. Heard no news. Returned in a carriage. Many of our passengers went up a foot. Hands all at work this Eve. Nothing of any interest this Eve.

> [March 31, 1862] We had a heavy shower this A.M. All hands busy getting boat over the bar. Feel very anxious to get off to the city. After a great deal of work, we got off again. We reached the Rock this Eve, & no news of any kind. Considerably lively by the moving of troops across the River. Spent the Eve up town.

For the crew of the *Rose Douglas*, April is going to commence with considerable excitement: soldiers on the move, an air of impending battles in the rumor mill, and devastating sights of wounded Confederate soldiers fresh from battle. Prices continue to soar, scarcity is the operative word of the month, and more defeats for Confederate troops are on the horizon. The heavy rains of April amply set the mood for the hardships of the corning months. Civilian traffic on the Mississippi is feeling the full brunt of the war.

April 1862

The Rock (Little Rock, Arkansas) is one of those frequent port stops where Gunther gathers news and loads provisions. By April 1, 1862, it was also in the eye of troop movements where Confederate soldiers are being ferried from location to location to try and prevent Grant's strategy of seizing the Mississippi and taking the last citadel on the river—Vicksburg. Many of these troop movements were poorly coordinated and in response to the onslaught of huge Union armies. The number of wounded increased exponentially and the mood of area residents in the small river towns was increasingly depressed. One such small town was Pocahontas, Arkansas, located along the Black River in Randolph County, Arkansas, named after the Indian maiden Pocahontas of Jamestown, Virginia, fame. In the very real American Civil War, Pocahontas saw immense damage. Its residents suffered shortages in food, livestock was appropriated by the residents, small farmers scattered to larger towns to avoid the fighting, and young men were impressed into the service. It exemplified the hardships being thrust on the small towns bordering the rivers of commerce.

> [April 1, 1862] The city is full of soldiers moving, & there is considerable stir in the streets. Panic prices are all the rage. Everything is very high, & hard to get. The *Key West* came down with a load of sick & wounded soldiers. Things look rough sure. See Columbus Jerome. We left this Eve for up the river 20 miles. Very heavy storm too night.

Mentioned several times in the diary, the *Key West* was a 170-ton sternwheel packet built in Pennsylvania in 1857. It was captured by Union troops near Van Buren, Arkansas, on December 27, 1862, and burned.

> [April 2, 1862] After footing on sand bar for some time, we got back to the Rock again at 12. A fight at Union City. C [Confederate] badly beaten. The city is more quiet most all the soldiers have left. All C. troops are now at Jacksonport &

Pocahontas. The West is given up, or rather eat out. We got off this A.M. & making good time down. Layed up 9 miles above Pine Bluff.

[April 3, 1862] This is a cloudy day. The atmosphere is warm. Reached Pine Bluff at 7 & off again at 8. The scenery along the river is fine—& the contrast great since the verdue [verdure] of spring has adorned the vegetation. Birds are signing [singing] & many things go far to remind me of home. But few passengers. Spent the Eve quietly.

Just as signs of springtime were emerging and glimmers of hope were peering through the new trees, bushes, and fruit-bearing limbs of Southern farms, the crew of the *Rose Douglas* were to receive news of the Battle of Shiloh. At Shiloh, Grant (after a tardy arrival) would land reinforcements at Pittsburgh Landing and save the Union from defeat. Confederate General Albert Sidney Johnston, considered by President Jefferson Davis as his best general at the beginning of the war, was killed at Shiloh on April 6, 1862, and thus became the highest-ranking officer on either side to be killed during war.

The siege of Corinth was to begin on April 29, 1862, and last until May 30. After Shiloh a cautious General Henry Halleck utilized offensive entrenchments, fortified trenches, and siege tactics to minimize casualties. Confederate General Pierre Beauregard, outnumbered two to one, used false information, Quaker guns, cheering troops every time a train went by, and buglers, drummers, and camp fires by the dozens to fool the enemy into believing he had assembled a vast army to counter any attack. These devious measures bought Beauregard's army time to escape undetected to Tupelo, Mississippi, and live to fight another day. While these military setbacks were forcing Confederate troops to retreat ever further from the border states into the Confederate heartland, Charles Gunther and his crew waited anxiously for the news while trying to maintain a semblance of hope for the future of their new country.

Images of Shiloh from Harper's Weekly, *May 3, 1862*

[April 4, 1862] We are making slow time laying up at night. We are now in backwater. All goes pleasantly & quiet, nothing to trouble me, plenty of everything. Got a lot of turkeys. The weather is fine & pleasant. The whole bottom is over flowed. Spent the Eve. reading & retired early.

[April 5, 1862] We layed up at Red Fork last night. We had a tremendous storm, thought the boat would blow off. Reached Napoleon at 10 o'clock, bound for Memphis. Am glad of it. We have but few passengers. The Miss. is very high. All the country is under water, running all eve.

[April 6, 1862] We are running up the Miss., making very good time. The weather is fine. We have a fine lot of people. All passes of[f] pleasantly. We had some fun this noon racing with the *New Moon* but can't come it. The whole country along—is overflowed. We reached Memphis at 10 o'ck.

On April 7, 1862, Charles Gunther learns that General Albert S. Johnston died. Rumors and "excitement" permeated the conversations aboard the *Rose Douglas* and in their ports of call. Ironclads are being readied by Confederate forces on the Mississippi and troops are being moved back and forth in an attempt to counteract the Union onslaught. Anxiety permeates the local populace as their homes, crops, means of getting goods to markets, incomes, value of currency, and in some cases the lives of their loved ones are at stake. Then suddenly the *Rose Douglas* is impressed into Confederate service as a hospital ship. Her freewheeling voyages of goods and passengers are suddenly halted by the exigencies of war. The next few weeks are tense for the ship and her crew as the cry of the wounded and the stench of death permeate the ship.

> [April 7, 1862] Exciting reports. Fighting at Corinth. The Fed's beaten. Gen. Johnson killed. There are many rumors & much excitement. Lots of reports. There are numerous gun boats at levee getting ironed, & much activity exists among the military authorities. All anxious to hear more news. Spent the Eve up with Lloyd.

> [April 8, 1862] We are impressed into government service. Got to carry sick & wounded. More fighting yesterday. The Feds reinforced & supposed ahead. Island #10 reported taken. The city full of rumors, & many long faces. Got my stores in, & left for Napoleon at 2 with a miserable load of sick. Things look rough,

> [April 9, 1862] We laid up last night—fear of storm. This is a cold miserable disagreeable day,—making good time down—all goes quiet—my passengers being but little trouble. Helena passed. All very anxious to get a paper. Reached Napoleon at 4. Got rid of all my sick, & lot of new "pass." & bound for White River.

The *Rose Douglas* was now ordered to proceed up the Cache River and rendezvous with Generals Van Dorn, Parsons, and Maury to assist them in moving troops and supplies. At this time, Van Dorn's Arkansas-based army had been ordered to join the Confederate army at Corinth, Mississippi. The troops and supplies were shipped by river steamer down the Cache and White Rivers to Memphis. The Cache River flows south-southwest through Arkansas, emptying into the White River just east of Clarendon. Nearby, the town of Maberry, founded in 1842, was an important shipping point for area cotton and timber both before and during the Civil War. In July 1862,

Hill's Plantation, located here on the Cache River, would become the scene of a clash between Union and Confederate forces ending in another Union victory. General Earl Van Dorn (1820–63), whom Gunther was to report to, had already suffered a defeat at Pea Ridge. He was a highly volatile and impulsive ladies' man whose dalliance with the wife of Dr. James Brodie Peters would end in his death on May 7, 1863. While an effective general with small commands, particularly cavalry, he faltered when in command of larger units. But at this time he was trying to mount an offensive against the incursion of Union troops and sorely needed Gunther's steam packet to assist in the movement of his small forces. During this time he was assisted, as mentioned by Gunther's orders, by General Mosby M. Parsons of Missouri, effective commander of the Missouri State Guard.

Dabney H. Maury, promoted to brigadier general after the Battle of Pea Ridge, had previously served under General Van Dorn as his chief of staff. Assigned a field command, he led a division at the Battle of Corinth and was promoted to major general in 1862, subsequently participating in operations around Vicksburg and later in the defense of Mobile. Charles Gunther would meet and get to know each of these pivotal figures in the Western theater of war.

> [April 10, 1862] We took in a large quantity of wood last night. We are up White River getting along very well. The whole country up to Mount Adams is submerged. Everybody on the shore wants to hear the news. Read most of my time. The woods look beautiful green—. We laid up during the night.
>
> [April 11, 1862] We get to Des Arc this A.M. It looks quite like a port. All the large Miss. boats laying at the way. There are but few troops here yet, bad roads being the fault. This place looks lively for once. No news. Gen. Price gone to Memphis. The troops look very hard & weather worn. Raining all day—mud awful.
>
> [April 12, 1862] The weather is some finer today & mud is drying up. The town is lively with more troops coming in. Got

Earl Van Dorn, courtesy Library of Congress

Dabney Maury, from Maury, Recollections

some stores from commissary. Got orders to leave & go up Cash [Cache] River. See Gen. Van Dorn, Parsons, Maury. No news. Line down. We are all anxious to get away. A lot of artillery came in this Eve.—went up town in the Eve.

The next few weeks are going to see the crew of the *Rose Douglas* following orders to transport troops and war material up the Cache and White Rivers. Their observations point out the desolation in people and activity in the still verdant and blooming countryside. War news is scarce and, when available, disheartening. They are already seeing the weariness in the eyes of the troops, experiencing the downcast expressions of the residents, and remarking on the seemingly endless confusion in the movement of Confederate troops. The increasing arms plying the rivers, the switch from civilian to military uses, and the endless maneuvering and placing of strategic troop concentrations mark the war as increasingly personal, close at home, and wearing on the people, the economy, and the spirits of all involved.

[April 13, 1862] We are off for down White River at daylight. The weather is fine __. Reached Clarendon at 2. Started up Cash [Cache] River—but had to return—too small for us—we are now laying here in this God forsaken place waiting for further orders. It is terribly dull here—only about 10 mail [sic] population left at home. All closed up—dryed up.

Clarendon, Arkansas, located in Monroe County, has hosted French hunters and trappers on its Cache River banks since 1799. The few male residents left in town attest to the success of Confederate recruiting efforts in this area as well as military impressments—the same fate that befell the *Rose Douglas*.

[April 14, 1862] This is a pleasant warm day—took a stroll out in the woods—all looks beautifully green—violets are in full bloom—. There are many things that turn my thoughts homeward—see a late Memphis paper—The Feds are at Huntsville. There are numerous boats going & coming down the River—a large fleet of boats up here—spent the Eve at boat—retired early.

[April 15, 1862] We got orders today to return to Des Arc. Howell & I took a buggy ride out in the country a little. The country backs looks miserable swampy & insects innumerable. The crew amuse themselves playing ball. There are many steamers coming down full of troops. We got of[f] at noon, broke wheel in the Eve. Layed up all night—at Lake Bluff.

The crew of the *Rose Douglas* looked forward to getting back to Memphis as it was a source of news, a large port with entertainment and a diversion from the monotony of the river, and possessed a feeling of home for the crew. Memphis, the county seat of Shelby County, Tennessee, saw a great deal of activity during the Civil War, highlighted by its being the headquarters of General Jeff Thompson after his defeat of Union ironclads at Plum Run Bend. Evacuated by General Pierre Beauregard on June 4, 1862, it became on June 6 the scene of the Battle of Memphis, where Union naval forces sank or captured all but one Confederate ship engaged. Shortly after, Union Flag Officer Charles H. Davis received the city's surrender, opening another section of the Mississippi to Union shipping and military control. Charles Gunther was a witness to this momentous part of the war in the Western Theater.

> [April 16, 1862] Reached Des Arc this A.M. Not many boats here. Several Regs. left during the day. The place looks quieter. We are taking on freight. No news. We had a fine shower this noon. Am anxious to get back to Memphis—Read some today—an old review. Spent the Eve on boat taking in freight all day.
>
> [April 17, 1862] This is a bad disagreeable day. Raining again—There but few boats here & not many troops move to come in. We were getting in heavy freight all day. Nothing new. News out of the question. We took a large lot of men on & started at 5 with a full trip—no fun—in that.
>
> [April 18, 1862] Laid up last night again. We are making slow time—& head up for wood. Our crowd take everything coolly & are very obedient to all commands & rules. I am vexed very much at my croweds [sic] for the table. Some of our lady passengers got off. Our whole cabin & floor is full of people this Eve. No beds—but war times, who cares.

Charles Gunther and his *Rose Douglas*, still under the control of the Confederate military through impressment, are ferrying troops, passengers, and war materiel up and down the White, Arkansas, and Mississippi Rivers. One of their ports of call is Helena, Arkansas, the county seat of Phillips County. Helena is nestled between the Mississippi River and the eastern side of Crowley's Ridge. Helena was occupied early in the war by Federal forces and was, in 1863, the site of the Battle of Helena, where Confederate forces made an unsuccessful attempt to oust Union troops and relieve some of the pressure on Vicksburg. Later, Helena served as the point of departure for Federal troops preparing to attack Little Rock, the state capital. Thus, the crew of the *Rose Douglas* was operating in a dangerous area where control shifted back and forth between Union and Confederate forces, where frequent skirmishing occurred, and where there was the ever-present danger of being captured and sunk.

> [April 19, 1862] O dear, more rain—rain all the time. All the rivers are overflowing to their banks. See nothing but water & drowned out places. A general desolation appears to be the prospects. It is enough to give a man the blues. We had to go up the Ark. River for wood & laid up all night again. Our passengers amuse themselves the best they know how. Retired at 10 o'ck.

> [April 20, 1862] This is a dreary cold, cloudy & chilly day. We got into the Miss. River at 6-1/2. The Miss. is very high. There are no indications of Sabbath to me, except I had to put on a boiled shirt. Parnlled [*sic*] passed us going up. All is quiet on board. We reached Helena at 7 o'ck. Got a late Memphis paper but no news.

Charles Gunther frequently mentions that he did not observe the Sabbath on his journey, either from the lack of nearby churches, because of other duties, or mere indifference to this religious duty in the face of war. While he did don a "boiled shirt" on Sunday as a sign of Sabbath recognition, neither he nor his crew demonstrated religious fervor while on the Mississippi. He does, however, attend church when in New Orleans, seemingly enjoying several prominent Southern-minded ministers. Perhaps the bleakness of war, the preoccupation with safely navigating the increasingly hostile rivers, or sheer indifference in the light of the ravages of war dampened his, and his crew's, religious attention to duty. War news certainly gave little to celebrate and praying to the Almighty did not seem to result in an increase of Confederate victories.

> [April 21, 1862] Laid up all night at Helena—got off early. Another

cold chilly day. I have much trouble giving meals. Many of the soldiers are out. Am very anxious to get to M [Memphis]. We are having more or less racing with the *Fair Play*. Beat her into Port. Am glad to get in. We up this Eve to see some of my friends.

[April 22, 1862] Memphis—Up bright & early. The sun shines beautiful for once again, & the muddy streets are getting better—All the Missouri troops are yet encamped around this city. The city is lively with soldiers. Reports—bombardment at both ends of the River & some fighting in N.C. Was up through the city considerable—bought some clothing. Spent the Eve with Lloyd, & Kriel.

While the Mississippi River saw increased military and naval activity, the port of New Orleans was still in Confederate hands—but not for long. Charles Gunther is beginning to hear rumors of fighting at Fort Jackson. Fort Jackson was located on the west bank of the Mississippi River and was a strategic point of protection south of New Orleans guarding the Confederacy's most populous city. On April 18, 1862, Federal gunboats under Commander David Farragut began bombarding the fort, nearly pulverizing it. Nevertheless, not until April 24 did the Union navy steam past the break in the river obstructions and capture (or sink) thirteen Confederate navy vessels. Thus, New Orleans lay open and vulnerable to capture, and a southern base was provided for Federal control of the Mississippi River. This must have further dispirited Gunther, for he was in Memphis as much of this was transpiring and his crew no doubt wondered what welcome they would receive upon their arrival back in New Orleans—or whether they would be seized by Union forces and impressed into Federal service.

[April 23, 1862] Our levee is just full of boats, & all in Gov. service—. The day is beautiful & the mud has dried up fast. I laid in my stores. All are anxious to hear the result from Fort Jackson, N.O. The fight yet goes on. The city is lively. All the Mo. troops being there. We got off at 5 o'ck. from Ark. River—but few passengers.

[April 24, 1862] We laid at Helena until this A.M. We are making a good run ___. I feel a little lonesome, & often think of home. War & my people are my continual studies. We reached Napoleon at 5. The whole place is under water, levee broke, all drowned out, and the whole river country—got off for Ark. River at 8 P.M.

While the swollen and overflowing levees desolated the countryside, they also hampered General Grant and Federal forces under his command from making great progress along the Mississippi. But not the same case existed further south, where the capture of New Orleans begun on April 25 was completed by May 1, when Fort Jackson and Fort Saint Philip surrendered and Union troops under Major General Benjamin "Beast" Butler occupied the city. Butler became the military governor of New Orleans, and while he did bring order to the city, his infamous Order No. 28, calling any woman of the city who offended Union soldiers a prostitute, earned him his nickname. Butler at times seemed more interested in appropriating Southern silverware. This awarded him his second nickname of "Spoons Butler" and the enmity of city residents who were merely confirmed in their notion of Yankee invaders as plunderers, thieves, and no-accounts.

[April 25, 1862] There has been another change of weather—cold—cloudy & windy—Ark. River is very high & the overflow great. We are going along finely. All is quiet. I amuse myself reading. We are in no particular hurry. Gov. service & no taste for carrying troops—no fun that. Laid up again during the night.

[April 26, 1862] We reached Pine Bluff this Eve, & stayed but a short time. This is another fine, warm sunshiny day. The banks of the river look beautiful with the verdure—after so long & dreary look of things all winter. But one passenger & all is very quiet. Amuse myself reading Shakespeare. Several boats passed down with troops. Run some this Eve & laid up again.

Charles Gunther finally receives an unconfirmed report of both the capture of New Orleans and the fall of Fort Pillow. The report of Fort Pillow's fall was premature—the Confederates didn't evacuate the fort until June 4—but the rumor reflected a result seen as inevitable. The engagement at Fort Pillow occurred just forty miles north of Memphis and the loss of this fort, just built earlier that year by General Gideon Pillow, coupled with the fall of New Madrid and Island No. 10, basically secured this stretch of the Mississippi for the Union army and gave General Grant an open river to Vicksburg. Fort Pillow would gain further fame on April 12, 1864, when Confederate General Nathan Bedford Forrest was accused of massacring black Union troops in his attack upon the fort. For the crew of the *Rose Douglas* the rivers were shrinking in their access to Southern shipping, becoming more hazardous for both crews and passengers, and making every trip synonymous with running a gauntlet of snags, hazards, and dangers. The simple shipment of goods and passengers was not so simple anymore, and Gunther knew his crew faced increasing dangers and that his family's worries about his safety would multiply.

> [April 27, 1862] Beautiful summer day. Reached Little Rock at noon. Some boats in port—no troops here at present. There is some exciting reports—N.O. taken & Fort Pillow evacuated—things are coming to a head if this is so—and many long faces are now to be seen, only report but we will see what we will see—time will tell— am not anxious to get to M[emphis]. Just at present. Went to church this Eve—the first for a long time.

> [April 28, 1862] Little Rock—all is quiet in this city & reminds me of some small towns I have seen before. The weather is fine, & the woods & hills in the distance look beautiful—after so long & dreary a look of the whole winter. We see no chance of getting off here—for below—still waiting for 'something to turn up.' Went up town with Howard in the Eve.

Gunther's friend and shipmate Howard Lane leaves the vessel for Van Buren, Arkansas. Van Buren is the county seat of Crawford County and is located directly northeast of Fort Smith. After its founding in 1819 by Daniel and Thomas Phillips, they constructed a lumber yard there that served as a fuel depot for river traffic and may explain Howard's business in the town—the securing of wood for the ship. Later in 1862 Union forces captured Van Buren, along with 100 Confederate prisoners, and ended the Confederacy's access to the lumber from the town. The stranglehold on this section of the Arkansas River was becoming more pronounced, depriving steam packets of their fuel supplies, restricting their ports of call, and reducing their cargo profits to the point that government impressment provided the only possibility of making a living—when, of course, they were paid. During this journey toward Little Rock, Gunther is still able to find joy in the spring countryside and relish the scenery of a more peaceful time when war did not scar the landscape and turn the rivers into avenues of death and destruction.

> [April 29, 1862] Bound for Little Rock up the river this A.M. Str. *Eliza G.* got in last night & the *Roane* N.O. certainly gone up—that's the report. We left at 9. Howard goes to Van Buren—so I must do the clerking & all—not much to do however. A fine day—the scenery is very fine on this part of the River, beautiful craggy hills—covered with Pine forests. Laid up for wood at Beaver Dam.
>
> [April 30, 1862] Wooding most all day—went up to Benedects, bought a lot of stores. See a late dispatch—all on the Miss. looks gone—the bottom of matters are knocked out—& the Feds going in—This is a very fine day—beautifully warm. Read Shakespeare at leisure, & take a stroll up this dull town. Went to Church in the Eve, for once—& things look natural—sermon only moderate.

"Beaver Dam" is a bar on the Arkansas River between Little Rock and Dardanelle. "Benedects" is probably the plantation of George Benedict, thirty-two miles upriver from Little Rock.

Diary
May–August 1862

Charles Gunther opens his May diary entries reiterating the food shortages, scarcity of transportable goods, and high cost of all life's necessities. Inflation has gripped the Confederacy along with the slow disappearance of those foodstuffs, fruits, and vegetables that made life more pleasurable. Oranges were selling for up to $5 each, which in today's currency is $500: a princely sum for a simple joy among the monotonous diets of corn meal, dried beef, and peas frequently encountered at this time in the war. Rumors still abound as to war news—probably more false than true—and more encouraging to Southerners than the reality they were experiencing.

Gunther reads *Harper's Weekly* when he can procure a copy. Subtitled the *Journal of Civilization*, this was a political paper published continually from 1857 to 1916. By the outbreak of the Civil War, it boasted a subscription base of 200,000. The journal developed a reputation for employing some of the best illustrators, including Winslow Homer, Granville Perkins, and Thomas Nast. So as not to upset its Southern readers, the paper took a moderate position on slavery but fully supported Lincoln during the war. After the war, *Harper's* became very supportive of the Republican Party and played an important role in Grant's election. Thus, Gunther viewed the paper as a fair source of truthful news with little offensive to Southern sensibilities.

May 1862

[May 1, 1862] May opens beautiful—could not be finer. Our levee is lively with boats, & some left for below. I was up town several times during the day—eatables in this place are getting very scarce, & everything is tremendous high. The Feds reported at Batesville—& also & flying rumor of Nashville being retaken &c. All false. Spent the on boat reading an old *Harper's*—anything takes now a-days.

[May 2, 1862] The weather continues beautiful—& some dust in the streets. I am getting tired of laying here—so dull, no news & lots of rumors. I walked over this place a good deal—& amuse myself reading & gossiping upon war matters. The levee is just full of steamboats & all stern wheelers. Spent the Eve. up town partly & at boat. Retired early as usual.

Batesville, Arkansas, the county seat of Independence County, is about eighty miles northeast of Little Rock. The second oldest city in Arkansas, it was formerly known by the names of Napoleon and Polk Bayou. By the Civil War, it was an important port on the White River and an entry point to the interior of Northern Arkansas. This area of Arkansas was noted for its extensive quarries of manganese ore, phosphate rock, sandstone, limestone, and marble. The river fronts of the White and Mississippi Rivers offer beautiful scenery, and at this time of the year the trees were blossoming, the weather was mild, and the smells of spring were pleasant as steamers cruised the rivers. Ever lurking, however, were the dangers of war, the threat of Union advances and confiscations, and the increasing burdens on the general population. The contrasts created by war transformed antebellum Arkansas, Louisiana, and Mississippi.

[May 3, 1862] Up early—& the good news that we were released from Gov. & going to start for Memphis tomorrow. I had a terrible time getting a few stores. No flour to be had, for love nor money.

Pine Bluff in 1874, from Leslie's Monthly Magazine, *May 1874*

Feel tired running around all day. Some 3 boats have gon(e) up to lay up for the time being,—spent the Eve. on boat & many are the thoughts on my mind upon the state of the country.

[May 4, 1862] I am very busy. The boat is just crowded with passengers deck & cabin—all bound for Memphis. All other boats afraid to leave. This is a terrible, ugly, rainy, morning. No news—the Feds in Jackson Co. Plenty of rumors. I am now filling 3 situations & keeps me busy. All goes well & pretty quiet on board. Reached Pine Bluff at 7 o'ck.

As the *Rose Douglas* finally reaches Memphis, the sad condition of this war-torn Mississippi River area became ever more visible. Crops are being destroyed to prevent their falling into Union hands and gunboats are patrolling the commercial water routes and posing an ever-present danger. Entertainment is still available, but it is of a lower caliber than before the war, and a general gloom and doom permeates the countryside. Charles Gunther is increasingly aware that river commerce is at greater risk than ever before and that his job is becoming more dangerous. He is keeping in touch with his family to ease their worries for his safety, but the tentative nature of mail delivery does not insure they will receive the letters. All talk is of Union encroachments on the peaceful river communities, the high cost of goods, and how tired the general populace is of war and sacrifice.

[May 5, 1862] Layed up at the Bluff all night. Had a chat with Ed Holland. Left early this morning—cloudy but no rain—We are making a fine run coming through into White River & up the Miss. We were a little apprehensive of some gunboats but came out all right & going up full tilt. River very high. All is quiet on board & running tonight.

[May 6, 1862] Up bright & early. Rather cold this morning—but sun came out fine. Made Helena by 7 o'ck. Nothing to note. See several boats going down & others layed up. War times & no go. We reached Memphis after supper & found the city very quiet & dull—nothing going on. Spent the Eve with Lloyd.

[May 7, 1862] The Feds are reported above Natchez coming up—no news. Sent a letter home via Louisville. Am glad that have got through all right. I was up over the city some streets are pretty badly—It is reported sugar & molasses & cotton was to be destroyed tomorrow. Spent the Eve walking up town with Lloyd & also visited a minstrel show—poor thing indeed—night beautiful.

All along the *Rose Douglas*'s return trip to Little Rock are signs of destruction—cotton being burned so as not to fall into Union hands, Union troops seizing more towns, gunboats harassing river traffic and bringing more Federal troops in to control the towns, and refugees appearing who used to be farm owners, ranchers, and middle class members of society. People were being displaced from their homes and hope was slowly lost for Arkansas as more land was slipping under Union control. Passengers aboard ship were trying to enjoy music and a few other forms of gaiety like card playing to pass the monotonous hours, but his diary entries indicate that Charles Gunther was trying not to think about future dangers and his eroding business. The diversions could not block out the sense of a creeping, impending doom.

[May 8, 1862] I was very busy all day receiving freight & attending to business on the boat. We will have a good trip up, & all our hands full. Boat crowded—thinking this the last chance for Ark. Everybody is greatly scared & the Fed boats are expected from all quarters. See Mr. B. & all & think it probable that I will not get back for some time. All goes down lively.

[May 9, 1862] This is a fine pleasant day. We are making good progress down. The passengers are all pretty quiet—but some sick. One gives considerable trouble. We reached Napoleon this noon, took on a lot more passengers & freight. Plum full now & no place to lie down. Some music this Eve by Anderson & some dancing by a few. Got to bed late after being routed out several times.

[May 10, 1862] The weather yet keeps fine & Ark. River has fallen very much. All the cotton on the river is being burnt. It looks hard to see so much distraction. I am anxious to get to the Bluff. I want to dump some of my passengers out to few for my taste.

> Reached the Bluff at 7, & many have got off to my great satisfaction. Howard got on today of the *Cadott*. See Ed ___.

His friend Howard goes off on the White River steamer *J. J. Cadot*, a small vessel of sixty-two tons, and he sees his friend Ed Holland.

The river traffic was still busy, passengers were still being taken to ports of call, Confederate troops were still being shipped to Corinth, and Gunther was still able to relax with his friends at both White Bluff and Little Rock. The *Julia Roane*, another stern-screw steamer built in 1859, is frequently mentioned as following the same general route as the *Rose Douglas* and experiencing many of these same problems regarding passengers and troops being transported to battle locations. This vessel was named after Julia Embree Roane (1807–70), a wealthy planter and sister-in-law of Pine Bluff's most prominent citizen, former governor John S. Roane. On January 10, 1863, Confederate soldiers W. H. H. and J. S. Shibley, writing to their parents, tell them of the capture of the *Julia Roane* "last Sunday," additional evidence of the dangers all of this shipping was exposed to by the ever-encroaching Federal army.

> [May 11, 1862] We run during the night as far as White Bluff. All glad to get up & no trouble at the bars. We reached the Rock by 5 o'ck. A great crowd down to hear the news & I glad to get rid of my passengers. The weather is fine. Howell & I took a walk up in the city in the Eve, & went into one church.

> [May 12, 1862] This is another fine day. The citizens are much scared here, & many are leaving the city. The Feds are coming & are expected at any time. The Gov. has fled for some other parts. Got in my stores this A.M., and we are off at 11 o'ck, & full of passengers again. Took on considerable wood & made but little running—& few lady refugees also came down.

After issuing a proclamation calling on Arkansas citizens to rally to the state's defense, Governor Henry Rector fled Little Rock with the state archives. This gave the editor of the anti-Rector newspaper in Little Rock, the *True Democrat*, the chance to embarrass the governor, sarcastically asking: "We would be glad if some patriotic gentleman would relieve the anxiety of the public by informing it of the locality of the state government. The last that was heard of it here, it was aboard the steamer *Little Rock* about two weeks ago, stemming the current of the Arkansas River" (*True Democrat*, May 22, 1862). Although Governor Rector returned to the capital later in May, the fiasco ruined his chances for reelection.

The periods of anxiety and worry aboard the *Rose Douglas* were punctuated by interludes of gaiety and laughter, competition and betting on the race with the *Julia Roane*, and calmly watching the beautiful countryside slip by. But never far behind was the ever present trickle of war news—another city captured, the Federal army getting closer, another ship seized, and another horde of refugees seeking shelter. War was always just over the horizon, and the simple enjoyments of the crew were a mask for the realities of a changing world.

> [May 13, 1862] All go's quiet with our passengers & plenty of card playing. The banks of the river look beautiful now. We reached Pine Bluff at 2 o'ck. There are plenty of Texans there—all wishing to go to Corinth—The *Julia Roane* came down also full—we did not take any— am very glad of it. I retired early this Eve—our boat wooding all Eve.

> [May 14, 1862] We made Napoleon today. Nothing new here—no boats corning down at all. We are bound for up stream having a race with *Julia Roane*, & a tight one it is too—. The race go's on with unabated vigor on both & the cheers from the boats are great. The weather is fine, & warm, & fine nights. All go's quietly among the passengers.

Rumors of Norfolk being taken were true. Confederates had held the Norfolk Naval Yard since Virginia seceded in 1861, but they were forced to abandon the yard, burn it to the ground, and surrender control to Union forces. This deprived the South of one of its major seaports, shipbuilding facilities, and supplier of naval stores. Thus the news being received by the crew of the *Rose Douglas* transcended local calamities and the war in the west, and eastern losses further dampened the future hopes of the crew for Southern independence. It was becoming increasingly difficult to distract themselves in infrequent moments of merriment when their hopes and dreams for an independent South were slowly fading.

> [May 15, 1862] The race still go's on, & we ahead. Race in the woods some last night. Made Helena at 6. News. Norfolk, Pensacola taken & the Feds at Little Rock. Both boats started out again—& all after each other. Everybody feels lively—& all goes pleasantly. Reached Memphis at 6-1/2. Am glad to get back again. Howell & I took a stroll up the city.

> [May 16, 1862] This is a beautiful and pleasant day—no news from anywhere—the city looks very quiet & nothing doing at all—the River keeps falling slowly—our levee is full of boats, but none departing. Times are truly lamentable. Everything is awfully high & scarce. This is Thanksgiving Day for the S.C. & is here generally regarded. I spent the Eve at a poor theatre at Oddfellows Hall.

Charles Gunther is now hearing more rumors of the Federal advance on Natchez and Vicksburg. Natchez, the largest city and county seat of Adams County, Mississippi, was the center of economic activity for the state before the Civil War. Situated strategically on the high bluffs on the eastern bank of the Mississippi River, it became a bustling port for packets carrying cargo to New Orleans. Natchez surrendered to Commodore Farragut shortly after Gunther heard the news. A famous memoir by Natchez socialite Ellen Shields stated that "Southern men, absent because of the war, were seen to have failed in their homes and in the wider community, forcing the women to use their class-based femininity and their sexuality to deal with the Yankees." Times were truly changing and Gunther was an excellent eyewitness to these social and military transformations.

[May 17, 1862] Expected to leave today but no go. So we have to layover here until Monday. That suits me. I was up over the city considerable there being some life on Main Street. The Feds reported above Natchez bound for Vicksburg. Nothing from Corinth or Va. Got in many of my stores & am ready to leave at any moment. Spent the Eve at theatre.

[May 18, 1862] There is a cold North wind blowing this A.M., & all looks gloomy. Howell & I went to Calvary Church. There is a good congregation out. I spent the afternoon at Lloyds. We have no news. The Feds have Norfolk & Portsmouth & made a demand for Vicksburg, getting closed quarters on the River—no news from above— spent the Eve on boat & retired early.

As the war news becomes even gloomier, people are deserting the cities where the new conscription law is easiest to enforce. After trying volunteer enlistments during 1861, the Confederate Congress passed a conscription law that was far-sighted in providing exemptions for skilled workers in essential trades and for large plantation owners with more than twenty slaves. The flaws in the Southern conscription process, which did alarm and anger many people, consisted mainly in overzealous conscription officers, too many exemptions that were widely abused, and the ease with which the wealthy could avoid service. Rebel soldiers, particularly the committed volunteers, hated the Conscription Act, thought it unfair, and believed it took the glory out of honorable service. Sam R. Watkins, serving in the 1st Tennessee Regiment, wrote home that, "… from this time till the end of the war, a soldier was simply a machine, a conscript. It was mighty rough on Rebels." With more Southern men leaving for war, the social control structure was lessened, black labor fled the fields, and Southern women had to fend for themselves against the dreaded Yankees.

[May 19, 1862] The word is—leave this Eve—no crew & my mind full of trouble. Plenty of people—but they will not go. Old Abe is too much in their mind. I bought my stores all today-& am ready to start. Full of passengers. No news. Skirmishing at Corinth. The Feds slowly approaching and intrenching. Spent this Eve up through the city, & at boat. The Conscription Law is scaring away many.

[May 20, 1862] Time of departure again postponed. No go until this Eve. Ugly, rainy day. I was running all over the city in the mud, hunting a chambermaid, & none wish to go—the niggers making big calculations on the Feds. We have a good lot of passengers, & too many for my own good. No news this Eve. Got off at 5, & making slow progress—poor wood—laid up all night for storm.

[May 21, 1862] The weather has brightened up again. The River is falling fast. The banks making their appearance again. Reached Helena at 11 & Napoleon at 8. Napoleon is completely played out. Started up slowly—poor wood—we laid up part of the night. I was up helping a lady off, Mrs. Longford. All goes quietly on.

[May 22, 1862] We are getting along slowly. Reached the Post at 12. Jack got off & several lady passengers came aboard for Richland. This is a hot day. Passed a gun boat laying above South Bend. Got hailed in by the *Kentucky*. No news. I have very little on my mind & nothing to trouble my mind except thoughts for my folks. Laid up at Col. Morton's Plantation.

While Gunther and his crew are experiencing greater peace of mind since no fresh news has reached them, the ever present worry for family and friends, the shortages of provisions, the danger of Union gunboats, and the movement of troops continue to foreshadow even harder times to come. The new Confederate Conscription Law continues to cause alarm among the younger males along the river, their absorption into Confederate service leaving fewer white residents and overseers to manage an increasingly restless black population, with slaves abandoning plantations, joining Federal camps as refugees, and weakening the

South's agricultural infrastructure. Gunther is viewing this slow disintegration of the Southern way of life from a front row seat, visiting many of the affected cities and small towns along the Mississippi.

> [May 23, 1862] O this is a terrible cold disagreeable rainy day—enough to give any man the blues. Steaming up pretty well. All is very quiet on board. I passed considerable time reading—having bought me a lot of old *Eclectic* Mag's, the finest of literature. We reached the Bluff by 5. There being a good many people here, troops &c.

> [May 24, 1862] We had a sad account. Mr. Griffin died last night at 10 from the effects of a dose of Morphine, taken by accident. I attended him to his last moments. We are progressing up finely—wood is scarce—& provisions more so. We had a quiet time of it all day—reached the Rock at 7. There are about 3000 Texans here, a gun boat & several steamers. Went over the city attending to matters for Mr. Griffin.

In the 1860s people commonly used morphine as we would use aspirin today. Occasionally the consequences of taking that pain killer were tragic.

The *Rose Douglas* has so far been able to keep her usual schedule with the noted exceptions of finding it harder to get good wood, provisions, and passengers. Troops are in movement repositioning themselves. News from the east, particularly the Richmond area, is discouraging, and even the weather frequently does not cooperate. Essentially, Gunther, feels his world, while continuing to move forward, is "dull and nothing doing." He has time on his hands to help with a friend's funeral, put his obligations in order for him, and stroll about town, enjoying the flowers, springtime, and reading before bed. These simple pleasures make up most of Gunther's days and evenings.

> [May 25, 1862] This is a beautiful day, & all is quiet in town but busy at the levee. See Ed Holland & others. We had a masonic fu-

neral for Mr. Griffin at 2 o'ck. A good attendance & all passed off very well giving satisfaction to all. News the Feds near Richmond, 7 miles. The *Roane* & *Kentucky* left for Memphis this noon. Howard & I took a stroll in the Eve. The flowers are all in bloom in the gardens, looking beautiful—reminding me of home.

"Howard" is Ohio-born John Howard Lane (1836–77), the clerk of the *Rose Douglas* and postwar merchant in Memphis.

[May 26, 1862] Go for Ft. Smith is the word to my great joy—glad to get a chance to see more of the country, taking in some more freight. Finished up my business. The Rock is lively today with soldiers. Conscript law go's in force today here. Some stir among the youngsters. Got off at 4-1/2 & steaming up finely. But a very few passengers—to my great satisfaction. Retired late.

[May 27, 1862] Ark. River above the Rock. We made a short run last night & getting along finely—the scenery is fine & great is the change from below—hills, mountains & valleys. Reached Lewisburgh at 9-1/2. A small one horse place, run on a sand bar at 11. We are making slow progress up, & nothing of any interest to mention. Run some at night, & then laid up. Nights cool.

Charles Gunther is exploring a new area of the Arkansas River (northwest of Little Rock) where the *Rose Douglas* usually did not go. He was eager to learn about new places, to explore parts of the river he did not know, to see new sights, and to meet new people. One such new stop was Dardanelle, Arkansas, located in Yell County and one of the oldest cities in Arkansas, officially incorporated in 1855. Located on the banks of the Arkansas River north of Little Rock, Dardanelle became a leading town by the start of the Civil War, hosting barges, boats, and steamships of all sizes and descriptions and serving as a transportation and business hub for the surrounding plantations. By 1862, Gunther sees the town not as a hub of activity, but as small and poor—a reflection of the economic ruin the war was bringing to this area of Arkansas and neighboring counties. As he says, the Ozarks "looked played out." Vibrant business activity has slowed to a crawl and the male citizens that fueled the port businesses had left for war.

> [May 28, 1862] Passed Dardanelle at 11. It is a very small place & looks very poor. Took a flat in tow. Passed Ozark & Ozark Mountains. The scenery today is beautiful. Ozark looks played out completely. We are making good progress up, got in sight of Van Buren in the Eve., but stuck on the bar all night. The country looks fine & well settled for a border country.

> [May 29, 1862] We made the riffle over the bar, but however Howard, Leroy & Ferd & I took it up a foot. The boat working along. We made VanB. after a pleasant walk. The town is small, but has the appearance of a business place in ordinary times, but at present it looks like all other places, very dull & nothing doing. We laid here all night, & I strolled up over the town making observations & . had to go to Fort Smith in the Eve. Horsebaer [sic].

Ozark, Arkansas, was another of the small towns Gunther visited on this trip beyond Little Rock. Ozark is one of the two county seats of Franklin County and is also the northernmost point on the Arkansas River, originally named Aux Arc by French explorers. During the time of Gunther's visit, Ozark was a supply drop off point for interior cities, and this supply mission was probably to bring needed articles aboard the *Rose Douglas*.

"Howard," "Leroy," and "Ferd" are mentioned as shipmates of Gunther's. "Howard" is John Howard Lane, the clerk (see May 25, 1862, note). "Ferd" is Ferd W. Hamilton (1845–98), who worked most of his life as a riverboat pilot. "Leroy" cannot be identified.

> [May 30, 1862, Fort Smith] Got to this place late last Eve., but transacted some business, put up with Col. Dilles at St. Charles.

> Got up early this morning. Went over the place some. Fort Smith is no doubt a good business place & has all the trade of all the Indian nations. See plenty of Indians, in all manners of dress. The old U.S. barracks look very well, but lack attention. Got back to Van Buren & was compelled to go over again at noon. Got back & bought a lot stores. Boat started for below, but stuck on a bar all night.

"Col. Dilles"—George K. Dills (1831–76), Colonel, 2nd Infantry, 6th Division, Missouri State Guard—settled in Arkansas after being driven out of Missouri by Unionists.

> [May 31, 1862] After sparring all night we got off to get on another at 6 this A.M. So at it again. We had a pleasant shower last night which cooled the atmosphere finely. The *Pine Bluff* & *Belvidere* passed up this A.M. Made a start and got down stream slowly, wooded considerable, managed to get a little butter, a scarce thing sure. All go's very pleasant and quiet. Layed up for the night at a wood pile. Good water very scarce.

June 1862
Charles Gunther opens his diary for the "first day of summer" with obvious disappointment at still being on the Arkansas River. The war is still going on with ever-increasing reports of territory lost, and there is excitement at the announcement of a new commander for the Confederacy. Troops are being moved from battle to battle, and shortages of food, fresh meat, good wood, and recent newspapers continue. Memphis is deteriorating under Union control, passenger lists are shrinking, and the landscape is forlorn, dilapidated, and depleted. Food and clothing are becoming luxuries and a general pall saps the hopes and aspirations of the Southern river people. Gunther sees no signs of events to be joyous about and more to worry about— particularly his absence from home and the welfare of his family. The new Confederate commander is General Thomas C. Hindman, a law-

Fort Smith and the Little Rock Arsenal, Harper's Weekly, *March 9, 1861*

yer and former congressman, who has been given command of the Trans-Mississippi Department. Chronically short of soldiers and supplies, he endeavored to play havoc with Union supply lines in hopes of slowing the Union army's advance.

> [June 1, 1862] The first day of summer finds me afloat upon Ark. River, contrary to my expectations. I long hoped & expected otherwise but so must it be. The day is fine. We passed Dardanelle & Lewisburgh & run on a sand bar again to lay up & work all night. No fresh meats on board, so go in on salt. The Eve got quite cool. Passed *Key West.*
>
> [June 2, 1862] Got off the bar again & making for the Rock. The day is cool & cloudy. Reached the Rock at noon. There is nothing new. The *St. Francis* is at the levee, & several small boats. Hindman is now Comm. in Chief of all the forces in the Trans-Miss.

Dept. Took a walk in the Eve with Howell. The place is very quiet & no stir in the Eve.

[June 3, 1862] —Little Rock—We had some ice today. The *Julia Roane* came up & brought some, also some late papers. Everything looks dubious about Memphis. The calaboose being torn down &c. The weather is hot. There is considerable stir since Hindman got here & active operations are going into. Orders for Napoleon tomorrow good—anything to get away. Retired early.

For the first time Charles Gunther is expressing his being tired of life on the river—the monotony, the shortage of goods and the lack of passengers and business that before the war held out the hope for a prosperous career. Instead of cotton and farm products the *Rose Douglas* is transporting raw recruits and hospital supplies. Towns are no longer bustling business centers but abandoned outposts that offer little to the traveler. The war has taken its toll on his business, his mood, and his dreams.

[June 4, 1862] Got off at daybreak, making a good run. Reached Pine Bluff at 2. There are a good many troops here, some 6 companies. The day is warm. We have but few passengers. Col. Dill & Mitchell got off at. News—at the Rock last Eve. Corinth taken & Fort Pillow. Created great feeling among all, & the things looks gloomy indeed for the Southern Confederacy at present.

[June 5, 1862] Laid up all night & started again at day break. This has been a hot warm day. Reached Napoleon at 2. The place looks fore lorn & terrible dilapitated. The river is in its banks again. The Fed gunboats expected at any time. The Miss. is gone up sure, but very few people here & nothing to eat or wear. Spent the Eve on boat.

[June 6, 1862] We are getting all the hospital things aboard. The weather is fine. I have no doubt but what the building will be burnt tonight. We got off at 11, & making a slow run, but doing better this Eve. Old Elliott & I don't get along very well. All go's pleasant on board, but few passengers. I am getting sick & tired of boating now. Run tonight.

The Union noose is slowly tightening around Gunther and his crew. Union gunboats are becoming an ever-present menace, and transporting troops for General Hindman is placing the *Rose Douglas* in a constant state of peril. Martial law has been imposed in this area and Gunther and his fellow rivermen are more frequently being pressed into government service. Guards now accompany the *Rose Douglas* on her military missions. Whatever semblance of antebellum order, commerce, and peace that Gunther had experienced had virtually disappeared. In this foreboding atmosphere, Gunther turns to thoughts of home, better times, the safety of family, longing for days gone by. The strains of war are intensifying.

> [June 7, 1862] The day opens warm. Got up early. Made a few landings & received a few more passengers. Reached Pine Bluff at 10, took on a company of 60 men for the Rock. They behave themselves very good for recruits. Pine Bluff looks played out—& is. We are going up this Eve as far as possible. Met Dodge of LaSalle & was very much surprised to find him a soldier. The nights are quite cool.

"Dodge of LaSalle" is probably Private Andrew J. Dodge of the 14th Arkansas (b. 1814), or his brother Tarpley T. Dodge (1839–1922) of the 27th Arkansas, both former residents of Illinois. Tarpley deserted from the 27th a month after this and later served in the Union army—either an indication of the divided loyalties of Northerners residing in the South, or an indication of how Northerners were forced into the Confederate army against their will. The Confederacy's payment voucher to the *Rose Douglas* shows they were paid $1,940 for transporting the soldiers—a considerable portion of the boat's income.

From Confederate Vessel Papers, Rose Douglas, *page 15*

[June 8, 1862] Laid up most of the night. We are getting along finely. Had a long conversation with Dodge, & talked much of home. He feels like myself—very anxious to get home again to see the folks. Reached the Rock at 5. Nothing new except news of a big gun boat fight at Memphis. Howard & I took a walk up town in the Eve. There is very strict martial law here.

Naval battle of Memphis, and Federal occupation of Memphis, Harper's Weekly. June 28, 1862

The facts that Gunther and his crew can get little news of the goings-on in the war and virtually no letters from home increase the worries of all aboard. General Hindman is intensifying military maneuvers in this section of the Mississippi and Arkansas Rivers. Union troops are reported in both Helena and Napoleon, two of the frequent ports-of-call for the *Rose Douglas*. This stress is obviously having an effect on Gunther, as he begins to feel ill more frequently, talks about taking pills, feels lonely and isolated, and complains of being attacked by mosquitoes and assorted "varmints." Conditions on board are deteriorating, as is the countryside that was so lively and abundant before the war.

> [June 9, 1862]—Little Rock—Orders first thing to take cannon & ammunition over the river, & then start for up the river for lumber. The day is fine & quite warm. We made a slower run & got up a piece & were compelled to lay up & return. We have 12 Texan soldiers as a guard. All go's pleasant. I feel & little out of trim, took a few pills this Eve. The nights are very cool.

> [June 10, 1862] Made an early start for the Rock. Am very glad we returned just suits me—feel like laying up for a short time & something to turn up, which I surely expect. Reached the Rock at 9, & layed for the balance of the day. Hindman is just pushing things in general, guards on every corner. Took a brief walk in the Eve with Howard.
>
> [June 11, 1862] We made a daylight start and making a good run. Reached the Bluff at 3, & have run downstream to Emerys Bar—could not get over, so returned for further orders. Layed at Bluff all night. Took a stroll all Eve. The Feds at Helena & supposed at Napoleon. John Barkeeper left on a flat yesterday eve. No news of any kind & it is hard telling what is going on.

As June gets hotter, the rivers subside, and the news becomes scarcer, Gunther and his crew try to relax by reading, walking through town, and scavenging for supplies. Most of the troops in the area who are now doing guard duty and imposing martial law belong to General John S. Roane's command. As with the crew of the *Rose Douglas*, many of these soldiers also heard very little news of the war around them and much of what they did hear—Washington being bombarded by Stonewall Jackson and McClellan's army being devastated, for example—were erroneous and mere wishful thinking. The fact that virtually no accurate reporting was available to Gunther not only agitated him but also increased his worry for family and friends at home.

> [June 12, 1862] Got orders per telegraph to proceed to bar again so we run down & layed at bank & light freight over bar with flats. There are 4 boats here. Got some fine milk this Eve. We feel awful lonely—cut off from all news of any kind whatever. No doubt history has been made since our last news. No fun—but kill time reading.
>
> [June 13, 1862] Dropped down on the East side. Took on a lot of Gov. freight. The weather has been quite warm, thou in shade 100

degrees. The soil is suffering for rain & Ark. water is hard to drink. The river being very low, but I am happy to note I am well, & enjoying the times considering. Spent the eve talking with crew.

[June 14, 1862] We got all our Gov. freight on & made a start for up the river. Had the good luck of making Pine Bluff without trouble. Layed there for the night. No news except extravagant rumors & reports of McClellan's army taken & cut to pieces & Washington bombarded by Jackson, & many believe it true. O! It is terrible to be cut off from all news.

Paraphrasing Shakespeare, Gunther is willing to trade his "kingdom for a paper." Wild rumors of the fall of Washington DC, Baltimore, and Louisville abound—almost all false or woefully exaggerated. Yet no accurate reports can be received. This is frustrating to Gunther and his crew as they can see the destruction around them—the burning of cotton, the movement of troops in near abandoned lands, and the scarcity of food, cargo, and passengers. While hoping for a respite in the information blackout, Gunther relaxes, reads a great deal, visits friends, and simply hopes no news is good news.

[June 15, 1862] Pine Bluff. See Ed Holland, now Q.M. clerk in *Roane*'s Brig. This is a very fine but warm day, & good water is so scarce & provisions scarcer. We started for up the river & got as far as Wildcat Lndg.—unable to get further. There a few good places in this neighborhood, but all are poor & got nothing to sell. Retired early.

[June 16, 1862] This is a terrible warm day. Thermometer 102 in shade. Went down to Mrs. Collwell's place in the morning. We manage to kill time very well. A lot of the boys were in swimming. I made me a lot of fine syrup for drink this noon. The *Era No. 7* & *Alamo* took a lot of our freight off this A.M. A fight took place & several shots were fired.

"Colwells"—probably the home of Lucy Ann Caldwell (1815–77), widow of James H. Caldwell (1800–58), who owned a huge plantation in Jefferson County.

> [June 17, 1862] Wild Cat Lndg. A rough name, but yet a very good one, & something is to be got to eat here. We are making the best of our time—doing nothing. Plenty to eat & no grumbling. I amuse myself reading &c. of news we are utterly deprived of any kind—& I am led to exclaim—a kingdom for a paper frequently. Retired in good season.

As news begins to reach the *Rose Douglas*, some of the war rumors are confirmed. Gunther has heard of the incursions of Union Generals John Frémont, James Shields, and George McClellan. General Frémont—explorer, Union major general, and 1856 Republican presidential candidate—commanded the Department of the West from May to November 1861, when President Lincoln removed him from command for emancipating slaves and seizing secessionist's property, and transferred him to the Mountain Department of Virginia, Tennessee, and Kentucky. On June 26, 1862, after being assigned to serve under General Pope, Frémont, in protest, left for New York, never again to exercise command during the war. Brigadier General James Shields commanded a division in the Army of the Potomac. Wounded at the Battle of Kernstown, he resigned from the army in 1863 after his promotion to major general was rejected, whereupon he moved to Mexico and operated mines. General George B. McClellan organized the Army of the Potomac and served as General-in-Chief of the Army from November 1861 through March 1862. A splendid organizer, he chronically overestimated enemy strength and failed to engage significant parts of his army when needed. Failing to move aggressively cost him the support of President Lincoln, who removed him from overall command. He subsequently ran against Lincoln for the presidency in 1864 on the Democratic ticket. These were the principal antagonists whom Gunther received rumors of during this hot summer of 1862 and whose exploits made great conversation at night with his crew.

John Frémont, courtesy Library of Congress

James Shields, Harper's Weekly, May 3, 1862

[June 18, 1862] Not much rest last night. Almost eat to death by mosquitoes. The night was quite warm. We had a fine shower during the night & it has cooled the air very much. Howard & I took a walk around to some of our neighbors trying to get a buggy. Varmints of all kinds are a terrible plague in this country. The Eve is cool, & prospects for a good sleep.

George McClellan, Harper's Weekly, December 5, 1862

[June 19, 1862] Paid off all hands today. The deck crew has left a foot to make their way to Memphis. Howard & I are after a buggy up to Raragens. Heard some news again from the reliable gent. Washington City taken. Louisville burnt, & also Baltimore taken.

Every lb. of cotton is being burnt by Gov. agents. Spent the Eve reading—mosquitoes are very numerous, to dread the night.

[June 20, 1862] This is a fine cool day. Some breeze. I am getting well used to our laying up place. I felt like retiring after running so long & working against all the disadvantages of the war. It feels like new life. Ferd, Howard & I played all noon, & some this Eve killing time. We are having good living.

While war news is as long as two weeks in reaching the crew of the *Rose Douglas,* they try to take their minds off of the monotony by playing cards, visiting, reading, catching turtles, and fishing. The days are long, hot, and mosquito-ravaged. The crew's loneliness and sense of being disconnected from the world is because of no news, little river business to keep them occupied, and a sense that the war is not going well. Their little world is ever shrinking to a shorter and shorter stretch of the Mississippi, Arkansas, and White Rivers, and that stretch is more barren, plucked clean of many food staples, and scarred by war.

[June 21, 1862] Got up rather early. This is a pleasant day. We all went over a pluming in the morning. We are all enjoying our rest & I feel as if I had a load off my shoulder. There is news of a fight at St. Charles. Our Confederate guns spiked &c. The *Little Rock* has layed up here today. Some company now.

[June 22, 1862] A fine day, rather warm. The boys are amusing themselves fishing—catching turtles &c. Chanced to see a late Rock paper. News authentic to the 9th. Heavy fighting in Va. Fremont, Shields & McClellan. I read the greater part of the day, & spent the Eve with Pat of the *Little Rock*. My thoughts are continually wandering homewards, but shall wait for something to turn up, & hope it may soon.

[June 23, 1862] This week opens again without any prospect of any change & the usual monotonous days at this place will be

The action at Saint Charles, Arkansas, from Harper's Weekly, *July 12, 1862. In this action a union naval squadron ran into Confederate defenses at Saint Charles and suffered severely. A Confederate shell burst the boiler of the Union ironclad* Mound City, *scalding to death over 100 sailors.*

passed—time is nothing but no news to be had makes it awful tedious. This is the first time in my life that I have been cut off from any news for any length of time, say 5 to 15 days. Spent spare time reading &c.

Travel on the Arkansas River is becoming harder during the dry, shallow summer months. Sand bars pose a frequent hazard and all of the riverboats are trying to help each other cope with frequent groundings and mechanical problems. Charles Gunther is extremely happy that he received his exemption papers from the Provost Marshall. Because of his occupation in the transportation of military goods, services, and personnel, he qualified for an exemption from the Conscription Law from the Confederate authorities. After all, the war was not going well and life on the river—even though infested with mosquitoes and "varmints"—was preferable to a private's life of marching, hardtack rations, wool uniforms, and sleeping in the trenches and fortifications for endless hours.

While Gunther frequently expresses displeasure with the weather and the bugs, he realizes he is lucky to be out of the army and enjoying the life of a river man.

> [June 24, 1862] The weather continues hot, & mosquitoes are a terrible plague. My bar is no protection whatever. We are troubled some for good water. Our well is stagnant & tastes bad. My syrup is a luxury & comes in good play. We make time pass finely at cards. We are having fine buttermilk for our dinners, & some vegetables of the season. Took a swim in the river this eve.

> [June 25, 1862] The river is rising. The *Little Rock* got up stream & got over the bar. Went up with boat as far as Barraques with boat for some vegetables. The day is very hot. We all took a very fine swim. There was a fine breeze blew up in the Eve making night cool. I am wishing I were at Memphis, & hope to get there before very long.

Named for French-born Arkansas pioneer Antoine Barraque, Barraque Township is in Jefferson County, north of Pine Bluff.

> [June 26, 1862] Another bad night of it. Fought mosquitoes all night again. The *Julia Roane* went up & also the *Era*. The Captain, Howard and self went up on her for the Rock. We travelled all day & got along very slow, had to pull the *Roane* off the bar in the Eve. This is a terrible night for varmints. Sleep up in the Pilot House to get out of their way. That thing however is hard in this country.

June 1862 closes with hot, humid weather, hordes of mosquitoes and assorted varmints attacking the crew, and the ever-present martial law still in place. Working on the river is exhausting in the 100-degree temperatures, and they are constantly seeking water of good quality. Provisions are available but in steadily decreasing quantities and at ever increasing prices. Charles Gunther and his crew are looking forward to fresh air, the absence of fevers and malaria, and being able to resume their trafficking on the rivers. They are to be sorely disappointed on all accounts.

>[June 27, 1862] This is a very hot day, & the *Era* a terrible poor boat for shade. As we went along—I was wishing I was going in some other direction. Reached the Rock at 10 o'ck. Things look very quiet. See Dodge. Martial law is in full force. I got my exemption papers from Provost Marshall—a good thing—these times. Slept on the *Little Rock*. Had a fine Mosq. bar.
>
>[June 28, 1862] Had a very fine sleep last night, the best for a week. Another scorching hot day. Made all my purchases & we got ready & left at 1 in our yawl. Rowing went terrible hard at first & the idea of 50 miles being before us made thoughts unpleasant. However we made good time & worked hard. Got a poor supper at Scrugg's & worked all night rowing down.
>
>[June 29, 1862] Rowed all night except 2 hours & then sleep in the open yawl on the soft side of a oak plank. Made off at daybreak & reached boat at 7 o'ck. Row glad. We were tired, hungry & sleepy. However made all things still after reaching boat. This is a very warm day. Thermometer 102 degrees in shade. Everything all right at boat. Took a good swim in the Eve & retired early.
>
>[June 30, 1862] Another fine day & quite warm. All go's pleasant on board. We worked all morning cleaning out the well above to improve the water. Never until now have I learnt the value of good water—why life is a misery without it. I read part of the day & took to the hurricane roof for a fresh breeze. My soda water is a luxury & all like it very much. Spent the Eve at a rough boat.

July 1862

The severe hot weather is beginning to take a toll on the health of the crew of the *Rose Douglas*. Gunther's complaints of a severe headache, fever, aches, and pains and the intermittent recurring of the symptoms, point to a possible case of malaria. The hot, humid, swampy Mississippi Delta frequently provided a breeding ground for malaria, typhoid, cholera, and yellow fever epidemics—the last killing General John Bell Hood in 1879. The pills Gunther was taking, Wright's Indian Vegetable pills, were developed by Philadelphia doctor William Wright in 1837. They were packaged using Native American vignettes, often used in the Civil War period to promote patent or proprietary medicines. As with many other "Indian remedies," neither Dr. Wright or his pills had anything to do with Native Americans and probably did little of what was advertised on the label as a general cure all for any ailment.

> [July 1, 1862] We had a fine excellent shower last night & it has cooled the air materially. Everything looks fresh, something very much needed by all growing crops. All goes quiet on board, good living & easy times. Kill most of my spare time reading. No news for a long time. It is awful getting along without knowing what is going on.

> [July 2, 1862] 1 got up pretty early & worked some. Took a severe headache & fever after & feel quite unwell all day. Took a dose of Wright's Pills, which operated freely. Some better in the Eve. I should hate to take sick in this place. It is then that one thinks of home. I would give anything to get out of this place to Memphis.

While not understanding the cause of his illness, Gunther continues to battle the symptoms, longs for home and the comforts of family, and wishes for an end to living in blissful ignorance of the war happenings, the fate of family back home, and the future course of business on the river. The days when no news was available now stretches into months during which little reliable information is received. To alleviate his worsening health condition, Gunther begins taking quinine along with the Wright's Pills. Quinine is a natural white crystalline alkaloid having antimalarial and analgesic properties. During the Civil War, quinine was frequently prescribed for malaria, fevers, and ague. It likewise played a significant role in protecting sailors engaged in transporting slaves from Africa and in protecting planters and overseers in the rice fields of South Carolina, Georgia, and Louisiana.

> [July 3, 1862] Heavy fever all last night & not much rest. Took some more phisic today. Feel quite unwell—fever, headache pains &c. all day. I am a little uneasy fearing I will be taken down. Went up the road with Howard to my injury I fear in the Eve. The weather is quite warm, & it just makes the sweat roll out.

> [July 4, 1862] Little do I know, see, enjoy or feel that this is the glorious old 4th. Sick all night & day, nothing to show any indications of this glorious old day. All passes off as usual on board. Had Mr. Mosby to come & see me. Feel quite well this noon. My thoughts of home are many but it is no use.

James Harvey Mosby (1817–67) was a wealthy planter in Jefferson County.

> [July 5, 1862] Heard some cannon on White River I think last night. Feel quite well most all day, but got headache & fever again in the Eve. The day as usual is very warm, but little air stirring. Read some. No news from any quarter. We are all longing painfully to hear something. We are now living in blissful ignorance, but we are living in hopes hope—a good thing for us about this time.

As the second week of July dawned, the remainder of the crew began to get sick with fever, headaches, and body pains. Gunther is beginning to realize that the lowlands of the Arkansas River, with their abundance of mosquitos, bad water, and scorching temperatures, is an unhealthy climate. Battling these symptoms with the few home remedies and scarce medical supplies is proving a challenging task. The crew is likewise depressed over the continued lack of war news and a feeling of isolation is creeping over the whole ship. Even ships like the *Tahlequah* have stopped going far north on the river. A ninety-two-ton sidewheeler, the *Tahlequah* frequently carried troops up and through the White River and the Mississippi River. For example, in May of 1861, the *Tahlequah* transported the Pulaski, Arkansas, Light Artillery (Woodruff's Battery) as they left Little Rock. At this time Miss Juliet Langtree uttered her famous charge to Lieutenant James Finley: "Take this flag and let your determination be like that of the Spartan's mother's advice when she presented her son with his shield: Come home with it or come home on it" (*Arkansas State Gazette*, May 25, 1861; *Arkansas True Democrat*, May 30, 1861).

> [July 6, 1862] This is another day of Thanksgiving & rest. But not for me. I have been laying down most all day—my fever still hangs on yet. The weather is terrible warm. Harry is quite sick. I am beginning to make up my mind that this is a very unhealthy location—in fact the whole river.

"Harry" is probably Harry Brazee, steamboat pilot and brother-in-law of Captain Maginnis.

> [July 7, 1862] Rested pretty well last night & felt quite well until this Eve, when my fever came on me again, and with a terrible headache. Harry took a fit. The Captain & Mrs. took him out to Mosby's. Frank sick too. It appears we are all going to have our turn. My only prayer is to get out of this country.

> [July 8, 1862] Rested moderately well last night. This is another hot day, although some breeze. I have no fever today, but a continuous headache. Am taking some quinine & more pills. The *Tahlequah* stopped going up, but not a particle of news—no news for 3 or 4 weeks now. Set up Eve's until about 9. Mosquitoes without number.

The first news received by the crew of the *Rose Douglas* concerned small engagements by Confederate general Albert Rust along the White River.

The news was disheartening, as several regiments were "cut up" and routed by advancing Federal troops. Originally colonel of the 3rd Arkansas Infantry, Brigadier General Rust (1818–70) fought at the Greenbrier River, Traveler's Repose, Corinth, and Winchester, as well as the White River. He spent from April 1863 to the end of the war operating with General Sterling Price in the Trans-Mississippi theater of operations. Unfortunately for Gunther and his crew, very little good news from the war front would reach them. Continuing Federal advances, the seizure of more of the Mississippi, and the eventual fall of river town after river town culminating in the taking of Vicksburg would turn control of the Mississippi over to Union forces and split the Confederacy in two.

Albert Rust, courtesy Library of Congress

> [July 9, 1862] There is quite a pleasant breeze today, but the sun shines very hot. Nothing of any import heard today. There are 3 on board now who are sick—had another fever this noon—quite to my anticipations after taking quinine all day. O! It is terrible to be in such a state. Have eat nothing hardly for 6 days.

> [July 10, 1862] Rested. Pretty well last night although my bar was full of mosquitoes. I feel much better—but it only lasts till fever time comes on again—some headache all the time. News of some fighting on White River. Rust got cleaned out. Several regiments got cut up. Quite cool & pleasant this Eve.

> [July 11, 1862] Commenced taking quinine at 4 & keep taking it until this noon. Thought to break off old fever, but he came on again but

not so severe. Frank is quite low. No doctor yet & have been expecting one for 4 days. A great country this for a man to get sick in sure. No appetite at all & as weak as a cat, & poor water to drink.

Mid-July saw news slowly beginning to arrive for the crew of the *Rose Douglas*. The news, however, was of constant Confederate retreats in the wake of Union advances. De Valls Bluff is evacuated by Southern troops and Confederate troops are withdrawing further south, ever closing the noose around Vicksburg and the middle Mississippi river towns. The miserable news just adds to the battle Gunther is fighting with malaria, dosing himself with ever increasing amounts of quinine. The hot, miserable miasmic days of summer added to the pallor of impending Southern defeat.

[July 12, 1862] It tried to rain a little last night but all turned out nothing, to our great disappointment. News today that the Army had fallen back from Devalls Bluff. The Feds are shoving up things. I feel very well today, but it is tremendous hot. Not a bit of air stirring, & no doctor yet. It is hard to be sick. Retired early.

[July 13, 1862] I see no difference in Sabbath from any other day. It is all one with us. I feel only moderate. The Dr. came at last. Am dosing down quinine today to break the fever & took a heavy sweat. The weather is awful hot. I think I broke the fever sure, & some hopes of getting well—God grant it. I sick enough for me.

[July 14, 1862] As usual this is a very warm day. The boat more like an oven than any thing else. Dr. Trundell called again. All are getting better. I feel very well myself. I read a good deal today in the *Eclectic Mag*. We are having plenty of vegetables, corn &c. but no appetite have I. The nights are moderately cool. No news at all.

Gunther's recovery from his illness is dampened by news of further Southern retreats and false rumors that McClellan's whole army had been captured. With the lack of credible news from the war front, these Southern setbacks and false Southern triumphs just establish a seesaw of emotions that unfortunately usually result in depression when accurate news is eventually received. In the meantime, the days pass slowly for the crew. They all battle their own illnesses caused by mosquitoes, high temperatures, and bad water, and loll away the days reading, visiting friends, and dreaming of home.

> [July 15, 1862] 1 had a fine sleep last night. This day as usual very hot. The *Tahlequah* went down. We learn today that our troops are all falling back further South. I feel quite well today although fever day. I taking down quinine again to keep her off, & did so. I think I have got it under now.

> [July 16, 1862] This is another hot day and to be spent like the balance loafing all day. The days appear awful long—& the time is hard to kill particularly when one is sick. No news except reports said to be true McClellan's whole army captured &c. Feds reported left White River. I read most of the day. Little harry is improving.

> [July 17, 1862] We had a little rain yesterday & some tonight, but this morning all is clear again. The day is nice & cool with a good breeze. I think my fever is over—able to eat again. A kingdom for a paper. Totally cut off from any news whatsoever. Don't even get a Rock paper. Howard & I visited Mrs. Burnell in the Eve a little while. I think the walk did me good.

"Mrs. Burnell" is probably Ann E. Bonnell (née Salley; 1818–1905), the wealthy widow of Stephen Bonnell of Jefferson County.

Transporting cargo and passengers on the Mississippi, Arkansas, and White Rivers has come to a virtual halt, and lazy summer days with little to do are the result. The war, movement of Union troops further south toward Vicksburg, and displacement of river families has left the crew of the *Rose Douglas* with idle days to occupy their time trying to find shade, visit friends, read, and play the banjo.

> [July 18, 1862] The day opens bright & clear, prospects a good hot day. Caught a big catfish first thing. I keep early hours. I am up every morning by 5 & 5-1/2 o'ck. There is nothing to note. I am neither sick nor well, but have some headache or unwell feeling more or less all the time. Manage to kill time reading & retire early.

> [July 19, 1862] As usual another very hot day, nothing to vary the change of life, manage to keep something to eat in the vegetable line. Howard & I took a walk out to Mosby's. Harry is better, but a very sore mouth. Mosby has a fine comfortable place & what is more some good water—a blessing. Got to boat at 9-1/2.

> [July 20, 1862] Another hot day. Thermometer above 100 degrees. Keep running allover the boat for a cool place—doors, roofs, etc. Jack & Will got here from DeWitt. All glad to see them. Learned from a soldier from the Rock that all those big reports about McClellan's Army are humbugs, fill back only. No news. A very warm evening. Bed early.

> [July 21, 1862] I am enjoying some good nights of sleep, notwithstanding the warm nights. One blessing—no mosquitoes. Manage to keep them out. It tries to rain every day by showers passing around but it appears God put a curse on Wild Cat Ldg. Run all over again hunting cool spots. Called at a neighbors in Eve & returned with headache.

The days of monotony continue on the river. Feelings of longing for days of past excitement, business, and the excitement of seeing new places and meeting new people dominate the thoughts of Gunther and his crew. Federal troops are moving to solidify control of the White River, Gunther and most of his crew are still sick with malaria and various fevers, and the weather remains exceedingly uncomfortable. Little Rock is under Union control, as is Memphis. New Orleans has fallen. Vicksburg is in the crosshairs of Ulysses S. Grant. Days pass slowly for the crew, and all members of the *Rose Douglas* continue to amuse themselves with reading, playing the piano, and visiting friends.

> [July 22, 1862] This another of those scorching days, hot as thunder. Thermometer 107 in shade. Was up on shady side of roof all noon. Some breeze, but as hot as caloric. Made out the best I could. Sleep & reading. A cool breeze in the Eve. We all long for rain—rain. Jack amuses us with banjo in the Eve.

> [July 23, 1862] It is some cloudy all day. Went down to Mosby's & stayed all day. It is quite cool & pleasant here, and everything comfortable. Had the ladies play some on the piano. It reverted my mind back to old times. We had an excellent dinner. Harry is improving. Returned to boat at 5. Feel fine today. Went up to Mrs. Burnell in the Eve. Squared up at 9 o'ck.

> [July 24, 1862] We had a cool night of it & slept well. Rob got a headache this morning. Dr. Cantrell was here this morning. It is reported the Feds are coming back on White River, causes some commotion. See no paper for a long time. Ark. paper of course no other for 2 months. Jack is with us yet. Sick people on board improving.

William Armour Cantrell (1824–1903) attended the University of Louisville Medical College prior to settling in Little Rock. He owned lands in Jefferson County. Medicines and treatments he would have prescribed for the crew, besides Wright's Pills and quinine, might have consisted of frequently used expectorants like antibilious pills, antidyspeptics like antacids, bitters, tinctures of blood root, cayenne, and cloves—all aimed at reducing fevers, indigestion, coughs, aches, and pains. Many masked the symptoms but produced little in the way of results, as evidenced by the long weeks of illness aboard Gunther's ship.

> [July 25, 1862] Well I feel much better today. Again, of course, this is not fever day. Get h—l tomorrow. Sat around on boat all day, reading and taking as good care as possible. Howard is now a constant patient on the sick list. Fever today. There are many in this section sick, over half white population ailing. Retired early.

> [July 26, 1862] As expected fever today again. Took some quinine non stop. Feel quite unwell all day. Joe Nicols & Dr. Cantrell were here, also the Capt. Harry is yet quite sick. Little Frank came back with the Capt. yesterday from the Bluff. Great sickness all along this River. Rain is all that is wished for. Larry is under the weather today.

> [July 27, 1862] 1 felt very unwell all day. Howard has got fever again. Jack started home this A.M. This is another hot day. There appears to be no intermission to the weather. All signs of rain though numerous pass off again without it. It appears to try but won't come. Another new one on the sick list. Johnson went up to Burnell's in the Eve.

One of the small joys left on the river runs was meeting other boats with crews who knew each other and shared their tidbits of war news, their stories of being trapped on sand bars, and their impressions of the chance for Southern victory. One such boat was the *Era*, officially the *Era No., 6*, which, like the *Rose Douglas*, was a steamer used to ferry supplies and personnel for the Confederate government. Facing capture later in 1862, it was burned by Southern authorities to prevent it falling into the hands of advancing Federal troops. This represented another loss of the old way of life and a forceful omen to the *Rose Douglas* of a fate that it too might encounter at any moment.

> [July 28, 1862] It is cloudy all day. Sprinkled a little, but am afraid it will not rain as usual. Little Frank & Johnson down with chills.

The *Era* passed up. Tom has a few young mockingbirds & it is amusing to see the old ones come & feed them in the cage. This is my fever day, but thank God, I have escaped it. Took a little quinine. Report of a fight at Vicksburg.

[July 29, 1862] There is nothing to note in the shape of a change in this monotonous place. We might as well all be in a penitentiary. See nothing, hear nothing, no papers, but keep reading old books, but good matter. I feel weak & feeble and look considerable poorer, no color, fever takes a fellow down sure pop every time. There indications of rain again this Eve. Hope it will come, & did so at 9 o'ck.

[July 30, 1862] O we had a blessed rain last night & this morning & is raining some this afternoon. The whole country must rejoice at this. All are suffering for it. Amidst my gladness I was again taken with a chill & fever this noon, caused by my door being open all night & rain & dampness coming in. I think. Lasted in all about 3 hours. Cleared up this noon again. The boys amused themselves playing at cards in the Eve.

[July 31, 1862] Rained last night again & is coming down this morning at intervals right goodhope it will rain for a week. I feel right smart today but weak as usual. Howard is better. I eat too hearty a dinner & feel much the worse for it all afternoon with fever & some headaches. The country around looks beautiful. There was a magnificent sun set this Eve. Feel better but the night is warm.

August 1862

August begins with the crew of the *Rose Douglas* still fighting their fevers and the extremely tropical heat. But some pieces of the war are beginning to intrude on the relative peace and quiet of the last two months. The steamer *Era No. 6* passed by with six Federal prisoners aboard, and

Federal deserters warn of impending advances. Rumors also abound that Federal troops are seeking to occupy Little Rock, further tightening the noose around navigable waterways.

> [August 1, 1862] Mosquitoes sang their symphony all night, my room being full with them. I was up during the night in consequence of taking a few pills, but slept pretty well the balance of the night. This is a bright fine warm day. Took quinine every two hours to break my fever, this being fever day, & succeeded in doing it I think. The *Era No.6* went down going to Helena with 6 Fed. prisoners on. The Eve is quite warm. Feel good myself. No fever.
>
> [August 2, 1862] Up bright & early. This is quite a hot day. I shifted myself to different quarters to some cool spot. The Capt. was down all day, & also the Madam came at noon. I feel quite well today. Took a few doses of quinine, read the *Eclectic Mag.* 106 all day. Frank & Larry are both down with the chills today. The Str, *Key West* went up in the Eve. Howard & I took a walk out to Mosbys in the Eve, & fine walk & cool-returned at 9 o'ck.
>
> [August 3, 1862] This is supposed to be Sabbath Day, but what evidence have we of it at Wild Cat Ldg? Were it not for the knowledge of it calanderical we would know nothing. Well, the day passed quietly, all the crew reading & hunting the coolest place to sit. Mr. Waters was here. Says he sees 6 Federal deserters at the Bluff. They report the Feds intention going to the Rock. The nights are cool.

It is amazing that Charles Gunther and crew can still obtain eggs, turkeys, and vegetables. By late summer of 1862 not only had scarcities begun to grip the Confederacy, but rampant inflation of Confederate currency had occurred. Additionally, businesses were beginning to refuse Confederate currency, banks and ordinary citizens were hoarding specie, and refugees were pouring in to towns and military camps already short on supplies. While food was being grown in sufficient quantities in the South, since cotton was purposely being withheld from markets to force Britain to recognize the Confederacy, the transportation system was poor, disrupted, or in some cases non-existent for getting goods to those in need. It is therefore a testament to the *Rose Douglas*'s crew that they were able to secure sufficient food to provide for their health.

The "Madam" is Mrs. Maginnis, born circa 1838 in Dayton, Ohio, as Mary Brazee. Her brother Harry Brazee worked as a steamboat pilot with James Maginnis. She married Captain Maginnis in Memphis on January 30, 1862, bringing into the marriage two children from a previous marriage to William A. Wandell. After her husband's death, she moved to Saint Louis to live with her son Harry Brazee Wandell, a newspaper editor in that city. She died there in 1889.

> [August 4, 1862] This is a warm day. The Capt. was up. My fever appears to have left me & I trust will never come back again. Johnson & Larry left for Memphis, in a skiff, sent a letter home. O how I should have liked to go along, if I thought it safe, but I will wait my time, & be on the safe side. See an old paper of the 12th last month, but all news to us. I am feeling first rate. The night very warm.

> [August 5, 1862] Thermometer 106 in shade today, but made the time pass very well. Hunted the cool places of the boat & read the greater part of the day. Howard & I take a game at cards for a diversion & break the monotony. Joe Nichols was here. He don't appear to approve of the present dynasty & policy. Had a few peaches today. Howard & I took a walk in the Eve to McCall's. Bought 5 doz. eggs & a fine turkey. Stopped at Mrs. Burnell's also. The Eve is cool & pleasant.

"McCall's"—The home of Ransom McCall (b. ca. 1817, Tennessee, d. ca. 1885), farmer and neighbor of the Mosby and Buck families.

[August 6, 1862] This is a fine warm day. Nothing going on. We go through our usual routine of business, reading & c. Am getting so I can play a few tunes on the melodion, anything for a change & pass time. I am now reading my next to last *Eclectic Magazine* of my lot.

Charles Gunther is almost fully recovered from his illness, as is the rest of the crew. Now their search for war news, even if from a Yankee newspaper, increases in intensity. They hear that General Theophilus H. Holmes is replacing General Hindman at Little Rock and they appear to welcome this change of command. General Holmes, born in 1804, rose to the rank of lieutenant general in Confederate service. Early in the war he commanded coastal defenses in North Carolina, fought with Beauregard at First Bull Run, fought with Robert E. Lee during the Peninsular campaign, and then became commander of the Trans-Mississippi Department. After failing to hold the Mississippi River or send troops to support Vicksburg, President Davis relieved him of command in March of 1863. His only other significant Civil War service was his participation in the Battle of Helena, Arkansas, after which he commanded reserve forces in North Carolina until his surrender to General Sherman on April 26, 1865. Obviously, his record did not comport with the enthusiasm he was first received with.

[August 7, 1862] No fever any more. Our whole crew is now nearly free from it. I am getting quite fleshy again. Keep taking some bitters. We are having good living—I enjoyed a fine turkey & vegetable dinner today. Am drinking nothing but river water (our well has got very bad). It is warm but sweet. Took a walk in the see a Rock paper of the 19 ult., but little news & such as it is.

[August 8, 1862] It is said Gen. Holmes supersedes Hindman at the Rock. All the people are glad of it. The *Era* went up just from Old Town & the Federal camp. Got a St. Louis paper of the 1st. All on board terribly pleased at seeing a Yankee paper & all listened to the news not much though. Read all market reports & everything else. The Capt. went up to the Rock. The *Key West* went down in the Eve. See Ferd Hamilton on her.

[August 9, 1862] This is a warm day but some breeze. The nights are cool & pleasant to sleep. The *Tahlequah* went up today with some corn. Howard & I passed time at cards, chequers & reading. After tea we took a walk down to Mosby's. Harry's leg is yet the same no better. I fear he will be crippled for life. Got back at 10-1/2, feeling better for the walk.

Theophilus H. Holmes, courtesy Library of Congress

Unfortunately for Gunther, his fever returned. While the quinine kept the fever at bay and masked symptoms, the malaria returned, aggravated by the high temperatures and muggy weather. He has added bitters and tonic to the quinine regimen in order to keep the fever at bay. Many of these pills and tonic sound today like the mixture of a quack doctor—snakeroot, horsemint, ginseng, bloodwort, extract of dandelion, and wormseed, just to name a few. While probably doing the patient little good, they did represent the cutting edge of herbal medicine for the Civil War era. Unfortunately for Charles Gunther, the effects of malaria sometimes lingered for years, intermittently attacking the body with fever and chills.

[August 10, 1862] Another Sabbath has rolled around & the month most half gone. Well we passed the day reading, no one coming near the boat. All very quiet. The *Era* came down & the Capt. on

> her. Got late paper but nothing new. The Feds are reported to be advancing in force for the interior. Look out for h__l. Howard & I took a walk in the Eve for the benefit of our health.
>
> [August 11, 1862] Up bright & early. Took a row in skift & launched off the bark (intended if necessary). Eat a hearty breakfast. Took much I think. Had some fever & a severe headache all the balance of the day—Read a little in Shakespeare & played some cards in the morning with Howard. Retired pretty late. Took some pills.
>
> [August 12, 1862] The pills brought me out before I intended. Some headache & some fever all day. It is very hot "Thermometer" for several days from 106 to 104. We have a kind of a spring at the foot of bank. It is very good in comparison to our others. The *Era No.6* went down. Got some fine melons the first of the season. The Feds reported on White River.

Charles Gunther is now witnessing an increased military presence and activity on the Mississippi and White Rivers. Rumors persist that the Union troops are advancing southward, that major Federal defeats are occurring around Richmond, and that the gunboat *Arkansas* was blown up. Amid all this excitement Gunther continues to battle his fever and malaria, adds emetics to his lists of medication, and tries to rest and recuperate from the sweltering heat and unremitting fevers and aches.

> [August 13, 1862] This is a warm day as usual. We have reports of the movements of the Feds in the interior. Took an emetic to break my fever, and I think succeeded well. It is the best cure in this country. Reading was impossible. Fell out of humor. Nursed myself all day. The nights are warm. I could relish a piece of ice nowadays if ever I could in my life.
>
> [August 14, 1862] I am continually taking some tonic to keep down fever. Feel first rate today. Enjoyed some fine muskmelon.

The *Tahlequah* came down & The *Era* later. No news, but I expect to hear news of a fight on white River every day. Things are moving in that direction. Took a walk in the Eve. I am doctoring Harry. He is quite sick—succeeding.

[August 15, 1862] This is a fine & as usual warm day, but a cool breeze part of the day. Spent the time reading Shakespeare & playing chequers with Howard. After tea took a walk down to Mosby's. Harry's no better. We had a fine melon today & I did justice to it. We are getting very anxious to get a little news, but we can't get any.

As he was just lamenting the fact that little war news was coming to their attention, word arrives that the warship *Arkansas* was blown up. The CSS *Arkansas* was a Confederate ironclad serving in the Western Theater during the Civil War. Laid down in Memphis, she was commanded by Capt. Isaac N. Brown. She gained notoriety for running through the Union fleet above Vicksburg on July 15, 1862, disabling the Union ship *Carondelet*, and inflicting severe damage and losses on the remainder of the Federal armada. At the 1862 Battle of Baton Rouge, the *Arkansas*, hampered by disabled engines, was scuttled by her crew, set adrift, and blown up in view of the attacking Federal fleet. Sadly for Gunther and his crew, this rumor proved true and was a major blow to the Confederate navy.

[August 16, 1862] This was quite a cool morning. Felt like sleeping after my walk last night. The day was passable. The *Tahlequah* went up. Spent all day reading Shakespeare & as usual a game with Howard. We had an excellent dinner & of course did justice as I am won't. Took a walk in the Eve. The nights are cool & sleep is easy.

[August 17, 1862] Up early. The day is bright & not very warm. The *Little Rock* went up. News. Another big fight at Richmond reported & the Feds whipped out again. Also, the blowing up of the gunboat *Arkansas*. I went to church this morning the first for a long time. A

CSS Arkansas, *from* Battles & Leaders of the Civil War *(1884)*

goodly number of people. The house filled with niggers. Sermon not much. Had dinner on the ground. Enjoyed some, returned home at noon. Prichard is in the boat. Took a walk in the Eve.

[August 18, 1862] I had an excellent night's sleep. The day is pleasant. We caught a fine fish this morning. We are spending the day variously. I read Shakespeare most all day. Was up at Mrs. Burnell several hours this A.M. Learned the Feds were at Clarendon but had left. Prichard on board yet. We are all enjoying good health now. Thank God. But keep taking bitters to keep fever off.

Gunther now observes masters moving their slaves from their former plantations to the safety of Confederate-held Little Rock. The presence of such large numbers of blacks was to be anticipated as slaves numbered 26 percent of Arkansas' population before the war. Additionally, the Confederate Conscription law, as well as voluntary enlistments, had depleted the number of white males available to police the slave population. The situation had become so acute that in October 1862 the Confederate Congress passed the Twenty Negro Law exempting from military service anyone who supervised more than twenty slaves.

[August 19, 1862] I was woke up this morning by the *Key West* whistling. Landed here. She is full of niggers going to the Rock. The day is pleasant & warm. We have no news of any kind— got used to it now—but the mere thought of former newspaper days awakened many regrets. We are having some nice peaches. They are plenty here. I see no chances of making home, as far off as ever.

[August 20, 1862] I started for White Bluffs at 8, after a long ride reached there, but did not succeed in getting what I went after. Stopped at several places coming back. Had some fine melons at Long's. The day is hot & roads very bad & dusty. Had a shower at noon, cooled the air. Here lots of war reports, but all lies. In my opinion, no reliance to be placed on anything you hear. Failed in getting what I went after.

[August 21, 1862] Up bright & early. The *Ben Coursin* went down with some niggers. We all-enjoying good health on board & are now having plenty of fruit to eat, peaches & melons. Our lines are set & hardly a day passes but what we catch some fish. Not a good season but still they eat good. Played some chequers & cards with Howard & retired early.

Continuing on his observations of runaway slaves, Gunther comments on how he nearly was attacked by "nigger hounds": dogs pursuing runaway slaves. It is obvious a great number of slaves are deserting their former masters and becoming contrabands of war.

[August 22, 1862] We had some rain this morning, something long wished for, but not enough to do any good. Only hope it will continue. The day is cool and pleasant. I killed the time reading Shakespeare & playing. We have heard no news for some time from the army in this state. Long to hear from home, but no prospect for some time to come. We have considerable fun playing poker for corn in the Eve—anything for amusement.

> [August 23, 1862] Up bright & early. The day is fine & warm. We have several very fine melons today. Went up to McCall's at noon. Came near being hit by nigger hounds. Learnt a little news, but all old. Jackson & Pope had their first battle. The *Extra* is so garbled that it is hard telling what the news is, but fighting continues & will for some time.
>
> [August 24, 1862] The Holy Sabbath Day, but there is nothing at this landing that awakens in me any of the old church going notions. Bells are out of the question. Spent the greater part of the day reading & Charlie & I went up & fished in a small bayou. Caught a turtle only. Retired early in the Eve. Night cool.

Charles Gunther hears of the first battle between Stonewall Jackson and John Pope. Thomas J. "Stonewall" Jackson was a corps commander under Robert E. Lee, most noted for his 1862 Valley Campaign. The report is of the Battle of Cedar Mountain, a Confederate victory. Jackson and Pope meet at Second Bull Run, where General Pope was trapped and forced to retreat. Pope was subsequently relieved of command and spent the remainder of the war in Minnesota. At the Battle of Chancellorsville on May 2, 1863, General Jackson was accidentally shot by his own pickets, causing an amputation of his arm that subsequently led to his death from pneumonia eight days later. This war news was some of the first Gunther heard that was a Confederate victory, giving him cause to rejoice.

> [August 25, 1862] The weather keeps warm. Thermometer ranges from 100 to 104°. Went down to Brodies Mill for flour but got none. I enjoyed the ride very much. No news & are now waiting for time & the events of the war to change our state of affairs, trusting in a speedy peace. Played at cards in the Eve. Some fun.
>
> [August 26, 1861). The times are passing as usual with us, but very little amusement through the day, but I enjoy reading Shakespeare more & more. The *Key West* came down this Eve.

Thomas Jonathan "Stonewall" Jackson (1824–63), courtesy Library of Congress

John Pope, from Harper's Weekly, *September 13, 1862*

Went up in the boat & boarded her. Got a late Rock paper. No news latter than 10th. Spent the Eve on the *Key West* & having a game of cards for amusement.

[August 27, 1862] Got up quite early. Fished a little & read some. Went up to Mrs. Burnell's. The Captain & Mosby were at boat. Report that Gen. Price has been defeated, but no reliance can be placed upon it. The day is warm. Thermometer 104 degrees in shade. We are having plenty of fruit (Peaches). We have some fun. Evenings playing poker for corn.

[August 28, 1862] Charley & I went out & stood for deer that a lot of others were driving—see more but party got three. The day is warm. Thermometer 104. Took a ride down to Brodie's Mill for flour, 75 lbs. This is all that can be bought in this country, so we will go it on corn. Good enough for me. I like it very well. O! For a letter from home. Spent the Eve playing with the boys.

The last days of summer are spent aboard the *Rose Douglas* reading, visiting friends, and treating Gunther's headaches and fever. He has added "oils" to his list of medicines. Frequently during the Civil War, oil of cloves, Bears oil, and olive or seed oil were remedies to deal with these ailments. The crew is obviously waiting for the arrival of autumn and the abatement of the 100-degree-plus temperatures, sweltering humidity, and teeming mosquito population.

> [August 29, 1862] Another warm day. I stayed on boat all day reading. No news of any kind. We know little how the world wags, so we will have to read it in the future history. We are all enjoying good health. We did a lot of cleaning today. Everything begins to look rough, but all bright again. Spent the Eve as usual.

> [August 30, 1862] Charley & I took boat & went a fishing below the Bayou. Caught a fine turtle & one large catfish. Saw 18 wild turkeys. The day is warm or rather quite hot. Stayed aboard boat all day reading, as usual. Seek the roof in the afternoon, where we get a breeze. No news of any kind, not even false reports, a wonder. It always takes a month to correct them.

> [August 31, 1862] I have got considerable of a headache all day_ Took oil, feel a little sick, & layed down part of the day. Read *Hamlet*. Thus has summer ended, in those sickly bottoms. I had my share of intermittants, but think it all over now, but there is no telling. September is a bad month here. I expected to be home ere this, but no telling now. I hope soon.

Diary
September–December 1862

Charles Gunther greets the arrival of fall with the news of the issuance of the Emancipation Proclamation. To take effect January 1, 1863, it decreed that all slaves in areas under Confederate control were free. Areas under Union control and border states were exempt, as Lincoln did not wish to give these states an excuse to leave the Union. Gunther is rightly alarmed at the impact this change will bring to the Southern way of life, a life he has (in part) adopted despite his German-Northern roots.

September 1862

[September 1, 1862] The first of Fall! Little did I think of being here at this season & how I long for home, not so much home, as to allay the fears & troubles of my folks, but I have great expectations. As usual may be disappointed again to an unlimited time. The day is warm. Went to Brodie's & did get 5 lbs. flour. Something new & good if it is poor. We played on the Eve for fun as usual.

[September 2, 1862] It has been trying to rain for some time more or less, but the desired & wished for has not come. Charley &

I went fishing. Caught a tremendous large catfish. It is fun hauling such ones in. We had considerable sport catching small catfish off the boat. Tom left for home this morning. The Capt. was up. Spent the Eve as usual. Went also to Mosby's.

Gunther hears rumors of General Buell's army being cut off, sending a wave of hope throughout the *Rose Douglas*. Union general Don Carlos Buell commanded Union forces at Shiloh and Perryville but was relieved of field command in late 1862, spending the next year and a half in Indianapolis in military limbo waiting for a hoped-for exoneration of his failure to pursue General Bragg after Perryville. Exoneration never came, and he resigned May 23, 1864.

Don Carlos Buell (1818–98), from Harpers Weekly, *April 12, 1862*

[September 3, 1862] Howard, Charley & I went fishing as usual this morning, but got nothing. The day is quite warm. All is very quiet. Some great reports again—universal emancipation in America by Lincoln, Buell's army cut off &c. If this is so it is a matter of life & death with the South. Went out for peaches this noon, got some very fine ones. Enjoyed a fine melon. Spent the Eve as usual.

[September 4, 1862] Got up early. Enjoyed good sleep. The nights are getting cooler, a shower yesterday Eve. We lack for nothing particular. I am rather boatless & no prospect to get any more. Went fishing this morning again—caught a large buffalo & cat. When I wear out my clothes now, there is no replacing them. So we will soon have to go in rags. Spent the Eve playing with boys.

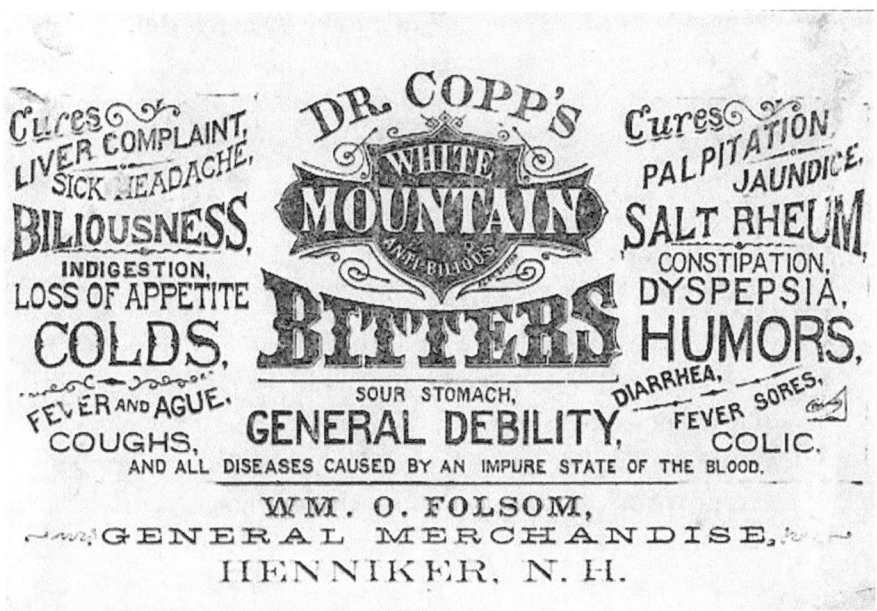

Dr. Copp's Bitters ad, 1883

[September 5, 1862] I am now enjoying good health again. Kept taking some bitters. Charley & I went fishing this morning again—caught 1 turtle & a catfish. I spent all afternoon rewriting my old diaries up with ink. I intend to finish them all. Have nothing else to do.

It was certainly good news for historians that Charles Gunther decided to rewrite all of his diaries in ink. This helped to preserve them for future generations and opened up a bit of riverboat history during the early war years that may have otherwise been lost. Charles Gunther is continuing to take medication to ward off his fever and aches. He has added bitters to his regimen of medicines. Bitters is an alcoholic beverage flavored with herbal essences and has a bittersweet flavor. During the mid-nineteenth century it was frequently marketed as a patent medicine (many times taken along with quinine) but really is a digestif (stomach-settler). Peychaud's Bitters and Dr. Copp's Bitters were two of the most popular brands.

> [September 6, 1862] I am getting to be an early riser nowadays for a man that has not more to do than I have nowadays. I stayed around boat all morning writing &c. After dinner Charley, Frank & I took yawl & went after melons to Colwells. Got a fine lot of them. I enjoyed the trip, had a good pull, fished some in the Eve, & played some after.
>
> [September 7, 1862] My feelings for the Sabbath were not great enough to walk a mile & a half through a hot sun & 6 inch dust to church. I enjoyed this morning writing a poem on the death of Mr. Buck. Little atla [sic]. She was a sweet little creature—a lovely child. We had a fine shower this noon. Commenced Byron. We are now feasting on melons, enjoying ourselves for war times.

Philip Buck (b.ca. 1826, Tennessee) and family, including young daughters, lived next to the Mosbys in Jefferson County.

> [September 8, 1862] We were surprised this morning by rain to our great joy. It has cooled the air much & makes it pleasant on the boat. We are utterly cut off from any news & don't know what is going on. Ignorance they say is bliss. Commence to think so now. Went to Mosby's in the Eve for some meal.

Again Gunther is bombarded with reports of another battle at Manassas and 20,000 Federal prisoners. Generals Pope and McClellan were reportedly killed also. These false rumors were not just random hearsay but frequently the product of legitimate newspapers and correspondents. The *London Times*, for example, saw Gettysburg as nothing more than a raid that ended in a draw. The *Richmond Enquirer* turned Antietam into a Confederate victory that would "immortalize" Confederate armies. And the *Chicago Times* ran editorials proclaiming an "inevitable" Southern victory. Thus is it any wonder that Gunther was able to believe that the South would ultimately be victorious, that the Mississippi

River would again flow with Southern cotton, and that the South would gain its freedom?

> [September 9, 1862] It rained this morning again. Spent the day fishing, reading, & took a walk up to McCall's. He has some fine nigger dogs & is going on a hunt tomorrow. I read an old Rock paper 13 ult. See a little news. I had some sweet home dreams last night & see some of the girls. Looked sweeter than ever. Spent Eve playing with boys.
>
> [September 10, 1862] The day is cloudy. Got up early. Charley & I went down the river fishing. Caught only two & one turtle. Read some Byron & all went out—Mason for some peaches, some very fine ones. It rained hard in the Eve. Heavy showers. The river is now very low. Frank is sick again. We are feasting on melons & peaches. We can get along at that.
>
> [September 11, 1862] The day is cloudy & cool. Also a small shower. It looks though Fall had come at last, but is making his way slowly. Days as hot as August yet. Heard news of another big battle at Manassas again. Feds cleaned out & 20,000 prisoners. Such are the reports here. If this is so goodbye to the Federal cause. Also McClellan & Pope killed. Oh! A kingdom for a late Memphis paper, or any other newspaper.

Gunther's days spent reading show a genuine affinity for the works of Lord Byron. Two of his favorites are *The Corsair* and *Lara*. *The Corsair* was published in 1814, a poem classified as a melodramatic-verse tale. Here pirate Captain Conrad risks all to rescue Gulnare, the chief slave in the Turkish pasha's harem. *Lara* has Count Lara, the haunted, gloomy, and doomed hero of Byron's 1814 poem, returning to his ancestral home bringing great secrets with him. Perhaps Gunther's identification with these poems related to his own longing to bring the secrets of river travel and the experiences of war back home with him. The Union would also rescue the slaves of the South—and Gunther was a witness to all of these human events just as Lord Byron had described them a half century before.

> [September 12, 1862] I am reading most all day. I find beauties in Byron I never knew before, and am favorable disappointed, from former opinion, based on what others had said. Read *The Corsair* & *Lara* today. The day is cool & cloudy & a coat is not uncomfortable. I had a dream of home again. Oh! how I love to have home dreams. It brings many fond recollections back.

> [September 13, 1862] I am now rising at 6 o'ck, and breakfast at 7. I am now enjoying a good appetite. The Capt. & family came aboard again for good. So we will have fair company again. The *Ben Coursin* went down, the first boat for a long time. River is yet very low. Fished some & caught nothing. This noon & Eve bright & fine.

> [September 14, 1862] I am in a great quandary all day. The *Tahlequah* is down, says Washington taken &c. Now can this be true, or possible. I have thought & wondered over it, & am waiting for further reports. All passed Sabbathetically on board. All very quiet. Read the greater part of the day in Byron, Corinth & others. *Manfred* is beautiful and sublime. I like it much.

While idling away his time to resume his river excursions, Gunther learns to shingle hair. Shingling is the process of cutting the hair in a series of tapers cut so evenly that they give a soft, sloping effect. He again hears rumors of great Southern victories, the last being Manassas. Second Manassas was fought August 28–30, 1862, between the Confederate divisions of Stonewall Jackson and Robert E. Lee and the Federal forces under General John Pope. After a stalemate on August 28, Pope launched a series of attacks the next day against Jackson's position with heavy casualties on both sides. On August 30, Pope renewed his attacks but was overwhelmed by the newly arrived General James Longstreet. The Union left was crushed and Pope retreated to Centreville. This time Gunther's rumor of Confederate victory proved correct—although it took two weeks to reach his ears.

> [September 15, 1862] Got up quite early. The day is beautiful. I went down to Mosby's this morning. Had a pleasant social chat & also went out to Hesters, a fine man rather enthusiastic. Rode a mule the first for a long time. Felt like a patriarch. Reports Feds on White River again &c. The longer I stay here, the more distant looks the time of deliverance from this lonely place. This is pastoral vesticity [*sic*] enough for me.

Wealthy farmer John B. Hester (b. ca. 1811, Kentucky) lived in Pine Bluff with his family.

> [September 16, 1862] I was woke from my slumbering by the sweet singing of a mockingbird nearby. I am getting so that waking up on mornings I must get out of bed. It has no charm for me to loll awake for hours. I spent all day reading on and off, and doing various small things. Cut Howard's hair, shingled it & did excellent if it is self-praise. No news. The family affairs aboard pass pleasant. Had some fine melons. My diary is getting very interesting to me again. Day pleasant & cool.

> [September 17, 1862] I am up bright & early before sun. We had quite a shower today but bright & clear this noon. The *Ben Coursin* & *Era No. 6* went up. Got a late telegram some account of a late fight at Manassas. Feds cleaned out again &c. Went over to McNeel's in the afternoon for some vegetables. Had a pleasant time. The people are in great ecstacies over the news. Washington, Cincinnati &c. taken.

Gunther is hearing increased reports of war news from the Eastern theater. Cincinnati is being threatened, Confederates are in Maryland, and

Alexandria, Virginia, and Washington, DC, are on the brink of falling to Southern forces. Again, as in the past, the rumors are largely baseless. The Maryland excursion Gunther alludes to was the Battle of Antietam, fought September 16–18, 1862. Here the armies of General Robert E. Lee and General George McClellan collided when General Joseph Hooker's corps attacked Lee's left flank. The resulting slaughter was the single bloodiest day in American military history. In spite of extensive casualties on both sides, Lee retreated south of the Potomac and McClellan chose not to pursue. Lee took his crippled army back to the Shenendoah Valley and, although the results were inconclusive, the Union claimed a strategic victory and Lincoln issued the preliminary Emancipation Proclamation. These false rumors of great Southern victories in disparate places caused Gunther to rely less heavily on unsubstantiated accounts of Confederate successes in the future.

"McNeel's" the home of Angus Frere McNeil (1832–63), a planter in Jefferson and Dallas Counties.

> [September 18, 1862] We had a heavy storm & rain last night but all bright & clear. I stayed aboard boat all day. Read some in Byron. Caught a fish. I am in pretty good spirits, notwithstanding my unpleasant position, and the circumstances which trouble the country. The river is rising fast. Am glad of it. Cut some of the boys hair, a shaved look set sure, but none know enough to cut mine.

> [September 19, 1862] The mornings are getting quite cold and a coat is comfortable. Heavy dews. Frank & I did some cleaning this morning. Read some. See some news. Feds evacuating all the lower country. Cincinnati in danger. Confederates in Maryland & at Alexandria. Washington as good as taken &c. H__l let loose &c. Anxious for more news. Caught two fine fish. Retired early.

> [September 20, 1862] Up bright & early. Quite cool, but hot all day. Helped Frank at some work. The appearance of Fall days are

commencing to show themselves. The late news makes matters for seeing folks more distant than ever. If I only could get a letter $10 no object. I went up to McCall's this Eve. I sat up some reading Mrs. Maginnis plays. Some music in Eve, making it consoling.

[September 21, 1862] Beautiful Holy Sabbath day. All is bright & fine. Spent the greater part of the day reading. There is a mocking bird that sings the whole day long on the trees beside us. I enjoy his company much. How cheerful yet he knows not our sorrows nor griefs. Mrs. Mosby & daughters called this noon. Fine people. Very. Tom got here last night from Dewitt.

While the war news continues to roll in, inflated yet as to the scope of Confederate successes, Gunther spends his days overhauling the boat, visiting friends, and reading—particularly Lord Byron, whom he feels captures the sentiments of his age. The poetry and stories of Lord Byron that Gunther was reading were written in the 1820s. *Werner, or The Inheritance: A Tragedy*, was written in 1822, followed in the next two years by *The Age of Bronze* and *Island*. His *Don Juan*, written 1819–24, consisted of seventeen completed cantos and comprise a satirical mock-epic in which Don Juan is portrayed as an innocent whom women fall for and try to seduce. The *Island* opens with the famous lines, "The morning watch was come; the vessel lay her course, and gently made her liquid way." *The Age of Bronze* contained the words, "No land of Canaan, full of milk and honey / nor (save in paper shekels, ready money; But let us not to own the truth refuse / was ever Christian land so rich in Jews?" Gunther enjoys all of these books and relates to the content, frequently interjecting sentiments that undoubtedly derive from the moods of Lord Byron's prose and poetry.

[September 22, 1862] This month appears to be passing very fast indeed and many are my thoughts on my folks, but it is no use. Report here that some of our troops are going up to Mo. & that Memphis had been attacked &c. The boat went through a general overhauling on deck, sewed all mattresses. Read Byron's "Werner" like it very well. Cain & others yesterday. Cain is a fine thing.

[September 23, 1862] Cloudy & a misty rain again. Charley & I went over to McNeill's this morning. Got some meat & vegetables. Articles all scarce in this section. In fact in the whole Confederate States. Read all noon. Byron's *Age of Bronze* & *Island*, both which I liked very much. My boots are giving out & no more to be got. Must go barefooted next I suppose. Rough times these.

[September 24, 1862] Something or other killed four of my chickens last night, a mink I suppose. This is a cool cloudy day. Rain most all day. Commenced *Don Juan*. No news yet & how anxious we are to hear it. Something has turned up there in Md. & Va. I have now resigned myself to my fate let come what will a strong heart & a good conscience will carry me through all troubles.

Charles Gunther's literary exploits continue as he more frequently thinks of home, and how his family may be in distress and he cannot get news of it. He also hears of the battles of Harper's Ferry and Fredericksburg—again hearing they are Southern victories. The Battle of Harper's Ferry took place September 12–15, 1862, when Robert E. Lee, learning that the post there had not been abandoned when he entered Maryland, placed artillery overlooking the town and prepared to bombard it. Colonel Dixon S. Miles then surrendered the garrison, although he himself was mortally wounded by the last artillery salvo fired. What Gunther labels a "fight" at Fredericksburg is either some minor skirmishing near Frederick, Maryland, or the September 17, 1862, battle of Antietam itself.

[September 25, 1862] This is a fine warm sunshiny day. I read a great deal of my time, intended going up to Mosby's but could not get a horse. Thought much of home this Eve. I know & feel that they are in trouble. I stuffed a big garfish. He looks well. Amused myself chatting over literary subjects in the Eve.

> [September 26, 1862] The day has been passed by me as usual. Feeling good, albeit I am looking pale. Went down to Brodie's & Mosby's & also to McCall's. Provisions are getting very hard to get. We will have to go it on corn alone by & by. Feel as if anything will do me nowadays. Appetite is good. Spent the Eve reading.

Scottish-born George Brodie (1809–79) headed a wealthy Jefferson County planter family in 1860.

> [September 27, 1862] I was fishing all morning & had bad luck. Caught nothing. Went down to Hawthorn's in the afternoon. There is a battalion of Texas cavalry camped there. They are a rough looking set & I think will make a good fight. Heard some news of a fight at Harpers Ferry & Fredericksburg, Confederates victorious. The men are busy on the roof. We read all Eve. Reading Byron's *Don Juan*.

Gunther has repeatedly complained about vermin overrunning the boat and causing him and the crew great distress. Mosquitoes, fleas, wood ticks, mites, chiggers, and flies were the unchecked constant companions of not only soldiers but men on the river and swampy areas of the Mississippi. These pests could drive Gunther to distraction, biting, and clawing at all hours of the day and night, not only carrying disease, but preventing a good night's rest, further weakening the body. This inevitable infestation also caused scratching, itching, and open sores that added to the pain and discomfort of soldier and sailor alike.

> [September 28, 1862] It looked misty this morning. Texas cavalry passed this morning. Dressed up & Howard & I went out to church out at Mason's. A small congregation, very poor singing & a moderately good sermon by a Texan. Eat dinner on the ground & remained for Eve service. After went to Bucks. Was introduced to Miss Williams, a moderately good looking lady. Took tea & was brought to boat by Mr. B. in buggy after night.

[September 29, 1862] A severe storm last night. Did not sleep well. Up early. After breakfast rode up to Barraques. Read all afternoon. Joe Nicols was down & a little tipsy. It is quite warm this Eve. There don't appear to be any rest for us. I am in continual misery & vexed mind. The confounded varmints of all kinds keep us scratching & itching all the time, no matter where you go they are after you. Thermometer 96 degrees.

[September 30, 1862] September has rolled around and gone. What sweet intoxications have I had to be at some other place ere this. But no telling now for the future. Have not seen a paper for a month or heard any news for a week such as it is. It is hard these stirring times, but are glad to get something to eat & be in peace here just now. Spent all day at boat reading Byron. Called up at Burnells. Weather warm. See some wild geese-the first this season.

October 1862

The war news being received by Gunther in early October presents both Union and Confederate sources claiming victories. Antietam (Sharpsburg) and Iuka have been declared victories by both sides, again reinforcing Gunther's belief of the unreliability of the news from the front and the distorted picture being painted by various newspapers. The Battle of Iuka, for example, occurred September 19, 1862, between the forces of Union general William S. Rosecrans and Confederate general Sterling Price. Upon arriving at Iuka, General E. O. C. Ord demanded that Sterling Price surrender. Price refused and ordered a withdrawal to join General Earl Van Dorn at Rienzi. During that march, Confederates engaged Ord's troops along a nearby ravine and ridge. Heavy fighting created a large number of casualties on both sides. Price finally completed his rendezvous with Van Dorn in preparation for an assault on Corinth. Thus, with heavy casualties on both sides, it was possible for both pro-Southern and pro-Northern papers to claim victory.

[October 1, 1862] October has opened warm & a slight shower this noon. Went down to Mosby's this morning. Left my old boots to be mended, am getting very hard up in the boot line. Never went with boots with toes out & no soles before, but all fair in war. See a Rock paper of the 27 ult. Feds claim big victories here. We had a rat hunt on the boat this noon. Spend the Eve's reading & retire early. Think of folks continually.

[October 2, 1862] To my satisfaction we are having rain this whole morning. Buck & Waters were here. I fished some & spent the balance of time reading. The *Corsin* came down, wooded here. We had a great time catching a mink that has been annoying us for some time. He made a powerful effort for his life, but there were too many for him. See news of a great battle at Sharpsburgh & one at Iuka. Feds claim victories, so do the Confederates, but it is evident the Confederates have left Md.

[October 3, 1862] Frank gone to the Bluff so have to do his chores. Went down to Mosby's on the pony & got my boots. Also at Sloan's. He made a good job of it, so I think I will get along now for some time on the boot line. The Feds are meeting with success in Va. from all accounts. Am very anxious to hear further. It is quite warm this Eve, thermometer 98 degrees. Conscript business is being again pressed forward in the state, who knows how we may turn out on the boat.

The Civil War was noted for many firsts, one of which was the national conscription of soldiers referred to by Gunther above. After Confederate setbacks at Pea Ridge, Shiloh, and Fort Donelson and engagements in the Eastern theater, recruits were far and few between. By April 1862, President Davis convinced the Confederate Congress to provide for the conscription of all able-bodied men between eighteen and thirty-five, exempting only skilled workers deemed essential to Confederate victory. Conscription was widely unpopular and violated, according to its opponents, the sanctity of States' Rights. It also illuminated the dwindling manpower resources available to the South and highlighted the danger felt by young men whose patriotism was now tinged with the fear of death on a remote battlefield. In Arkansas, General Hindman was especially remorseless in enforcing the conscription law.

> [October 4, 1862] I got up early & went to Mrs. Burnells for milk, a walk early in the morning is very pleasant. We are all getting along very well. We had a great time shooting some very large gars, who would come & try & take a large buffalo I had caught in this morning. Some tremendous fellows indeed. Read some in Byrons Miscl. poems. Got our sale boat rigged & took our tril [sic] trip. Go's first rate.

> [October 5, 1862] Rainy & misty this morning but warm & fine at noon. Stayed on boat all day. Took a good bath. Read some & finished Byron's work completely. I hardly know what to note or write. My thoughts are in a perfect state of apathy, except that I am continually more or less thinking to get away from here, but the time looks as far distant as ever but my mind is quiet & nothing troubles me.

> [October 6, 1862] News from home. How much pleased I am all day. Feel happier & easy all things pass pleasant. Mrs. Smith arrived from Memphis & brought us all news. Mr. Lane calls Ed to see folks & sent word all well & easy. She has much to say. Has had a terrible time in coming through, of a determined character & I honor her for her spunk. The capt. is quite sick. Was carried to carriage & gone to Mosby's. Since hearing from home I long the more to see all & time will be harder to kill now than before for some time.

Gunther receives news of a fight by Parson's regiment up in Missouri. This is probably the September 30 Battle of Newtonia, although Col. "Wild Bill" Parsons' 12th Texas Cavalry (which earlier in the summer had operated near Pine Bluff) did not participate in the battle. This type of news is interspersed with simple tasks of reading, fishing, and visiting friends to relieve the boredom from the restricted river traffic and opportunities for traversing the Union-held portions of the Mississippi and White Rivers.

> [October 7, 1862] I was woke up last night by the *Corsan* corning up at 11. No news. The Capt. got quite sick & was taken out to Mosby's last night. Howard & I took a sail this noon. Had a fine breeze. Mrs. McGinnis & Mosby & daughters were here this Eve. Made myself useful. Wrote a letter home & one to Bohlen to be taken through by Mrs. Smith. The day warm.

> [October 8, 1862] I took a trip down the River for a fish. Caught a fine catfish but had him taken by a tremendous gar. Howard & I took a walk out to Mosby's at noon for Mrs. Smith. There is a report that Parson's Regiment had a fight up in Missouri. We have had considerable showers today. Read some & wrote lines to Jennie in the Eve.

> [October 9, 1862] Up bright & early. Mrs. Smith started for Memphis. Sent letter home & one to M__. I pray to the Lord that she may get through safe. We had a fine dinner today on wild ducks. I enjoyed them much. Pigeons are flying plenty, but ammunition is scarce. Went over to McNeel's in the Eve. She is in great distress—had two brothers killed at Sharpsburgh. Spent the Eve playing.

Gunther has finally dispatched two letters home by Mrs. Smith who he hopes will safely get through Union lines and be able to mail the letters North. He again experiences a second tragedy of war—the loss of two of Mrs. McNeil's brothers at Sharpsburg. Mrs. McNeil was not alone. After the Battle of Antietam (Sharpsburg, Maryland) the town's 1,300 residents were outnumbered four to one by the number of dead soldiers littering the fields around the town. Gunther also announces the election of Harris Flanagan as governor of Arkansas. Flanagan (who married Marsha Elizabeth Nash) served as the Confederate governor of Arkansas from 1862 to 1865.

> [October 10, 1862] We had a tremendous rain storm all night and day and the weather is cold. I had to change clothing. Got on a heavy coat. We are hard up for news, hearing nothing for a long time. Man from Rock says Flanagan elected Governor of this state. I read most all day Whateley on *Rhetoric*. I am enjoying health & appetite & go in on corn & sweet potatoes. Our life here.

> [October 11, 1862] The night was pretty cold, but day clear & sun shining. Warm again. I read all forenoon & went out to Mosby's in the afternoon for more news. Helena again reported evacuated but I don't believe it. I am getting very anxious to hear from Virginia. Nothing now since Sharpsburg fight. Captain sick yet & out at Mosby's. Arkansas troops reported in Missouri now. Spent Eve playing with boys.

> [October 12, 1862] Oh! This has been indeed a very dull Sabbath for me. A fire was comfortable this morning, the first this season. Took a walk & read *Ivanhoe*. I am fondly hoping Mrs. Smith will have no trouble, and that folks will get letter. I am getting so I don't know what to make of this. I am in continual hopes for a relief from here, but from reports it looks more distant than ever.

Besides Lord Byron, Gunther enjoyed the novels of Sir Walter Scott. *Ivanhoe*, written in 1819, was set in twelfth-entury England. It is the story of one of the remaining noble families of Norman lineage who, in 1194, are witnessing the return of the Crusaders from the Holy Land. Modern conceptions of Robin Hood (Locksley) and his merry men grew out of their characterization in this book. While romantic and historical novels greatly appealed to Gunther, he must have also realized that he was living through a crucial period of American history and himself witnessing events that would be written about for hundreds of years.

[October 13, 1862] The day is clear and pleasant. The river is rising fast. I took a walk up to McCall's. I spent the balance of the day reading *Ivanhoe*. It is the first of Scott's novels I ever read, and am much pleased with it. There is true humanity in it. The Captain & family came aboard again this Eve.

[October 14, 1862] The men were out last night taking our wood. The river has come up very much and is now of respectable size. The *Ashley* & *Julia Roane* went down. It looked natural to see a good boat run again. I only wish we were going also & bound for Memphis. A bright day this. Pigeons flying thick. Had a fine dinner & as usual enjoyed it much. Holmes has established another price list for the state. No news yet. Heaven help us.

Faced with rampant inflation, and families unable to afford breadstuffs, Confederate military authorities in Arkansas issued orders decreeing fixed prices for food. General Holmes's attempt at price controls "were the subject of considerable complaint both on practical and constitutional grounds and appear to have been ineffective."[1]

[October 15, 1862] Got up this morning early. The weather foggy, but fine at noon. Was up at Mrs. Burnell's & after took a ride out to Mosby's. Can't learn any news. Heard none since the 18th ult. I was surprised seeing a lot of Northern Meadowlarks this morning. They sang beautiful & gayly. They are on their migratory tour, but got astray in the fog. There are none in this section. Pigeons, geese & ducks are flying plenty. River is still rising. Read all afternoon.

Gunther is finally to receive some war news concerning the Battle of Corinth. Fought October 3–4, 1862, between the armies of Union general William S. Rosecrans and Confederate general Earl Van Dorn, it began when Van Dorn attacked Union entrenchments. On the first day he was successful in pushing the Yankees back, opening a breach in their lines, and attacking with Sterling Price's force. Waiting until the next day to finish off the Federals proved to be a mistake, as Rosecrans regrouped and Van Dorn was forced to retreat, giving up Corinth. Gunther is not only depressed at the Southern defeat at Corinth but sees this loss and the subsequent tighter Union grip on the Mississippi River and northern Mississippi as further impeding his chances of resuming productive river business.

> [October 16, 1862] News of a fight at Corinth, a Confederate victory of course, but nothing from Virginia. I am very anxious to hear from there. None for a month. Took a walk up to McCall's this morning and spent the balance of the day reading. The river is rising yet. It looks very much like the Mississippi now. The day has been fine. Our life is dull & monotonous & getting more so every day with no better prospects.

> [October 17, 1862] This has been a fine warm day. Gallenippers are getting plenty & are annoying us tremendously again. I read pretty near all day. Some extracts from London *Punch* collection—very good indeed. The river is falling again. Pigeons are flying thick. Reports today: Feds, a big victory at Corinth. I am of the opinion that our residence will be prolonged here for the winter. Sorry for it, indeed.

> [October 18, 1862] The river is receding again pretty fast. The *Ashley* came up. The Captain & lady gone to the Rock. The day has been bright. I read part of the day, Burns. Some of his poems are beautiful, their beauty lying in their simplicity of diction and his subject—that of the suffering poor; he being one himself. I wrote a poem on news from home in honor of Mrs. Smith for running the blockade to bring us news but I am unable to do justice to it today.

Charles Gunther is sensing an urgency to leave his present landing and get back to business. He is finding the leisure time reading, visiting, and playing cards to be relaxing but not productive. His ambition is stifled, his prospects for the future are limited by his present confinement at the landing, and boredom is beginning to take its toll. This, coupled with increasing Confederate setbacks and a realization that Southern papers are increasingly optimistic despite the facts, enable him to envision himself as one of Burns's "suffering poor."

> [October 19, 1862] This has been a very quiet Sabbath day with us. I read all morning & Howard & I took a walk at noon. I have thought over many things of home & the future don't appear to trouble my mind the least. Except the small matter of our getting away from this landing & get started in business again.

> [October 20, 1862] It was cold this morning. We had a fire for some time. The *Ashley* went down. The *Bracelet* & *Key West* went up this Eve. I read some & wrote a rhapsody. Howard & I took a walk up to McCall's, learnt the Feds at Helena yet. News is hard to get from any section. None from Virginia.

> [October 21, 1862] I take a walk every morning before breakfast nowadays. The mornings are fresh, no frost yet, but heavy dews. I read some & Howard & I took a walk out to Sommers. Heard of a fight in Kentucky. The Feds victorious. Bragg & Buell I suppose. Money no object for a paper nowadays. A rare delicacy to read one indeed.

In August of 1862, Confederate general Braxton Bragg, who successively commanded the Army of Mississippi and the Army of Tennessee, brought his forces to Corinth and was charged with improving the poor discipline and morale of Confederate troops in this area. In August 1862, Bragg invaded Kentucky, hoping to solidify Confederate control of the state. He won a tactical victory at Perryville against General Don Carlos Buell, although the invasion of Kentucky was a general failure. This was the battle that Gunther had heard of and he was correctly informed that it was a Federal victory. General Bragg later commanded at Stone's River and Chickamauga, but by 1864 his increasing unpopularity and lack of battlefield success precipitated his recall to Richmond to serve as a military advisor to President Davis.

[October 22, 1862] I see a Rock Extra of the 20th. Fed news 13th particulars of fight at Corinth & some account of the battle in Kentucky. Confederates in Chambersburgh, Pennsylvania. I am very anxious to hear further. Was out at Mosby's for meal. Took dinner with them. A good one & enjoyed it of course. I think there will be a stir in this state before long. Day fine.

Braxton Bragg (1817–76), courtesy Library of Congress

[October 23, 1862] This is a fine day. The *Little Rock* went down with a lot of Federal prisoners on—going to Helena. Howard was gone around with them. The Captain & Lady got back. I walked out to Mosby's with the madame at noon. We got a Chicago paper of the 15 ult. I read it with great attention. It is a long time since I have had the pleasure of perusing one. Reports of Buell's Army being annihilated in Kentucky.

Chambersburg, a borough of south-central Pennsylvania, was the scene of an October 10, 1862, raid by 1,800 cavalrymen under Confederate general J. E. B. Stuart. They destroyed $250,000 of railroad property and seized 500 guns, hundreds of horses, and at least "eight hundred young colored men and boys." They failed however to accomplish the main target of the raid—the burning of the railroad bridge across the Conocoheague Creek at

Scotland, Pennsylvania. The Chicago paper Gunther was reading was the *Chicago Times*, which began publication in 1854 and eventually merged with the *Chicago Herald* in 1895. Founded by James W. Sheahan with support from Illinois Senator Stephen A. Douglas, it took on a decidedly Copperhead point of view after 1861, supporting Southern Democrats and denouncing Lincoln's policies. General Ambrose E. Burnside suppressed the paper in 1863, but the ban was lifted shortly afterward by Lincoln.

> [October 24, 1862] The night was cold. I got up pretty late. I miss Howard considerable. I spent nearly all morning up at Mrs. Burnell and read all the balance of the day. Some of *Harper's* old magazines. The *Ashley* went up. Prospects now are very poor to get home this winter. I think. Read my *Chicago Times* over again, markets & all.

> [October 25, 1862] There is a hard cold wind all morning, with some sleet & snow, an extraordinary day for this country. I never got off the boat. Stayed around the stove all day reading & mending up old pants, something we got to do nowadays for want of better. Buying anything being out of the question. The *Tahlequah* went up.

> [October 26, 1862] A heavy frost last night. The leaves are now commencing to fall. The sun shone all day, fine & clear. I am sorry to say this day was a very dull one to me. My thoughts were in a perfect state of melancholy. Have no reason for it. Read some to kill time. Only fragmentary reading would suit me to muse with the poets. Mrs. McGinnis came aboard this noon.

Charles Gunther has been reduced to re-reading old papers and magazines, as news is still extremely hard to come by. It is obvious that life aboard the boat, without cargo or a definite plan of business activity in the future, is becoming dull and monotonous. Small spats are breaking out among some crew members; others are taking short trips to Little

Rock in hopes of breaking the tedium, but Gunther is staying with the boat, hoping for an improvement in both war news and the weather, and missing home and friends terribly.

> [October 27, 1862] A beautiful fine day. Passed the day reading & taking a walk at noon after pecans. See late paper of the 23d. Confederates claim victories in Kentucky at Perryville. I am in a gloomy state of mind on account of a quarrel with Harry. He is wholly to blame & I am going to stand on my dignity & self-defense. Captain & Howard are on their trip to Helena yet. See some Northern Blue Birds on their migratory tour.

> [October 28, 1862] Got up rather late. Mornings cold. I spent all day reading over an old bound volume of *Rollow's Pictoral* & took a short stroll towards Eve down to the Bayou. The day is fine & warm. I feel lonesome since Howard is gone. I feel the time more for a week past than ever and hope that my time of imprisonment will soon end, at least I feel such. Retire early.

Rollow's Pictoral probably refers to *A Picture Book for Rollo*, one of a series of popular children's novels written by Jacob Abbott (1803–79).

> [October 29, 1862] Manage to get up by 7 & 6-1/2 in mornings. I was up at Mrs. Burnell's this A.M. Buck & others have gone out a hunting. I am anxiously looking for the Little Rock from Helena. I am anxious to hear some news. I spent balance day reading some old bound *Harpers*. The day is fine & warm.

> [October 30, 1862] A beautiful warm day. Went down to Mosby's this morning & also up to Burnell's. The *Key West* went down this morning, landed here, no news. Looked for the *Rock* sure today, but didn't come. I don't feel alright for a few days past. Headache. The river is quite low again. I feel piqued at not going around on the *Little Rock* &c.

[October 31, 1862] Thus has October past & yet I am no better off & prospect no better than six months ago for my ever getting away from here. Getting more tiresome than ever. Looking for the Rock up, no hopes that I see. The river is falling & very low. A fine day. I stayed on boat all day. Buck was down to see us. Read my Chicago paper over again & *Harpers* all day.

November 1862
November opens with Charles Gunther again bemoaning the lack of news, as it has now been over three anxiety-filled weeks since the last paper got through to the boat. While he is anxiously waiting for news of the war, he is expanding his usual pursuits of reading, visiting, and fishing by taking up writing rhapsodies, poems, and short stories. But more significantly, he makes his first mention of making taffy candy—a practice that will, after the war, lead him to Europe to perfect his skills in candy making, and then to Chicago, where he will found the Gunther Candy Company.

[November 1, 1862] November has come in bright & warm, a summer day. I went up to Mrs. Burnells this morning. Stayed on boat & read some. Wrote a poem "Beauties of Plum Bayou." We are all anxiously for our folks from Helena, 10 days out now. No news for 30 days. Oh! What a world, country rather.

[November 2, 1862] I passed the Sabbath very quiet, reading & writing all day. All has passed pleasant aboard. Mrs. McGinnis fixing up old scrap book. We are yet without any news. The Captain & Howard not back yet. Now 11 days out. No news for 22 days. Oh! What a life, but they say ignorance is bliss. It won't hold good in my case, but I think there is a good time a coming.

[November 3, 1862] Cold & chilly this morning. Not anything to note today. Have not been off the boat. Fine and warm at noon. I spent the greater part of the day writing "Leolela," & I think if I

> make all as good as the first it will do. We are making some Taffy candy, i.e. the madam. No news today again. Let her rip.

When Gunther finally receives newspapers from New York, Cincinnati, Saint Louis, and Chicago he reads each of them cover to cover, trying to absorb the real state of affairs beneath the biased rhetoric of the source. After a thorough reading, he begins to look at the cause of the South in more dubious terms, clearly wondering what the fate of his new nation might be.

> [November 4, 1862] Got up nowadays at 7 & sometimes a little before. I spent all day aboard boat again writing "Leolela" average about 180 lines a day, besides other work, which is not much. Mrs. McGinnis has gone to Colwells. The *Era* went down with some ammunition. No news again. A kingdom for a paper again. We must make the best out of it like it or not.

> [November 5, 1862] A pleasant day. All quiet on board. We were much surprised by the entering of Howard just from Helena. All pleased to hear the news, and had the pleasure of seeing paper of the 24 ult. of New York, Chicago, St. Louis & Cincinnati. We had a great time reading them, a rich treat indeed and which may be well imagined. Breakers ahead.

> [November 6, 1862] Got up early. The morning cold but sunshine all day. Read papers all day nearly. Went down to Mosby's for meal. See many things new to me and names familiar with old times. The state of affairs look dubious to me, so we must look out for the future. Things no telling will come on us. Read until late.

An avid reader, Gunther finally gets to read some of Leslie's magazines. *Frank Leslie's Weekly* was an illustrated literary and news magazine founded in 1852 and continuing in business until 1922. Throughout its publishing career, the weekly provided illustrations and reports, first with woodcuts and daguerrotypes, later with more advanced photography, of wars and military actions from John Brown's raid at Harper's Ferry and the major battles of the Civil War to the Spanish American War and World War I. During the Civil War it took a strong pro-Union stance.

Image of Frank Leslie's Weekly, *from 1857*

[November 7, 1862] I sat around on boat all day writing. Finished "Leolela" and reading. The weather is pleasant. Went up to McCall's this Eve. See a late paper, but nothing new particular. Things commencing to be pressed in this state. The Feds are coming in at all points. It appears. Sat up late in the Eve reading.

[November 8, 1862] This month appears to be passing very fast. Time is indeed short to me. The Captain & madam are out at Mosby's yet. I see a prairie chicken this Eve—the first I see for a long time. Game is very plentiful but no ammunition. I see more pigeons yesterday than I ever see before in my life. We had two good pigeon dinners yesterday & today. Barker was up today. Read some of *Leslie's Magazines*.

[November 9, 1862] This has been a quiet day with us. It is pretty cool but warm this Eve. I read most all morning. Howard & I took a walk this noon. My mind is occupied by war thoughts only, and many are my thoughts how this & that might be done, but of course all castles built in the air and imaginary battles fought in the brain.

Charles Gunther makes the interesting comment that prairie chickens and game of every sort is readily available, but ammunition is scarce. Obviously appropriated by the military for battle usage, it spared the local flocks of pigeons, chickens, and other animals that might otherwise have been killed and eaten. It was more important to kill Yankees than to hunt dinner! He also begins speculating how battles and engagements should be fought and won, suggesting that he and the crew with whom he frequently discusses war events are becoming increasingly disillusioned with the current crop of Confederate commanding generals. This questioning of current military strategy, coupled with increasing inflation and a devaluation of Confederate currency, as well as the scarcity of commerce and a way of supporting himself is alarming Gunther and stirring thoughts of depression regarding the war's outcome.

> [November 10, 1862] This week opened with a fine & pleasant day. I read around on the boat all morning & after dinner. Howard & I went down to McNeel's, bought a lot of eatables. Everything is at an enormous price nowadays beyond any former belief of prices possible in America. Captain & family are all aboard again for a few days rest.

> [November 11, 1862] The weather has clouded up some & prospects of rain. I was up at Burnell's this morning—rode a mule out to Mosby's. Took dinner and had my hair cut close—to nothing I might say. Feel better now & something I long desired. There is no news, but all the talk is what they are going to do if the Feds come. Everybody for themselves. Some have curious notions.

> [November 12, 1862] I had some very pleasant dreams last night of home of course & many things were vividly brought to my mind. This is a disagreeable cloudy day. Barker was up. I wrote

considerable, copied "Leolela" in ink. The river is very low yet. I am more anxious every day to leave & get away from here.

Gunther receives the news that General William S. Rosecrans has replaced Buell. Rosecrans, a graduate of West Point, an engineer and inventor, achieved early successes during the Civil War in West Virginia and at Iuka and Corinth. He likewise defeated Bragg at Stone's River. His strategic movements caused Bragg to abandon Chattanooga, but his pursuit of Bragg ended at the Battle of Chickamauga, where his unfortunately worded order mistakenly opened a gap in the Union line and he and one-third of his army were swept from the field. Rosecrans was subsequently relieved of command by Grant and reassigned to the Department of Missouri. This would have been the news Gunther heard and was in conjunction with news of the flight of many area residents to avoid Federal intrusions. Gunther observes this flight of area residents, along with their slaves and is apprehensive about what this means for himself and his crew, stranded at the landing.

[November 13, 1862] This is a fine warm day, fine November weather. I went out to Bucks on business. No news for some time now again & of course we are thinking something must have turned up ere this. We are fixing up the boat & expectations are that we will run again as soon as we have water. Hope so anyhow.

[November 14, 1862] We manage to get breakfast by 7 nowadays. We had some duck traps set last night, but nary duck this morning. I was out to Buck twice. See a Rock paper of the 8. News Rosecrans supercedes Buell & that is about all I can see. Feds up at Fayetteville and many of our neighbors are making preparations to leave for other quarters, with niggers, as soon as the Feds come.

[November 15, 1862] The Captain started for the Bluff this morning. The day is fine and all very quiet. We have nothing new but much talking about leaving this section if the Feds should get

General Rosecrans (1819–98), from Harper's Weekly, November 8, 1862

up this way at all. It appears to be the general topic. Read some & walked up to McCall's in the Eve with Howard. I am a little uneasy about the future.

War news continues to arrive at the *Rose Douglas*, but even as Gunther speculates, much of it is false. News of the final recognition by Britain and France of the Confederacy proves to be just another rumor. Despite numerous insinuations in the British and French press hinting at possible recognition, neither country went beyond declaring neutrality during the war and neither formally recognized the South as a separate nation. Likewise, news of an armistice is wishful thinking that, while talked about in the North by Copperheads and some Democrats and in the South by those hoping to avoid further bloodshed, never approached a serious stage of negotiations. Only the 1864 election, still in the future, held any hope for a truce to end the bloodshed.

[November 16, 1862] As usual a very dull Sabbath to me. Of course there is nothing in our surroundings that would inspire anyone, but only the thoughts of the past and what the Sabbath has been to me once. The chimes of the bells and the well dressed tidy people & stillness of all business is not seen here, but the same from day in to day out. Read some & wrote a couple pieces of poetry.

[November 17, 1862] The day is rainy but warm & no fire is necessary. The men are getting the boat ready for business when water comes. I was on boat all day reading &c. Not doing anything particular. No news. Some talk of an armistice again, but as usual, humbug, I suppose. I don't know what to think hardly, but something will turn up in my favor before long, I believe.

[November 18, 1862] I got up during the night in a heavy thunderstorm & rain. The boat moved about considerable. It has continued to rain on & off all day. The Captain got back last night. News that England & France had recognized the Southern confederacy. Said to be a fixed fact this time. Feds at Holly Springs moving down. I read some old magazines all day & wrote some. Some prospect of moving now. The river coming up. The *Corsan* gone down.

The crew of the *Rose Douglas* is spending considerable time now readying the boat for a renewal of commercial trade. Rugs are being scrubbed, the wheel polished, and the decks cleaned. Clearly this is being done in hopes that the ship again can resume plying the rivers as before its current mooring. Gunther receives a late newspaper reporting the previous rumors of an armistice and recognition as false—and again is beginning to sense his own future may be caught up in the success or failure of the Southern confederacy. This is further amplified by shortages of food, powder, ammunition, and hope. But the crew persists, and the *Rose Douglas* is ready to resume sailing the Mississippi and White Rivers.

[November 19, 1862] The day has been continually blustering & rain. The river is coming up slowly. Salley at Burnell's is very sick. I spent the greater part of the day reading, went up to McCall's in the Eve. I see any quantity of game but we have no powder to shoot. Johnny Jones got up from Pine Bluff this Eve. Read till late this Eve, night cool.

[November 20, 1862] Went up to Burnell's early this morning. Got horse & went to Mosby's for meal. Had a pleasant chat. Took dinner. Mr. Reeves was also there. See some late papers. News up to the 5th inst. Heavy movements in Tennessee. Nothing from the state. Armistice & recognition humbug again. The day is cold & windy. Spent most all day absent from the boat.

[November 21, 1862] This is a fine bright summer day. We took up carpets & scrubbed overhead. Hard work to me but enjoyed it & I always am able to eat a hearty meal after doing a good day's work. Salley is yet very sick. The *Tahlequah* went down this A.M. We are getting ready to run. Read some & retired early.

Gunther is finally realizing his dream of leaving the landing and heading back to river travel. The boat has been thoroughly cleaned, the crew certainly rested, and provisions stored. While war news is depressing, and a battle looms large at any moment, the *Rose Douglas* finally pulls out of port and heads to Colwell's Landing. At Colwell's Gunther buys a load of peanuts (the only crop available) and goes on an expedition searching for corn, butter, and eggs. While supplies are still available, prices continue to rise due to inflation and sheer scarcity. The river crew, however, is still experiencing more luck in securing food than the hungry Confederate soldiers continually on the march. Gunther realizes this and is happy that supplies are still available and his crew well provisioned.

[November 22, 1862] Up early & at it. Frank & I did a big days work. Cabin looks fine & clean. We have no news of any kind. Getting the wheel up today. This is another very fine day. We had a very good dinner, some fresh beef, a luxury nowadays. I am some now on corn & like it very well, it being 2/3 of what we eat.

[November 23, 1862] I slept well last night. Had some home dreams. I put down carpet this morning again and all looks natural. Salley died last night at 8 o'ck. He was a fine man & had much suffering with disease for years. Learnt today that ___ stole a march on Hindman & a battle is expected at any hour. Matters look critical in this section. Went up to Burnell's in the Eve.

The deceased was William H. Salley (b. ca. 1812, South Carolina), a relative of Mrs. Bonnell.

> [November 24, 1862] Set up with Salley's corpse all night in company with Bell. I layed myself down for a sleep this A.M. at 5 & got up at 9. Busy all day cleaning & helping below all hands pitching in. We got steam up in the Eve & dropped down to Mrs. Colwell's landing. The day has been very fine. I feel quite tired this Eve & retired early.

Finally the *Rose Douglas* begins to journey up river with a sizeable contingent of blacks aboard. Her sister ships, the *Bracelet* and *St. Francis*, passed them with large contingents of soldiers on board, being shipped downriver to Arkansas Post. Troops are being shifted in this area, the Union fleet has not yet secured Vicksburg and completely closed the river, and commerce and movement of soldiers and blacks is providing a substantial portion of the work available to the boats.

> [November 25, 1862] This has been another very busy day with all of us. Working in general and getting ready for the corn. Howard & I went down to Mrs. McNeal's this noon. Bought a lot of peanuts. Could get nothing else. No news of any kind for some time & it is hard telling what is going on. Some ladies were down this noon. Retired early.

> [November 26, 1862] I took a long trip today. Started early this morning for the Clear Lake regions in a mule cart. Had a good time through a rough country. See any quantity of game, some fine deer. Was very successful in my trip. Got plenty of butter & eggs &c., but high prices. The boat was loaded by 9 o'ck. & all ready to start.

> [November 27, 1862] We got started by daylight on our trip. Plenty of niggers aboard & are steaming up slowly. The *Bracelet*

& *St. Francis* went down with a lot of soldiers for the Post. We expected to get to the Rock this Eve but could not make it. Too much head wind. Layed up below Fouch Bar for the night. Retired early.

Gunther closes out November with thoughts of the gloom pervading most of this river area. Soldiers are seemingly directionless and wandering about, no real offensive is being mounted against Union intrusions; prices of clothing, food, and lodging are soaring—a shirt cost approximately three weeks' pay and a hotel room approximately a week's pay. An aura of defeat hangs in the air, and Gunther and his crew sense the impending doom of military setbacks to come.

[November 28, 1862] Made an early start & reached the Rock by 9. Nothing new. Many former reports turn out untrue. The city looks natural and considerable stir amongst the Quartermaster & Commissary Departments. Commenced onloading but made poor progress. I walked allover the place, visited the newspaper offices & stalked over town in general.

[November 29, 1862] Little Rock. The weather continues fine. I met many old acquaintances today—also accidentally run across Bradshaw of Searcy. Was very glad to see him. Learned much news from him of Searcy County matters. Walked over town a good deal. The *Era* came up from the Post. We run up to the mill this Eve to unload, bought me two shirts this Eve. Paid only $10 each. Retired early.

The Searcy County news Gunther refers to regarded Searcy County, Arkansas, established in 1835 and named for Richard Searcy, the first clerk and judge of the Arkansas Territory. During the Civil War, Searcy County provided two companies of soldiers to the Confederacy, although a Unionist Peace Society was also formed in the county. Nearly a hundred of these Union sympathizers were rounded up and forced into

Confederate service under Colonel John S. Marmaduke of the 18th Arkansas. After the war, Union veterans took control of the county and have held it for the Republican Party ever since.

For Bradshaw, see the diary entries for January and February 1861.

> [November 30, 1862] Howard & I went up to church this morning. The day is fine. Everything is selling very high. Boots $40 & $50—& clothing such as it is at an exorbitant price. Provisions the same. Board at hotel $4 per day. I was up at the Anthony House this noon and see a good many soldiers. Some people stirring & all looks gloomy and dead. I spent the Eve reading.

At $40-$50, boots were selling for ten times the price they sold for prior to the war.

Located on Merchant Street, the Anthony House was described by a Little Rock newspaper as "the principal hotel in Little Rock."

December 1862

While the *Rose Douglas* is again plying the rivers, Gunther is still finding time to read and relax. He is dining with friends, writing letters, absorbing false reports of Confederate victories, and trying to maintain his active life style. One of the new novels he is reading is *Women in White.* This was an epistolary novel written by Wilkie Collins in 1859. The story is a detective yarn, fictional in character, in which the hero, Walter Hartright, a drawing teacher, is employed by Mr. Fairlie to teach his niece and heiress Laura. Walter and Laura fall in love, but Laura is promised to Sir Glyde, her father's friend. A strange lady in white appears after Laura's sudden death in London (a staged death where Laura was locked in an asylum to gain control of her fortune). Laura eventually marries Hartright and later they inherit their own estate and become wealthy. Gunther's romantic longings take center stage with this novel and, based on his previous literary efforts, show a definite bent for this type of love and romance novel.

[December 1, 1862] We got unloaded this noon. I am up town all morning. See Bradshaw. Sent two letters up the country & paid him $10.00 for Asa Hoffman. Some false reports about the street again about a battle in Va. Nothing going on below that we know of. Got started this noon & got only as far as Fouch Bar. Wood here and retired early. Some rain.

[December 2, 1862] Got an early start but made poor time running down, hitting some snags. The day is cold & some rain. Got to Colwell's Landing after dinner. I am glad we have got a horse. I can now ride around some. Mrs. Caldwell got severely hurt this noon by the team running away. All is now quiet again on board & will probably lay here some time again.

[December 3, 1862] The day has been very fine and pleasant. Took our horse off and rode up to McCall's. Took dinner at Burnell's, and at noon rode down to Slover's. All hands loading boat again. River falling yet. Am very sorry. Love to keep a going again. Active life what suits me. These times & love to get where we get some news.

[December 4, 1862] I went up to Hawthorne this morning. The day is cold, cloudy & windy. Took all of Mrs. Caldwell's corn on. I did very little myself today. Read some to kill time, Wilkie Collins's *Women in White*. A very good tale. I am in a kind of unquiet state of mind for a few days past and I never feel happier than when I am engaged writing something.

For the next several days, Gunther and his crew spend time repairing the boat, hunting wild game, and loading cargo. But behind this seemingly calm exterior lies the crew's uneasiness that Yankees are approaching, the river will be shut, and their way of making a living will be destroyed. This disquietude is pervasive and Gunther's melancholy comes through in his writing, his overhearing much talk of Yankees invading, observing slaves fleeing the war zone and abandoning plantations, and of the real threat they may be captured or sunk by Union gunboats. Despite these fears, Gunther and his friends go about routine tasks with at least the external appearance of hope and an expectation of better conditions ahead.

> [December 5, 1862] There was a white mantle of snow over everything this morning, the most snow I see for two years or more. The sun came out clear and warm & all melted again. I went down the river some 6 miles on horseback for tar, but failed. No news again for some time and it is hard telling what has taken place. I wrote some this Eve of a dream.

> [December 6, 1862] Another bright day overhead, but muddy underfoot. I was up at Hawthorne's this morning. Found one of the Missourian's laying in the wood severely hurt by being thrown from a horse. Nothing of any interest to note, but looking out for something ahead. There is much talk about the Yankees among the people. Some think they will get here.

> [December 7, 1862] A bright & fine day. Went down to Mosby's this morning. See some late Rock papers with dates up to the 20 ult. reliable. Nothing but preparations appear to be the order of the day. Something very shortly will turn up in my opinion before very long. Lots of niggers down on the boat today. Spent the Eve reading & retired early.

Gunther and his crew are enjoying an interlude in their loading cargo and keeping their ship trim. They have the opportunity for the first time of watching horse races with some of the Missouri soldiers they are ferrying. Horse racing was a popular sport among soldiers (as was racing lice). Bets were common on these events and they all provided a peaceful respite to the sights and sounds of the battlefield. Gunther also makes an insightful comment on the condition of the people in the bayou country—people who are thin, sallow, and cadaverous. The war has obviously taken a toll on the health of area residents due to a lack of food and a healthy variety in diet. Additionally, many able-bodied men were off to war, leaving the sickly and unfit behind to tend the meager crops.

> [December 8, 1862] I went up to Mosby's this morning. Fixed up his Post Office account current. The day is very fine. The bayou is very full of ducks & wild fowls of all kinds & the woods full of game, but no ammunition. The weather continues fine. Howard has gone to the Bluff & returned making a ride of 45 miles & doing business with our new horse. Very good I think, under the circumstances.

> [December 9, 1862] We had considerable sport today. Two horse races by our neighbors, the Missourians, a jolly gay set of men & full of fun, healthy & able-bodied, something we don't often see in this section. There is always some complaint of some kind among the men, or a wan cadaverous look about them in all these bottoms. Day bright & very fine. Read in the Eve.

> [December 10, 1862] Another race this morning & considerable fun but an accident this noon which has stopped the sport for the present. Man & horse hurt severely. I went up to Mrs. Burnell's this noon and rode around considerable on Texas. He paces very fine & I think the captain made a good bargain in my opinion. There is speed in him. It is very pleasant to have a horse here, to go out & ride around the country.

For the first time Gunther mentions the effect of the Union blockade on Southern ports. He is longing for some of the food and drink that was imported prior to the war. The diet of corn and small game is getting monotonous and depriving him and his crew of those few luxuries that made life on the river enjoyable. He also speculates that there are increasing Federal troop movements on the Mississippi, that McCulloch's Division is heading for Vicksburg (a rumor which proved false), and that there is momentum in troop movements that signal some pressing war developments—all of which he agonizes over because of his inability to get war news, especially accurate news.

> [December 11, 1862] A beautiful day. The Captain & Howard have gone to the Rock this A.M. & the men a hunting. I stayed aboard boat all day reading & writing. The *Tahlequah* went down to the Post. I am very contented in mind nowadays, and am looking & thinking of many things of the war—but all castles in the air. I am afraid.

> [December 12, 1862] Got up early and as usual did little of nothing all day. Reading some. It is very lonesome aboard. All gone away. It tried to rain some but rained very little. Frank caught a very large fish. We had some fine ducks for dinner. I am getting so that I am forgetting a good deal about the blockade—thoughts sometimes rise for something to eat & drink of old.

> [December 13, 1862] Weather continues very pleasant & warm. Comfortable without fire. It was very quiet on board today. I read most of the time. Tom & Jack got up from DeWitt this morning & the Captain & Howard from the Rock. See some papers with dates up to the 25 ult. Late news for this country. We are about 3 weeks behind the age. It is hard but nevertheless true.

One of the newspapers Gunther manages to get hold of is the *Saint Louis Republican*. It began operating in 1848 and became the first paper in the Missouri-Arkansas region to publish a Sunday edition. After the great Saint Louis fire of 1849 and the cholera epidemic, some ministers said God had visited Saint Louis with fire and pestilence because the newspaper was violating the Sabbath with its Sunday edition. During the war, however, it continued to publish extensive war accounts and was read by area residents who desired news, albeit slanted, of the outcomes of events and battles. Gunther never limits himself to one publication however, and is a voracious reader of any paper he can obtain.

> [December 14, 1862] A dull, rainy Sabbath. Everything as usual on board. Reports say Hindman had a fight on the 5th & cleaned Feds out. Nothing but preparations appear to be the order of the day among the Feds & by this time there must have something taken place. No news since the 25th ult. I don't know what to make of it in this state, but time will tell. McCullough Division gone to Vicksburgh.

Here Gunther hears a garbled version of the Prairie Grove campaign, in which Hindman's Confederate army, after an initial success, was forced to retreat.

> [December 15, 1862] It has rained heavy all night & this morning. The river is rising to our great delight. Commenced loading this noon & intend to start in the morning. I rode down to Williams for butter all afternoon. The roads are very bad. Any quantity of niggers working at the corn, also tonight. I retired early feeling very tired.

> [December 16, 1862] Got started by 1 o'clock & wooded until 11-1/2. All aboard feeling good & ready for operations. The river is rising fast. A beautiful day. Got up stream some 15 miles below the Rock. Layed up for the night. All is very pleasant aboard. I am very short of a crew, but pitch in myself, anxious to hear some news.

The *Rose Douglas* is again working for the Confederate government. This time they are on a mission delivering supplies to General Hindman's forces in northwest Arkansas. This necessitates a trip up the Arkansas River, past Little Rock and Dardanelle, on to Norristown, and finally to Fort Smith. Norristown, now standing as a single, weather-ravaged log cabin and the remnants of a native stone chimney, was, during the Civil War, one of the most important towns between Little Rock and Fort Smith. It became a hub of river and steamboat traffic with sugar, salt, hardware, and dry goods going upriver and cotton going down to New

Orleans. Lewisburg, then the county seat of Conway County, is situated on the north bank of the Arkansas River. Spodra Bluffs, Arkansas, is located in Pope County also and was part of the area consisting of Norristown, Lewisburg, and Dardanelle that comprised the marketplace of this transriver county. Thus, the crops and supplies available in these river centers became an important supply source for Western Confederate armies.

> [December 17, 1862] Made the Rock by 10. Run over the place some & had considerable trouble getting stores for boat out of commissary. See a late paper of this place but no news. Nothing later than the 25 ult. That is hard but I must stand it I suppose. We are ordered up to Fort Smith with our load to Hindman's army. Satisfactory to us. I want to go up to the seat of war. Layed up for the night above the Rock.

> [December 18, 1862] We got along rather slowly. See nothing of interest to note. The river is falling slowly. We have some fears we will not get up. All are lively aboard & living very good for these times. I think the *Ashley* gone up with General Holmes. Made Lewisburgh in the Eve & layed up for the night. Stayed aboard all Eve.

> [December 19, 1862] The weather continues fine. Made a very good run. Passed Dardanelles & Norristown & also a couple of boats. Everything looks very dull & dead. A good many movers at the ferries. See a lot of Marmaduke's [Confederate] Cavalry pass down the road. Layed up for the night a few miles below Piney. Retired early.

Gunther's travels on the Arkansas River ferrying troops and supplies have gotten him in the war spirit and now, for the first time, he is dreaming about being on the war front. Perhaps he feels this is the only way to get accurate war news, or perhaps he is feeling the need to witness accounts first-hand so he knows they are true and he does not have to get his hopes up regarding Confederate victories or read about them three weeks later. He cruises down to Frog Bayou Bar, where that bayou flows into the Arkansas River. Frog Bayou is usually navigable from late fall through mid-spring and is bounded by dense strands of pines, oaks, elms, pecan, and walnut trees covering narrow mountains that border the scenic bayou. These small landings are frequented by Gunther and, perhaps because of the beautiful scenery, engender thoughts of home and loved ones.

> [December 20, 1862] Made an early start again, but made only some 60 miles. Passed Spodra Bluffs. Took on a passenger. We hear nothing new. All quiet above. We are living very good for these times. The whole country around here is eat out. Several boats passed us this Eve, after tying up. Some of our passengers got on smaller ones. I retired as usual early.

> [December 21, 1862] It looks a little like rain. The river is yet falling. Got on a snag—but no damage. Had considerable trouble all day & made only 25 miles. Tried to pull the *Arkansas* off but was ineffectual. Had to burn rails for wood. None to be had. Managed to get a late *Saint Louis Republican* of the 2nd inst. Was very glad to see it & read it with pleasure. See some news. Made Ozark in the Eve.

> [December 22, 1862] We made but a short run today, some 15 miles—rubbing the bars considerable—and of the opinion we will not get up. Nothing of any importance. Learn that the army is on the south side of the river. I am anxious to get up. I want to see some life again. So long since I seen any. No news now for 20 days. Something taken place ere this I imagine.

Gunther's ample diet of fresh meat, vegetables, and fruit has given way to subsistence on corn and an occasional fish caught from the river. There is no ammunition left to hunt with, and area residents are approaching the boat begging for food and looking starved. The river folk lack even the basic necessities of life, and this depresses Gunther in the rapidly approaching Christmas season. Home, family, and the horrible deprivations from the war are weighing on his mind and making this Christmas season a lonely and sad event.

As Gunther's diary makes clear, the Confederate supply line along the Arkansas River depended on riverboats that constantly ran aground. Ultimately, these delays in delivering supplies doomed Hindman's campaign to retake northwest Arkansas.

> [December 23, 1862] Got pulled off a snag yesterday eve and got up to Frog Bayou bar, where we are compelled to lay waiting for a boat to be lightened up. Made only two miles. Some rain this morning, but having no effect on the river. No news yet & feel very anxious now. But getting used to it some. Very much like last summer. Several small boats passed down. Young & Tucker gone up on the *Arkansas*.

> [December 24, 1862] Weather cleared off fine again. The river has fallen some 6 inches since we came here, and are now doomed to stay here for some time. O what a misery this laying here at Frog Bayou Bar to spend a Christmas. Home comes back again with renewed feelings. I know my parents are feeling for me.

> [December 25, 1862] O what a Christmas at Frog Bayou. Truly lamentable. See nothing at all day except two deer—all is dull & gloomy & as usual living on corn—the staple of life nowadays. I fret for home & folks again today. I know Mother is feeling for me, but I will make it up some future day. We are now waiting for water & then for Fort Smith. A good many citizens called & begged for a bushel of corn, nothing to eat. Retired early.

Finally Confederate forces are evacuating the Arkansas River hamlets frequented by Charles Gunther. There have been numerous small skirmishes over the last year in this area, but the forces of Union general James G. Blunt have finally broken through, caused a general Confederate retreat south, and burnt military supplies, wagons, and boats. General Blunt (1826–81) was a physician and abolitionist who attained the rank of major general. In 1857 his ardent views led him to join a force against the proslavery territorial government—a force including John Brown. He began the Civil War as colonel of the 2nd Kansas and by April 1862 was given command of the Department of Kansas. He subsequently fought at the First Battle of Newtonia, the Battle of Cane Hill, and the Battles of Prairie Grove, Honey Springs, and Westport. After the war he again practiced as a physician and a lawyer, but by 1879 was admitted to an asylum due to his increasingly erratic behavior. Gunther, however, considered him a friendly man and accompanied him up north in a fine carriage, observing the debris of war and the devastated landscape as they went.

> [December 26, 1862] The river has risen a few inches. We got up steam & made about 2 miles & 1/2 and as usual on a log. A great country this. People say the Feds are some 40 miles from here, but we will look out for No.1. There is a great deal of sickness around here. And, the decidedly poorest people I ever saw, not even the necessaries of life—dull Christmas week, but there is nothing like living on hope—and hope it is. Rob. Lewis looks on & says he won't fight.

> [December 27, 1862] We got underway again & ran to Van Buren Bar—where we stuck as usual. Several boats passed. The confederates are evacuating all this country as far as Spodra Bluffs. Everything is ordered below. Weather is fine and bracing. There are several aboard sick. Hear reports of the Feds getting whipped lately. Burnside & Lee at Fredericksburg. Sparing [sic] off this Eve.

> [December 28, 1862] Van Buren Bar. Howard & I went up to town for medicine & to our great surprise the Feds were skirmishing just above here, who came rushing in town capturing

5 boats, wagons, men &c. See several skirmishes and lively times in general. To our great joy we are once more in the land of freedom—am bound for home now—sure very much unexpected—but thank God I am free again to speak my opinion.

James G. Blunt, courtesy Library of Congress

General Blunt's forces unexpectedly swept down on Van Buren [December 28], brushing aside a weak Confederate guard. Blunt's troops captured the town, the sick and wounded Confederates convalescing there, and a store of supplies the Confederates desperately needed. Blunt also captured several river steamers, among them the *Key West*, the *Frederick Notrebe*, the *Era No. 6*, the *Van Buren*, the *Violet*, and the *Rose Douglas*. The Confederates burnt two other steamers to keep Blunt from capturing them. According to one report, the *Rose Douglas* carried a cargo of corn, sugar, and molasses when captured.

For Charles Gunther and the *Rose Douglas* the war is over. He is again heading home to the "land of freedom." He obviously is rejoicing at the opportunity to see his home and family, leave the devastation that has been brought to the Arkansas and Mississippi River towns, and again express his apparently pro-Union sentiments. He makes fast friends of General Blunt and is pleased to leave the boat and go home.

His views expressed earlier in his diaries, which seemed so outspokenly Confederate, are now brought into question: Did Gunther believe in the Union cause all along, or has he become a sudden convert as the tide has turned in the Union's favor?

> [December 29, 1862] Van Buren. We worked hard to get the boat up at 3 o'ck. The place is lively and any quantity of men—a different looking set from the Confederates. We packed up everything and made preparations to leave. Took up my quarters with Gen. Blunt, a very fine man indeed. I have fell in the hands of friends—All the boats were burnt and troops are moving out for camps at Cane Hill.

This final area Gunther is passing through, Cane Hill, is a ridge eight miles long and five miles wide in the southwest corner of Washington County, Arkansas. The Boston Mountains, in a high and deeply dissected plateau located in northern Arkansas and Eastern Oklahoma, are the source of many rivers and streams that flow from the mountains in all directions, including the White River, Buffalo River, and King's River. This will be the last area traversed by Gunther as he arrives at Blunt's headquarters at Rhea's Mills and begins his long journey back home.

> [December 30, 1862] We left this morning very early for the up country with the General. The country here is very rough and in a very desolated condition. All the troops are moving up for Fayetteville. We have a very fine old coach to ride in and all are well satisfied with it. Stayed for the night in an old house.

> [December 31, 1862] Moved along again. Crossed over Boston Mountain and passed through Cane Hill, a very small hamlet. All this country around has been the scene of many struggles in this war and we see many indications of it along the road. We arrived at Headquarters at Ray Mills in the Eve. There was quite a stirring scene music &c. All lively and full of fun. Sleep in a camp.

Gunther's diary ends here, in Rhea's Mill. His eagerness to return home was tempered by the fact that he was stranded in the hills of northwest Arkansas, hundreds of miles from the nearest railroad. Issued a horse, he rode with the withdrawing Union army back to its base at Fort Scott,

Kansas. From there he took a "liberated" (i.e., captured) coach to Fort Leavenworth, from where he arranged travel back to Illinois via river steamer and railroad. After a brief three-day reunion with family and friends, Gunther took a position with a bank in Peoria, Illinois, but only lasted there a short time, as he had a job offer in Chicago to become a traveling salesman for C. W. Sandford, a large wholesale confectionary house. This job became the starting point for a career that, according to one observer, made Gunther a fortune, made the name Gunther "a synonym for [the candy] trade," and founded the historical collections of the Chicago History Museum.

Notes

Diary, January–April 1861

1. Ralph Leland Goodrich diary, courtesy Arkansas History Commission.
2. William D. Baker, *History and Architectural Heritage of Searcy County*, Arkansas Historic Preservation Program, 9–10. Available at http://www.arkansaspreservation.com/pdf/publications/searcy_county.pdf [accessed May 24, 2012].
3. William H. Russell, *My Diary, North and South*, 2 vols. (Boston, New York: T. O. H. P. Burnham, O. S. Felt, 1863), 305.
4. *Memphis Appeal*, March 16, 1861.
5. John Hallum, *Diary of an Old Lawyer* (Nashville, Southwestern Publishing House, 1895), 225.
6. "Fanchon, The Cricket," *Memphis Appeal*, March 27, 1861.
7. *Memphis Appeal*, April 7, 1861.
8. Hallum, *Diary*, 152.
9. Marcus J. Wright, diary entry for April 23, 1861. Available at http://docsouth.unc.edu/fpn/wrightmarcus/menu.html [accessed May 28, 2012].
10. Russell, *Diary*, 309–310.

Diary, May–August 1861

1. Memphis Chamber of Commerce, First Annual Statement (1861), 9. Available at http://docsouth.unc.edu/imls/memphis/memphis.html [accessed May 27, 2012].
2. R. Lockwood Tower, ed., *A Carolinian Goes to War: The Civil War Narrative of Arthur Middleton Manigault, Brigadier General, C.S.A.* (Columbia: University of South Carolina Press, 1992), 78.
3. *Peru, Illinois, Centennial, May 25–26, 1935: Commemorating One Hundred Years of Peru's Existence* (Peru: Historical Committee, 1935), 7, 8. For more on the ice trade, see Gavin Weightman, *The Frozen Water Trade: A True Story* (New York: Hyperion, 2003).
4. *Macon* (Georgia) *Telegraph*, June 11, 1861.
5. Russell, *Diary*, 322.
6. James I. Robertson, *Stonewall Jackson* (New York: MacMillan, 1997), 247–251.
7. David Hinze and Karen Farnham, *The Battle of Carthage* (Campbell, CA: Savas Pub. Co.,1997).

8. Hallum, *Diary*, 225.
9. See Hughes and Stonesifer, *The Life and Wars of Gideon J. Pillow* (Chapel Hill: University of North Carolina Press, 1993), 180–181 for more on this proposed move—which never took place.
10. Elliott Ashkenazi, *The Civil War Diary of Clara Solomon: Growing Up in New Orleans, 1861–1862* (Baton Rouge: LSU Press, 1995), 273.
11. Stanley F. Horn, *The Army of Tennessee: A Military History* (Indianapolis: Bobbs Merrill, 1941), 28, 432.

Diary, September–December 1861
1. Memphis Chamber of Commerce, 1861, 16.
2. Russell, *Diary* for June 19, 1861, 325.
3. Terry's Texas Rangers website, http://www.terrystexasrangers.org [accessed May 28, 2012].
4. *Tennessee State Gazetteer and Business Directory for 1860–61* (Nashville: John L. Mitchell, 1860), 105.
5. Ibid., 249.
6. Ibid., 302.
7. Russell, *Diary*, 325.
8. *Tennessee State Gazetteer*, 16.
9. Russell, *Diary*, 326.
10. Ibid., 230.
11. Ibid., 234–235.
12. Mark Twain, *Life on the Mississippi* (Boston: James R. Osgood & Co., 1883), chapter 16.
13. See Bruce Allardice, *Confederate Colonels: A Biographical Register* (Columbia: University of Missouri Press, 2008), for more on Terry.

Diary, September–December 1862
1. Dougan, *Confederate Arkansas*, 97.

Select Bibliography

A Biographical History, with Portraits, of Prominent Men of the Great West. Chicago: Manhattan Publishing Company, 1894.

Abbott, Henry G., *Historical Sketch of the Confectionary Trade in Chicago: Compiled from Various Authentic Sources of Information.* Chicago: Jobbing Confectioners' Association, 1905.

"About the Building." In *Chicago History Museum,* 2008. Available at http://www.chicagohs.org

Alexander, Edward P. *Fighting for the Confederacy: The Personal Recollections of General Edward Porter Alexander.* Gary W. Gallagher, ed. Chapel Hill: University of North Carolina Press, 1989.

Allardice, Bruce S. *Confederate Colonels: A Biographical Register.* Columbia: University of Missouri Press, 2008.

Ashkenazi, Elliott. *The Civil War Diary of Clara Solomon: Growing Up in New Orleans, 1861–1862.* Baton Rouge: Louisiana State University Press, 1995.

Baker, William D. *History and Architectural Heritage of Searcy County, Arkansas.* Historic Preservation Program (n.d.). Available at http://www.arkansaspreservation.com/pdf/publications/searcy_county.pdf

Buenger, Nancy. "Gunther, Charles Frederick." In *American National Biography Online,* April 2003. Available at http://www.anb.org

"Charles F. Gunther," *Chicago Tribune,* August 1, 1908, 2.

"Charles Frederick Gunther." In *Dictionary of American Biography* vol. 26. New York: Charles Scribner's Sons, 1958.

"Charles Frederick Gunther." In *National Cyclopaedia of American Biography.* New York: J. T. White, 1910.

Curry, Josiah S., *Chicago, Its History and Its Builders.* Chicago: S. J. Clarke Publishing Company, 1918.

Dougan, Michael. *Confederate Arkansas.* Tuscaloosa: University of Alabama Press, 1990.

Goodspeed. *A Reminiscent History of the Ozark Region.* Chicago: Goodspeed Brothers, 1894.

Gunther Death Certificate, Cook County no. 7457 (1920).

Gunther Papers, Chicago History Museum.

"Gunther's New Building." *Chicago Tribune*, May 15, 1887, 17.

Hallum, John. *Diary of an Old Lawyer*. Nashville: Southwestern Publishing House, 1895.

Hinze, David and Karen Farnham. *The Battle of Carthage*. Campbell, CA: Savas Pub. Co.,1997.

Hoffman, U. J. *History of La Salle County, Illinois*. Chicago: Rand, McNally, and Company, 1906.

Horn, Stanley F. *The Army of Tennessee: A Military History*. Indianapolis: Bobbs Merrill, 1941.

Huddleston, Duane, *Steamboats and Ferries on the White River: A Heritage Revisited*. Conway, AR: University of Central Arkansas Press, 1995.

Hughes, Nathaniel and Roy Stonesifer. *The Life and Wars of Gideon J. Pillow*. Chapel Hill: University of North Carolina Press, 1993.

Illinois State Census for 1865 and 1866. Available at "Illinois State Census Collection," http://www.ancestry.com

Keating, John M. *History of the City of Memphis, Tennessee*. Syracuse: D. Mason and Company, 1888.

Knutson, Ted. "Believe It or Not, Museum Collections Tell a Story." *Chicago Tribune*, July 27, 1984, LF16.

Memphis Chamber of Commerce. First Annual Statement (1861). Available at http://docsouth.unc.edu/imls/memphis/memphis.html

Moses, John, *History of Chicago, Illinois*. Chicago and New York: Munsell and Company, 1895.

Mullen, William. "Finding True History amid the False." *Chicago Tribune*, July 5, 2007, C1.

National Archives, Washington, DC. Gunther passport application, 1867.

"Pneumonia Ends Active Career of C. F. Gunther." *Chicago Tribune*, February 11, 1920, 17.

Robertson, James I. *Stonewall Jackson*. New York: MacMillan, 1997.

Russell, William Howard. *My Diary North and South*. Boston, New York: T. O. H. P. Burnham, O. S. Felt, 1863.

Silvestro, Clement. "The Candy Man's Mixed Bag." *Chicago History*, Fall 1972.

Select Bibliography

Ship's passenger list, *Herculean*, 1842. Available at "Passenger Lists," http://www.ancestry.com

Stanton, Donal, Goodwin F. Berquist, and Paul C. Bowers, eds. *The Civil War Reminiscences of General M. Jeff Thompson*. Dayton, OH: Morningside Books, 1988.

Tennessee State Gazetteer, and Business Directory for 1860–61. Nashville: John L. Mitchell, 1860.

Terry's Texas Rangers, http://www.terrystexasrangers.org

"The Bloody Evidence." http://www.chicagohistory.org

"The Palace of Sweets," *Chicago Tribune*, August 23, 1872, 6.

Tower, R. Lockwood, ed. *A Carolinian Goes to War: The Civil War Narrative of Arthur Middleton Manigault, Brigadier General, C.S.A.* Columbia: University of South Carolina Press, 1992.

Twain, Mark. *Life on the Mississippi*. Boston: James R. Osgood & Co., 1883.

United States Census for the years 1850–1940. Available at "US Census Records," http://www.ancestry.com

Warner, Ezra J. *Generals in Gray: Lives of the Confederate Commanders*. Baton Rouge: Louisiana State University Press, 1959.

———. *Generals in Blue: Lives of the Union Commanders*. Baton Rouge: Louisiana State University Press, 1964.

Waterman, Arba, *Historical Review of Chicago and Cook County*. Chicago and New York: The Lewis Publishing Company, 1908, 1035.

Weightman, Gavin. *The Frozen Water Trade: A True Story*. New York: Hyperion, 2003.

Wendt, Lloyd, "Civil War Round Table," *Chicago Tribune*, February 29, 1948, B8.

Wright, Marcus J., diary. Available at http://docsouth.unc.edu/fpn/wrightmarcus/menu.html

Index

Adair, John K., 34, 35
Adams Bluff, Arkansas, 196
Algiers, Louisiana, 175, 187
Antietam (Sharpsburg), Battle of, 292, 294, 296, 297, 299, 300
Arkansas Post, Arkansas, 221, 246, 315, 321
Arkansas, C.S.S., 278-280
Ashley, William, 24
Augusta, Arkansas, 181, 182, 184, 197, 199

Ball's Bluff, Battle of, 149, 150
Barker, John Butler, 192, 309, 310
Barraque Tp., Arkansas, 262, 296
Batesville, Arkansas, 238
Baton Rouge, Louisiana, 172, 178, 187, 192, 201, 204, 280
Bean, Chauncey, 159
Beauregard, Pierre G. T., 106, 213, 224, 276
Belmont, Battle of, 156-158
Big Bethel, Battle of, 89, 90
Blunt, James G., xvii, 326-328
Bohlen, Mr., 48, 52, 54, 64, 69, 73, 84, 139, 143, 144, 151-153, 158, 169, 217, 220, 299
Bohlen, Phillip R., 53
Bohlen, William, 53
Bohlen, Wilson & Co., xii, 44, 52-54, 61, 70, 141
Bonaparte, Jerome, 111, 112
Bonnell, Ann E., 269, 271, 272, 275, 280, 283, 296, 298, 301, 305-307, 310, 313-315, 318, 320
Boonville, Battle of, 94, 95
Bowers, Peter, 79, 80
Bowling Green, Kentucky, 134, 138, 181, 203
Brack, J., 158
Bradshaw family, 30, 32, 316, 318
Bragg, Braxton, 286, 303, 304, 311
Brazee, Harry, 266, 270, 272, 275, 277, 279, 307
Breckinridge, John C., 110, 111
Brodie, George, 295
Brodie's Mills, Arkansas, 282, 283, 285
Brooke, Walker, 105
Brownlow, William G., 99
Brownsville, Tennessee, 151
Buck family, 288, 295, 311
Buck, Philip, 288, 296, 307
Buckner, Simon B., 138, 210, 204, 205
Buell, Don Carlos, 286, 303, 304, 311

Burnside, Ambrose, 221, 305, 326
Burrowville, Arkansas, 31
Butler, Benjamin F., 90, 233

Cairo, Illinois, 65, 68, 73, 78, 110, 130, 199
Caldwell, Mrs. Lucy, 258, 318
Caldwell's, Arkansas, 257, 258, 288, 308, 314, 315, 318
Cameron, Simon, 192, 193
Campbell, John, 35, 36, 40
Cane Hill, Arkansas, 327, 328
Cantrell, William A., 271, 272
Carnifax Ferry, Battle of, 132
Caskey, Thomas W., 62, 63
Chambersburg, Pennsylvania, 304
Chicago, Illinois, xii, 81, 86, 307, 308, 326
Christy Minstrels, 50, 51
Clarendon, Arkansas, 46, 180, 181, 226, 229
Clinton, Arkansas, 28, 40-42
Coapland, Joab, 28
Coates, George, 50, 129
Columbus, Kentucky, 113, 115, 129, 130, 138, 141, 142, 144, 155-157, 159-161, 167, 210, 213
Conway, Arkansas, 25
Corinth, Mississippi, 145-147, 220, 224, 226, 227, 246, 252, 267, 296, 301-304, 311
Crockett, Jacob V. J., 33, 40

Dardanelle, Arkansas, 235, 248, 249, 251, 322, 323
Davis, Jefferson, 66, 107, 121, 133, 134, 155, 206, 224, 276, 297
De Vall's Bluff, Arkansas, 180, 181, 184, 185, 196, 200, 268
Des Arc, Arkansas, 46, 180, 181, 183, 184, 196, 200, 227, 229, 230
Dickerman, Henry, 31
Dills, George K., 249, 250, 252
Dodge family, 253, 254, 263
Donaldsonville, Louisiana, 207
Douglas, Stephen A., 86, 87, 305

Election for Governor of Tennessee, 103, 113
Election for Mayor of Memphis, 97
Election for Secession of Arkansas, 40
Election for Secession of Tennessee, 42, 43, 88
Elkhorn Tavern (Pea Ridge), Battle of, 216, 227, 297
Ellsworth, Elmer, 81, 82, 87
Etheridge, Emerson, 99, 101
Eunice, Louisiana, 185

Index

Falling Waters, Battle of, 101
First Bull Run (Manassas), Battle of, 106-110, 122
Flanagan, Harris, 299, 300
Florence, Alabama, 145
Floyd, John B., 131, 132, 136, 204, 205
Foote, Andrew, 201, 205
Fort Donelson, Battle of, 109, 200, 201, 203, 204, 206, 213, 297
Fort Harris, Tennessee, 73, 76, 77
Fort Hatteras, Battle of, 124, 125
Fort Jackson, Louisiana, 232, 233
Fort Pickens, Florida, 68, 163, 164
Fort Pillow, Tennessee, 165, 199, 234, 252
Fort Randolph, Tennessee, 68, 69
Fort Smith, Arkansas, 212, 235, 248-251, 322, 323, 325
Fort Sumter, Battle of, 62
Fouch Bar, Arkansas, 212, 213, 222, 316, 318
Fredericksburg, Battle of, 294, 295, 326
Fremont, John C., 120, 127, 156, 258-260
Friars Point, Mississippi, 46
Frog Bayou Bar, Arkansas, 324, 325

Gayoso Hotel, Memphis, 108
Gilbert, Dr. Samuel, 116, 117
Grand Junction, Tennessee, 147, 148
Grant, Ulysses S., 156, 210, 203-205, 209, 210, 223, 224, 233, 234, 237, 271, 311
Graves, James R., 112
Gunther, Charles F.
    Birth, xi
    Caramel business, xii-xv, 328
    Conscription, 245, 246, 280, 297
    Debt collection, 143-151, 158-161
    Early life, xi, xii
    Family, xi-xv, 87, 89, 123, 325, 327
    Freemasonry, 21, 37, 51, 58, 65, 84, 92, 96, 97, 103, 106, 144
    Goes to theater, 55, 117, 123, 136, 137, 140, 155, 158, 175, 211
    Ice business, xii, 19, 44, 52-55, 58-143, 151
    Later life, xii-xv, 329
    Melon sales, 112, 117, 120, 122, 124, 127, 130, 135
    Odd jobs in Arkansas, 19-45
    Purser on the Rose Douglas, vi, 165-326
    Thoughts on the war, xvi, xvii, 57, 62, 66, 92, 152, 182

Halleck, Henry, 224
Hamilton, Ferd W., 249, 260, 277
Harmstad, Lawrence, 164, 220
Harpers Ferry, Virginia, 90, 294, 295

Harris, Isham G., 74-76, 103, 110, 113, 114
Harris, Thomas A., 185
Hatchett, King, 28, 41
Helena, Arkansas, 169, 226, 230, 231, 233, 240, 244, 246, 255, 256, 274, 276, 300, 303, 304, 306, 308
Hester, John B., 291
Hickman, Kentucky, 128-130, 168
Hicks, William, 42, 43
Hindman, Thomas, 77, 92, 250-253, 256, 276, 298, 314, 322, 323, 325
Hoffman, Asa, 19, 22, 24, 27-34, 36, 38, 73, 318
Holland, Edward C., 211, 212, 240, 241, 247, 257
Hollins, George N., 144
Holly Springs, Mississippi, 148, 313
Holmes, Theophilus, 276, 277, 301, 323
Hughes, Dave, 176, 202
Humboldt, Tennessee, 149, 150, 161

Island No. 10, Siege of, 214, 218, 226, 234
Iuka, Battle of, 296, 297, 311
Ivy Mountain, Battle of, 161

Jackson, Claiborne, 90, 94, 103, 104, 108
Jackson, Thomas J. "Stonewall", 101, 257, 282, 283, 290, 291
Jacksonport, Arkansas, 181, 182, 197, 223
Johnson, Andrew, 99
Johnston, Albert S., 133, 134, 138, 224-226

Kesner, George W., 36, 39, 40
Kriel, Andy, 158, 161, 232

La Grange, Tennessee, 148
Lane family, 138
Lane, Howard, 197, 234, 235, 241, 248, 249, 254, 256, 260, 262, 265, 269, 270, 272-275, 277-281, 286, 291, 295, 298, 303-310, 312, 317, 320, 321, 326
Lee, Robert E., xiv, 136, 141, 276, 290-292, 294, 326
Leslie, Sam, 29, 35, 40
Levy, Abraham S., 56
Lewisburg, Arkansas, 248, 251, 323
Lexington, Siege of, 137
Lincoln, Abraham, xiv, 51, 55, 64, 67, 75, 80, 101, 110, 112, 113, 120, 186, 258, 285, 286, 292
Little Rock, Arkansas, 21-25, 40, 181, 184, 213, 213, 217, 222, 223, 244, 235, 242, 244, 247, 248, 251, 252, 255, 256, 262, 263, 269-271, 274, 276, 277, 280, 281, 283, 296, 300, 307, 316, 317, 321-323
Lloyd, Stephen, 48, 50-52, 55-57, 60, 77, 83, 98, 114, 122, 144, 151, 154-157, 163-165, 195, 219, 226, 232, 240, 241, 245

Lovell, Mansfield, 187, 189, 191
Lyon, Nathaniel, 76, 94, 117-120, 12

Maginnis, Capt. James L., xvi, 165, 175, 220, 262, 266, 272, 274, 277, 283, 286, 290, 299-301, 304, 307, 309-311, 313, 321
Maginnis, Mrs. Mary Brazee, 266, 274, 275, 293, 299, 302, 304, 306-308, 311
Manassas, C.S.S., 168, 169, 179
Manassas, Battles of, See First, Second Bull Run
Mason, James, 161, 162, 186
Maury, Dabney H., 226-228
McCall, Ransom, 275, 282, 288, 293, 295, 301-303, 309, 312, 313, 318
McCarthy, Harry, 100, 102
McClellan, George B., 104, 105, 112, 256-260, 268-270, 288, 289, 292
McClure, Lydia, 47, 48, 69
McCrory, Ludwick, 24, 36
McCullough, Ben, 102, 119, 195, 216
McDowell, Dr. Joseph N., 74, 108
McElroy, Gashum, 43
McNeil, Angus F., 292
McNeill family, 291, 292, 294, 299, 310, 315
Melton family, 24, 25, 27, 29-35, 37, 38, 41, 70, 102
Memphis, Tennessee, xii, xvii, 19, 39, 44-143, 151-158, 161-165, 172, 184, 185, 215, 217-220, 225, 229-232, 234, 238-240, 244, 248, 250, 254, 255, 259, 262, 264, 271, 289, 293, 299, 301
Memphis, Naval Battle of, 230, 254, 255
Militia (local), 105, 112, 114, 115, 140
Miller, Joe, 73, 83, 135
Mill Springs, Battle of, 193
Mitchell, Maggie, 55
Monks, Joe, 60, 61
Mosby, James H., 265, 266, 270, 271, 274, 277, 279, 283, 286, 288, 291, 293-301, 306
Moss, Jonathan, 69, 72, 74, 128
Mound City, U.S.S., 183, 261

Napoleon, Arkansas, 169, 170, 180, 194, 200, 210, 216, 218, 221, 225, 226, 233, 241, 243, 246, 252, 255, 256
Natchez, Mississippi, 170, 171, 186, 201, 208, 240, 244, 245
New Madrid, Missouri, 115, 118, 168, 214, 216, 218, 234
New Orleans, Louisiana, xvii, 88, 116, 140, 141, 144, 167, 172-177, 180, 182, 183, 187-191, 201-204, 206, 207, 213, 231, 232, 234, 235, 271, 322
Nonintercourse Order, 120
Norristown, Arkansas, 322

Oxford, Mississippi, 147, 148
Ozark, Arkansas, 249, 324

Palmer, Benjamin M., 189, 190
Paris, Tennessee, 149, 150
Park, John, 97
Parsons, Mosby M., 226-228
Parsons, William H., 298, 299
Payne, Robert Garnett, 111
Pea Ridge, Battle of, See Elkhorn Tavern
Pensacola, Florida, 56, 143, 164
Perryville, Battle of, 286, 303, 304, 307
Peru, Illinois, xi, xii, xvii, 37, 52, 54, 60, 64, 80, 84, 85, 87, 89, 106, 107
Pike, Albert, 195, 196
Pillow, Gideon, 66, 108, 109, 112, 156, 234
Pine Bluff, Arkansas, 21, 211-213, 215, 217, 218, 222, 224, 233, 239-241, 243, 247, 252, 253, 256, 257, 274, 298, 313, 320
Plum Run Bend, Battle of, 229
Pocahontas, Arkansas, 223, 224
Polk, Leonidas, 91, 103, 104, 108, 112, 118, 129, 133, 156, 158, 165
Polk, William H., 103, 109, 110, 113, 114
Pooley, James, 130, 131
Pope, John, 214, 258, 282, 283, 288-291
Prairie Grove, Battle of, 322, 327
Price, Edwin W., 185
Price, Sterling, xvi, 137, 156, 197, 203, 227, 267, 283, 296, 301
Prior, Mr., 51, 52, 55, 66, 69, 74
Pritchard, Reese, 280
Pyne, Michael, 54, 55, 74, 81, 83, 102, 105, 116, 121-123, 128, 131, 134, 136, 142, 144

Quinby & Robinson Foundry, 73, 139

Rector, Henry, 242, 243
Rice, Dan, 58-60
Ringo, Daniel, 180
Rogers, David, 45
Rose family, 29
Rosecrans, William S., 131, 132, 141, 196, 301, 302, 311, 312
Russell, William H., 68, 93, 94, 122, 146, 150, 160, 167, 173
Russellville, Arkansas, 34, 36, 38
Rust, Albert, 266, 267

Salley, William H., 313-315
Santa Rosa Island, Battle of, 143
Schmal, Jonathan, 55, 86, 100
Scott, Charles, 84, 92
Scott, Winfield, 66
Scruggs, Phineas, 62, 63

Searcy, Arkansas, 44
Secession of Tennessee, 74, 75, 88
Secession Referendum in Tennessee, 42, 43, 88
Second Bull Run (Manassas), Battle of, 282, 288-291
Sharpsburg, Battle of, See Antietam
Shaw, Abel B., 116, 117
Shaw, Ellen Maclean, 116, 117
Shields, James, 258-260
Shiloh, Battle of, 224, 225, 286, 297
Slidell, James, 161, 162, 186
Small, J. T., 78
Spodra Bluffs, Arkansas, 323, 324, 326
St. Charles, Arkansas, 184, 185, 192, 196, 200, 260, 261
St. Charles, Battle of, 183, 260, 261
St. Charles Hotel, New Orleans, 173, 174, 188
Steamboats, civilian
    Acacia, 216, 218
    Admiral, 47
    Alamo, 257
    Alice Dean, 149
    Anna Perret, 204
    Arkansas, 324, 325
    Belvidere, 250
    Ben Coursin, 281, 290, 291, 296
    Bracelet, 303, 315
    Capitol, 50, 52, 53, 60, 61, 64, 78-80, 88, 89, 143
    Chester Ashley, 218, 301, 303, 305, 323
    Citizen, 65
    Cotton Plant, 217
    Dickey, 68
    Eliza G., 204, 235
    Era No. 6, 272-274, 276-279, 291, 308, 316, 327
    Era No. 7, 211, 257, 262, 263
    Fair Play, 232
    Frederick Notrebe, 327
    Frontier City, 21
    General Price, 198, 199, 203
    George Foreman, 68
    Hartford City, 76
    J. J. Cadot, 241
    Jno. Walsh, 80, 186
    Julia Roane, 235, 241, 243, 248, 252, 262, 301
    Kennett, 218
    Kentucky, 80, 157, 246, 248
    Key West, 223, 251, 274, 277, 281-283, 303, 327
    Lady Jackson, 65

    Little Rock, 261-263, 279, 304, 306
    Manchester, 72
    Natchez, 152
    New Madrid, 46
    New Moon, 225
    Perry, 76
    Pine Bluff, 250
    Prince of Wales, 80
    Quitman, 179
    Rose Douglas, xvi, xvii, 165-326
    St. Charles, 77
    St. Francis, 251, 315, 316
    Star of the West, 66
    Tahlequah, 265, 266, 269, 1277, 280, 290, 306, 314, 321
    Trent, 207
    Van Buren, 327
    Violet, 327
    Washington, 79
    William M. Morrison, 179, 180
Stedman, James O., 73, 74
Stephenson, Andrew R., 35

Tappan, James C., 161
Terry, Benjamin F., 147, 176, 178
Thomas, Richard, 99, 100
Thompson, John Baker, 23
Thompson, M. Jeff, 115, 136, 154, 229
Trenton, Tennessee, 150, 151
Tuscarora, C.S.S., 163, 164
Tuscumbia, Alabama, 145

Van Buren, Arkansas, xvii, 161, 223, 235, 249, 250, 326-328
Van Dorn, Earl, xvi, 226-228, 296, 301, 302
Vicksburg, Mississippi, 53, 54, 170, 179, 193, 200, 203, 204, 209, 210, 227, 234, 244, 245, 268, 271, 273, 276, 280, 315, 322

Wandell, Harry Brazee, 275
West Point, Arkansas, 39, 43-45, 121
Wildcat Landing, Arkansas, 257, 258, 270, 274
Wiley's Cove, Arkansas, 29, 30, 40
Williams, Thomas, 112, 116, 118, 128, 131, 132, 141
Wilson, George, 102, 121
Wilson, Victor F., 53, 54, 158
Wilson's Creek, Battle of, 119, 122

Zollicoffer, Felix, 193, 197

www.ingramcontent.com/pod-product-compliance
Lightning Source LLC
Chambersburg PA
CBHW020352080526
44584CB00014B/990